Khyruddin Akbar Ansari, Ph.D., P.E. & Bonni Dichone, Ph.D.

An Introduction to Numerical Methods Using MATLAB

SDC
Publications

SDC Publications
P.O. Box 1334
Mission, KS 66222
913-262-2664
www.SDCpublications.com
Publisher: Stephen Schroff

Copyright 2018 Khyruddin Akbar Ansari and Bonni Dichone

Examination Copies
Books received as examination copies are for review purposes only and may not be made available for student use. Resale of examination copies is prohibited.

Electronic Files
Any electronic files associated with this book are licensed to the original user only. These files may not be transferred to any other party.

Trademarks
MATLAB and Simulink are registered trademarks of The MathWorks, Inc. See mathworks.com/trademarks for a list of additional trademarks. Other product or brand names may be trademarks or registered trademarks of their respective holders.

ISBN-13: 978-1-63057-245-7

ISBN-10: 1-63057-245-4

Printed and bound in the United States of America.

This book is dedicated to the following:

The memory of Khader Mohiuddin Ansari, the first author's father, who constantly reminded him that the pursuit of knowledge for the sake of knowledge itself is never in vain.

The memory of Khaja Mohiuddin Ansari, the first author's uncle, a mathematics professor and a great teacher, who instilled in a young mind the love for the study of mathematics and its ever-fascinating applications.

Fatima Ansari, the first author's wife, a constant source of support in all his endeavors.

Paulo Dichone, the second author's husband, who never ceases to be supportive and loving and who knows far more about programming than she does.

About the Authors

K. Akbar Ansari, who has been a professor of mechanical engineering at Gonzaga University in Spokane, Washington, since 1986, received his bachelor's degree in electrical engineering from Osmania University, Hyderabad, India in 1964, his master's degree in mechanical engineering from the University of California at Berkeley in 1965 and his Ph.D. degree in engineering mechanics from the University of Texas at Arlington in 1972. He did his doctoral thesis work in the area of nonlinear vibrations of rotating blades under the guidance of the late Professor Nils O. Myklestad. Professor Ansari has many years of varied industrial, teaching and research experience, having been associated in the past with such organizations as Bell Helicopter, Westinghouse Electric , Bell Aerospace, Brown and Root, King Fahd's University of Petroleum and Minerals and Battelle Pacific Northwest Laboratories. At Gonzaga University, Professor Ansari has been involved in the teaching of courses in the areas of engineering mechanics, numerical methods, advanced engineering mathematics, vibrations, system dynamics and controls, and machine design. His research, which has been varied, has resulted in several published articles and contributions to books including chapters in the Encyclopedia of Fluid Mechanics and Developments in Offshore Engineering. Professor Ansari is a life member of the American Society of Mechanical Engineers and the American Society for Engineering Education. He is also a registered professional engineer.

Bonni Dichone is an Associate Professor at Gonzaga University in Spokane, Washington in the Department of Mathematics. She received her Bachelor's degree and Master's degree, both in Mathematics, from Eastern Washington University in 2003 and 2005, respectively. She completed her Ph.D. in Applied Mathematics from Washington State University in 2011. The work of her dissertation, entitled "A Nonlinear Stability Analysis of Vegetative Turing Pattern Formation for an Interaction-Diffusion Plant-Surface Water Model System in an Arid Flat Environment", was featured in *The Economist* in 2012. Dr. Dichone has taught mathematics at the university level since 2003 and, as an applied mathematician, enjoys teaching and working with students across discipline, especially those in engineering and biology. She recently co-authored a textbook entitled "Comprehensive Applied Mathematical Modeling in the Natural and Engineering Sciences", with David J. Wollkind, published by Springer in 2018. She is a member of many mathematical societies, including the MAA, AMS, SIAM, SMB, and AWM. You can learn more about her and her work through her Gonzaga website: http://connect.gonzaga.edu/dichone.

Preface

This book, which is designed to be used in a first course in numerical methods in a computer science, mathematics, science, engineering or engineering technology curriculum, had its beginnings in notes that I generated over several years, since 1997, in the process of teaching a sophomore level course in numerical methods at Gonzaga University with MATHCAD as the supporting software. Over time, these notes were recast in the form of a textbook entitled "An Introduction to Numerical Methods using MATHCAD" and published by Schroff Development Corporation of Mission, Kansas. Twenty years later in 2017, Gonzaga University's School of Engineering and Applied Science decided to replace MATHCAD with MATLAB as the main computational program for use in the undergraduate engineering curriculum. To this end, I invited Dr. Bonni Dichone of our Mathematics Department, an expert in the use of MATLAB, to join me as a co-author, in an endeavor to undertake a revision of the MATHCAD version of my book that would employ MATLAB as the software and programming environment and provide the user with powerful tools in the solution of numerical problems. I am very happy and proud, indeed, to have Dr. Dichone as my co-author, because, without her involvement, this book would still be wishful thinking.

In the opinion of the authors, this book should also provide a reliable source of reference material to practicing engineers and scientists and in other junior and senior-level courses such as dynamics, machine design, vibrations, and system dynamics and controls, where MATLAB can be effectively utilized as a software tool in problem solving. A principal goal of this book, then, is to furnish the background needed to generate numerical solutions to a variety of problems. Specific applications involving root-finding, interpolation, curve-fitting, matrices, derivatives, integrals and differential equations are discussed and the broad applicability of MATLAB demonstrated. The material contained herein should be easily grasped by students with a background in calculus, elementary differential equations and some linear algebra and, when utilized in a mathematics, science, engineering, computer science or engineering technology course sequence, it should give a good basic coverage of numerical methods while simultaneously demonstrating the general applicability of MATLAB to problem solving.

Although this book is not meant to be an exhaustive treatise on MATLAB, MATLAB solutions to problems are systematically developed and included throughout the book. The first chapter discusses MATLAB basics while the second gives a general introduction to numerical methods in science and engineering and presents the computation of numerical errors along with the Taylor series as a basis of approximation in numerical analysis. Chapter 3 offers a coverage of the popular methods of finding roots of equations such as Bisection, Newton-Raphson, Secant and Iteration. Solutions to systems of nonlinear algebraic equations obtained by the iteration method are also presented. The applicability of root-finding to practical problems such as those that occur in column design and control system analysis is demonstrated. In the fourth chapter, matrices and linear algebra are dealt with along with the solution of eigenvalue problems. Applications to the field of vibration engineering and stress analysis are also discussed. Chapters 5 and 6 focus on numerical interpolation and curve-fitting respectively. The common techniques of interpolation and the functions generally resorted to in engineering for curve-fitting of data are covered quite thoroughly. The applicability of these to the analysis of scientific and engineering data such as stress-strain, load-deflection and fatigue failure is presented. Chapters 7 and 8 address numerical differentiation and integration. The concept of finite differences is introduced and the common methods of differentiation and integration, such as the interpolating polynomial method, trapezoidal and Simpson's rules and Romberg integration are covered. Applications of numerical differentiation and integration such as determination of velocities and accelerations from given displacement data and computation of the moment of inertia of a cross section are included. The last chapter, which is the ninth one, deals with coverage of numerical solution of ordinary differential equations, and although it does not discuss each and every technique that is available, it does focus on the popular ones such as Taylor series method, Euler, modified Euler and Runge-Kutta methods. A variety of practical applications of numerical procedures are included in this chapter, ranging from the response of an electric circuit to an input voltage to the effect of damping on the response of a control system. Partial differential equations is a topic that is typically dealt with in detail only in graduate level courses and, therefore, we did not think it very appropriate to introduce it in this book which is really aimed at the needs of undergraduate students. MATLAB files and scripts are generated and examples showing the applicability and use of MATLAB are presented throughout the book. Wherever appropriate, the use of MATLAB functions offering shortcuts and alternatives to otherwise long and tedious numerical solutions is also demonstrated. At the end of every chapter is included a set of problems to be solved covering the material presented. A solutions manual that provides solutions to these exercises can be made available to instructors.

Although MATLAB is a very powerful and versatile tool that can do complex computations and plots, several figures and sketches in the book had to be done using AutoCad. The help provided by Carlos G. Alfaro earlier in generating these figures and Ryan Lambert later in making some additions and modifications to them is gratefully acknowledged. The authors are also thankful to those of our students who have so kindly made useful suggestions and pointed out errors and mistakes in the manuscript. Their input and feedback have certainly been helpful. The first author is grateful to Drs. Claudio Talarico and Timothy Fitzgerald for their help with the MATLAB solution of various problems. Last but not least, the authors are indebted to their spouses, Fatima and Paulo, for their patience, support and understanding during the preparation of this book.

Users of this book are welcome to e-mail any comments and suggestions to the authors at ansari@gonzaga.edu and dichone@gonzaga.edu, and, of course, we will be pleased to address these in subsequent versions/editions.

K. Akbar Ansari
September 2018

Contents

Chapter 1
Basics of MATLAB

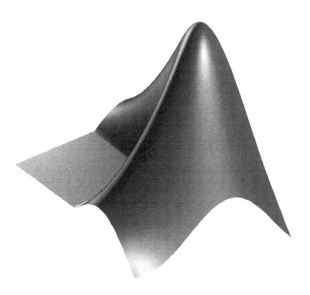

1.1 Introduction

MATLAB is a programming language developed by MathWorks. It is primarily used for mathematical operations involving matrices and arrays. With MATLAB, we can plot functions and data, implement algorithms, and create iterative processes. In this text, we will use MATLAB primarily for numerical computing; however MATLAB does have some symbolic computing ability which we will use lightly.

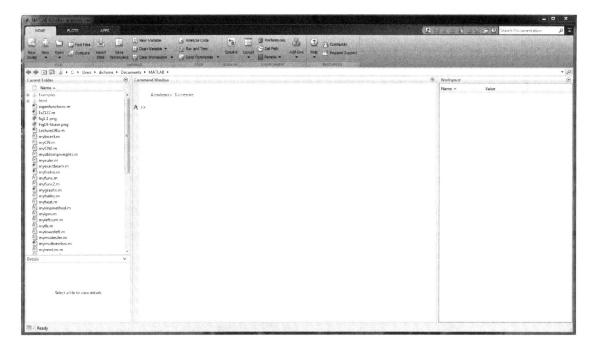

Fig. 1.1: MATLAB Screen

1.2 The MATLAB Screen

When you first open MATLAB, you will see some version of the screen shown in Figure 1.1. We will begin by entering commands in the Command Window.

1.3 Entering Vectors

In MATLAB, data is typically entered as a matrix, or array of numbers. Vectors are examples of matrices with only one row or one column. A row vector with n elements has dimension $1 \times n$ and can be entered as follows:

```
v = [1 2 3 4 5 6]
```

When you hit "enter", MATLAB will print out the vector in the Command Window:

```
v =

     1     2     3     4     5     6
```

Notice that we separate the elements of a row with spaces. You can also separate the elements with commas.

A column vector with m elements has dimension $m \times 1$ and can be entered as follows:

```
u = [7; 8; 9; 10]

u =

      7
      8
      9
     10
```

Notice that we separate the elements of a column with semicolons.

You can access an entry in a vector with:

```
u(3)

ans =
      9
```

You can change the value of an entry with:

```
u(3) = -14

u =

      7
      8
    -14
     10
```

You can extract a "slice" of a vector with:

```
u(2:4)

ans =
      8
    -14
     10
```

You can transpose a row vector into a column vector and a column vector into a row vector:

```
w = v'

w =

      1
      2
      3
      4
      5
```

```
        6

z = u'

z =
        7       8     -14      10
```

There are shortcuts to create vectors whose elements are a set distance away from each other:

```
x = -2:.1:-1

x =
    -2.0000    -1.9000    -1.8000    -1.7000    -1.6000    -1.5000
        -1.4000    -1.3000    -1.2000    -1.1000    -1.0000
```

For this definition of a vector, the first number is the starting element, the middle number is the step size between elements, and the last number is the ending element.

Also:

```
y = linspace(0,1,9)

y =
        0    0.1250    0.2500    0.3750    0.5000    0.6250
        0.7500    0.8750    1.0000
```

In the *linspace()* command, the first input is the starting element, the second input is the ending element, and the last input is the desired number of elements in the vector. MATLAB will then use an appropriate step size to evenly divide the given range into the given number of elements.

1.4 Plotting Data

Let us enter some data:

```
x = [5 15 20 30 42];
y = [-3 0.5 2 -1 5];
```

Notice that by putting a semicolon after the definition of our vectors, MATLAB doesn't print out the vectors.

To plot the data:

```
plot(x,y)
```

Which produces the following figure:

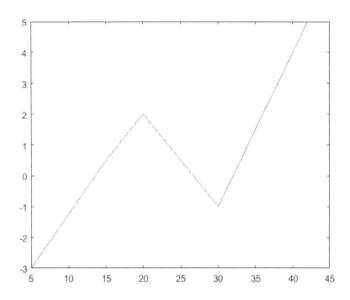

Notice MATLAB produces a graph with the data connected by lines. This is not always the best way to represent discrete data, so you can plot the data as individual points, represented by symbols:

```
plot(x,y,'*')
```

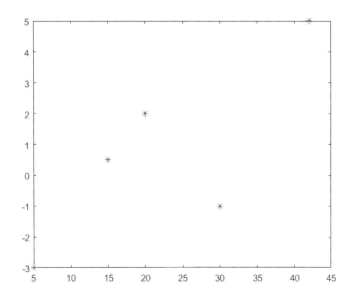

There are other symbols that can be used, like 'o', '.', 'd' and others. For a complete list and explanation, you can enter:

```
help plot
```

which will display an explanation of the command *plot* and its inputs.

1.5 Built-in Functions

MATLAB has many built-in common functions, like *sin()*, *cos()*, etc. We can use these to find values of these functions:

```
sin(0)

ans =
     0

cos(pi)

ans =
    -1

exp(0)

ans =
     1
```

The built-in functions can also operate on vectors, which can then be used to produce plots (see next page):

```
x = linspace(0,2*pi,8);
y = sin(x);
plot(x,y)
```

Notice that this plot is not as smooth as we know the plot of a sine function should be. Remember, MATLAB is simply plotting a discrete number of data points and then connecting the data with straight lines. To get a more smooth and continuous curve, we should increase the number of data points, like this:

```
x = linspace(0,2*pi,100);
y = sin(x);
plot(x,y)
```

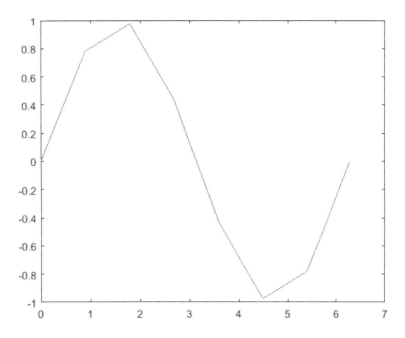

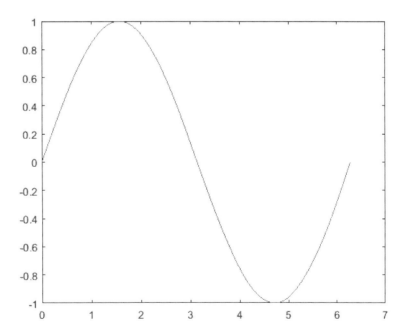

1.6 User-Defined Functions

Should we wish to define a function that is a polynomial or a combination of built-in functions, we will use an "Anonymous Function". An anonymous function is not stored as a program file. It can accept inputs and returns outputs, just as a built-in function does.

We enter an anonymous function as follows:

```
f = @(x) 2*x.^2 - 3*x + 1
```

Notice the syntax. We name the function f, followed by the equals sign (=). That is followed by the at symbol (@) and then the input of the function in parentheses (x). Finally, we have the function itself, in this case, the polynomial $2x^2 - 3x + 1$.

We can evaluate the function at a single value or for a vector of values.

```
f(2.4)

ans =

    5.3200

x = -1:.5:1;
f(x)

ans =

     6     3     1     0     0
```

You may have noticed in the definition of our function, we used $*$ symbols every time we multiplied, but also, more importantly there was a . in before the $\wedge$ This is not a typo, but a very important indicator to MATLAB that it is not a scalar operation, but a vector operation. This is what allowed us to evaluate the function for an entire vector. By using a . in front of different operators, like $\wedge$, $*$, and /, MATLAB will perform those operations entry-wise for each component of the vector. For example, consider the following two operations, one with the . and one without:

```
[1 2 4 5].^2

ans =

     1     4    16    25

[1 2 4 5]^2

Error using  ^
Inputs must be a scalar and a square matrix.
To compute elementwise POWER, use POWER (.^) instead.
```

The . example performed the squaring operation on each element. The ^ example produced an error because it was attempting to multiply the 1×4 row vector by itself, which is not possible because the inner dimensions do not match. (In order to take the product of the vector times itself, one would need to multiply using the transpose.)

Lastly, we can use the anonymous function to plot, just as with the built-in functions.

```
x = -5:.1:5;
y = f(x);
plot(x,y)
```

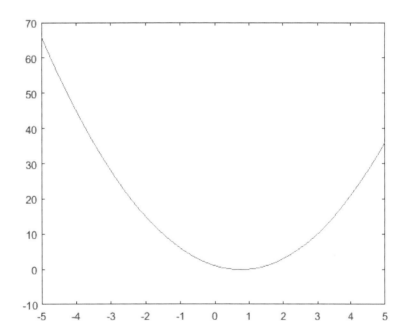

1.7 M-Files

Programs in MATLAB can be saved in files called *M-files* and have the extension .m. Generally speaking, there are two main types of M-files: *functions* and *scripts*.

1.7.1 Function Programs

Click on the new script icon, located in the upper left hand corner of the command window interface. This will open up a new window, that looks like this:

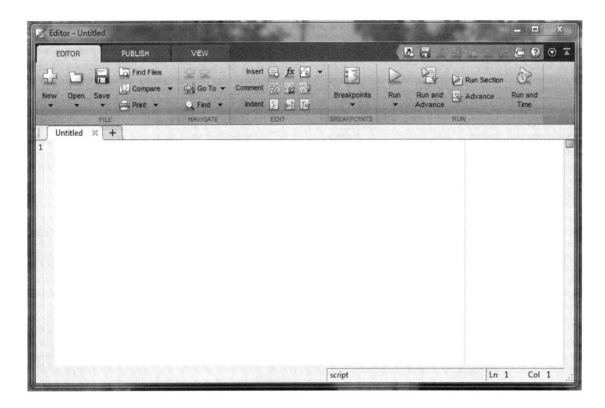

Before we create a function file, there are four important things we should know about function files:

- All function files begin with the word "function".
- There must be an input and an output.
- The output, name of the function, and input all follow immediately after the word "function" in the first line, like this:

```
function output = FunctionName(input)
```

- Somewhere in the body of the program, the output must be assigned a value.

With these items in mind, let's create out first function file:

```
function y = myfunc(x)

y = 3*x.^2 - 2*x + 1;
```

Notice the output is "y", the function name is "myfunc" and the input is "x".

Save the file as myfunc.m in your working directory. Cautiously, you must save your M-file with the same name as what follows the equals sign in the first line of your function. This will be important when we call the functions from the command window (or another script or function file).

Now, let's use your function file, by calling it in the command window. Make sure that the path in your command window points to the same working directory in which you saved your file. If it is not the right path, you will get errors. Now, let's call the function and plot the results:

```
x = -5:.1:5;
y = myfunc(x);
plot(x,y)
```

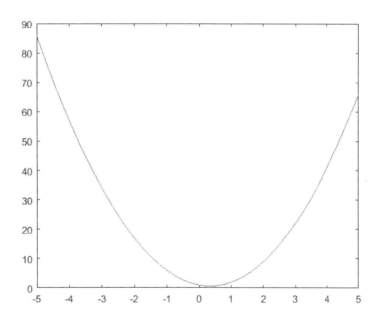

In the command window, we can name the input and output anything we want. It does not have to match the names used in the definition of the function file. Notice that the following yields the same results:

```
z = -5:.1:5;
cat = myfunc(z);
plot(z,cat)
```

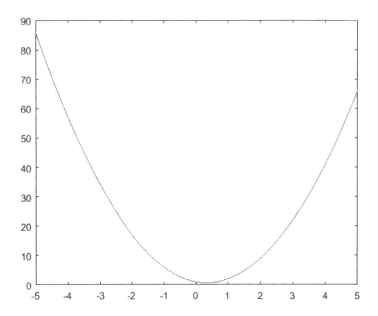

Functions can be multivariate in both input and output. Consider the following two function files, dblinput.m and mypowers.m:

```
function z = dblinput(x,y)

z = 2*exp(x.*y) + x.^2.*y.^2;
```

```
function [x1 x2 x3 x4] = mypowers(x)

x1 = x;
x2 = x.^2;
x3 = x.^3;
x4 = x.^4;
```

The first has two inputs (x,y) with a single output z. The second has one input x and outputs a vector [x1 x2 x3 x4].

In the command window, we see how these files are called, executed, and used.

```
z = dblinput(0,1)

z =

     2

x = 3;
```

```
[x1 x2 x3 x4] = mypowers(x)

x1 =
      3

x2 =
      9

x3 =
     27

x4 =
     81

x = -5:.1:5;
[x1 x2 x3 x4] = mypowers(x);
plot(x,x1,'black',x,x2,'green',x,x3,'red',x,x4,'blue')
```

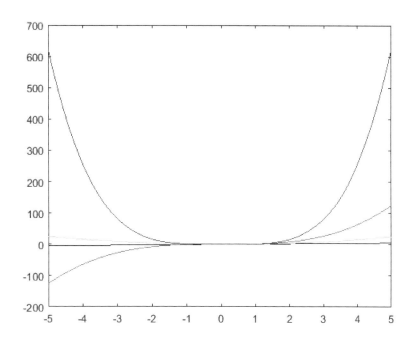

Notice in the last plot, we could plot each of the different vectors separately, but repeating the input with various parameters for each of the vectors.

1.7.2 Script Programs

Script programs differ from functions in several ways. The key difference is that scripts do not have inputs or outputs. Also, a script can use and change variables in the workspace.

Let us begin by creating a script that essentially does the same thing as the mypowers.m function we created previously. We name it mygraphs.m.

```
x1 = x;
x2 = x.^2;
x3 = x.^3;
x4 = x.^4;

plot(x,x1,'black',x,x2,'green',x,x3,'red',x,x4,'blue')
```

Now, in the command window, we can call our script. Notice, first we define a range for *x*:

```
x = -1:.1:1;
mygraphs
```

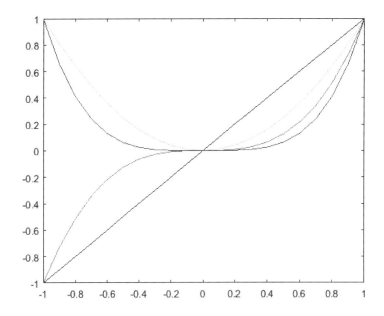

Both our function and the script produced the same result; however, the script is reusable. We could pass it a different range for *x* without having to retype all of the commands to find the powers or to plot. For this reason, scripts are often used for routine calculations that require typing multiple commands in the command window.

1.7.3 Comments and Documentation

Now that we can save both functions and script files, it is important that we properly document our code, by "commenting" on what different commands within our programs perform. In MATLAB, anything that follows the percentage symbol (%) is considered to be a comment and will not be ignored by the compiler.

You should always include comments at the top of any .m file that includes the name of the file, a basic explanation of what the file does, and, for a function, what the inputs and outputs are. It also helps to add comments after different commands, explaining what a certain line of code executes. This is an important and helpful tool so that later, if you come back to a program you can easily remind yourself what the program does.

The following is an example of how we could comment the script we wrote in the previous subsection.

```
%% Script: mygraphs.m
% Plots the graphs of x, x^2, x^3, and x^4 in different
   colors

%Fix a range of x
x = -1:.1:1;

%Calculate the powers of x to be plotted
x1 = x;
x2 = x.^2;
x3 = x.^3;
x4 = x.^4;

%Plots each of the graphs on the same coordinate axes
plot(x,x1,'black',x,x2,'green',x,x3,'red',x,x4,'blue')
```

1.8 Publish MATLAB Code

At the top of the editor window, where you create scripts and functions, you will notice a tab named "Publish". Click on it and you will see a new menu bar at the top.

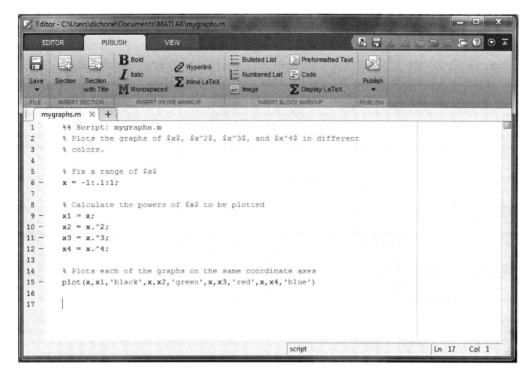

We will now publish our script mygraphs.m by clicking "Publish". In the figure, you can see our code (with some modified LaTeX) on the left and on the right is the resulting published PDF file.

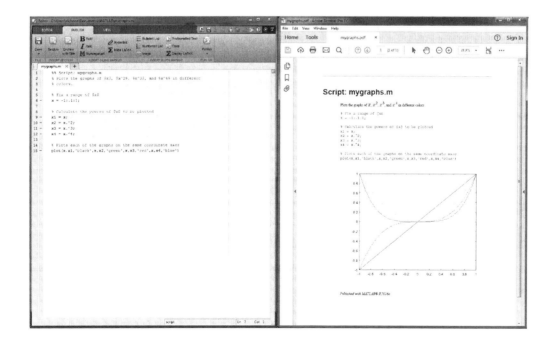

The first time, your file may publish in a different format, like HTML or XPS. You can change the output in the "Edit Publishing Options" menu. We will not go into great detail here about all the different features of Publish. As you work through this text and produce examples and programs of your own, you will discover the different features necessary if and when you choose to use the Publish feature in MATLAB.

Problems

1.1. Create a table of data. Input it as vectors and plot it. Turn in the graph.

1.2. Create an anonymous function $f(x) = x + \cos(x^2)$. Plot it on the domain $-5 \leq x \leq 5$, with a step size of 1. In what way does the graph incorrectly represent the function? What can you do to make the graph properly represent the function? Fix it and turn in both plots.

1.3. Write a function program for the function $x^2 e^{-x^2}$. Include adequate comments in the program. Plot the function on the interval $[-5, 5]$. Turn in the program and graph.

1.4. Write a script program that graphs the functions $\sin(x)$, $\sin(2x)$, $\sin(3x)$, $\sin(4x)$, $\sin(5x)$, and $\sin(6x)$ on the interval $[0, 2\pi]$ on the same set of coordinate axes. Include comments in the program. Turn in the program and the graph.

Chapter 2
Introduction to Numerical Methods

2.1 The Use of Numerical Methods in Science and Engineering

Analysis of problems in engineering and the physical sciences typically involves four steps as follows.

(1) Development of a suitable mathematical model that realistically represents a given physical system.
(2) Derivation of the system governing equations using physical laws such as Newton's laws of motion, conservation of energy, the laws governing electrical circuits etc.
(3) Solution of the governing equations, and
(4) Interpretation of the results.

Because real world problems are generally quite complex with the generation of closed-form analytical solutions becoming impossible in many situations, there exists, most definitely, a need for the proper utilization of computer-based techniques in the solution of practical problems. The advancement of computer technology has made the effective use of numerical methods and computer-based techniques very feasible, and thus, solutions can now be obtained much faster than ever before and with much better than acceptable accuracy. However, there are advantages as well as disadvantages associated with any numerical procedure that is resorted to, and these must be kept in mind when using it.

2.2 Comparison of Numerical Methods with Analytical Methods

While an analytical solution will be exact if it exists, a numerical method, on the other hand, will generally require iterations to generate a solution, which is only an *approximation* and which certainly cannot be considered exact by any means.

A disadvantage associated with analytical solution techniques is that they are generally applicable only to very special cases of problems. Numerical solutions, on the contrary, will solve complex situations as well.

While numerical techniques have several advantages including easy programming on a computer and the convenience with which they handle complex problems, the initial estimate of the solution along with the many number of iterations that are sometimes required to generate a solution can be looked upon as disadvantages.

2.3 Sources of Numerical Errors and Their Computation

It is indeed possible for miscalculations to creep into a numerical solution because of various sources of error. These include inaccurate mathematical modeling, wrong programming, wrong input, rounding off of numbers and truncation of an infinite series. Round-off error is the general name given to inaccuracies that affect the calculation scene when a finite number of digits are assigned to represent an actual number. In a long sequence of calculations, this round-off error can accumulate, then propagate through the process of calculation and finally grow very rapidly to a significant number. A truncation error results when an infinite series is approximated by a finite number of terms, and, typically, upper bounds are placed on the size of this error.

The true error is defined as the difference between the computed value and the true value of a number.

$$E_{True} = X_{Comp} - X_{True},\tag{2.1}$$

while the relative true error is the error relative to the true value

$$e_r = \frac{X_{Comp} - X_{True}}{X_{True}}.\tag{2.2}$$

Expressed as a percentage, the relative true error is written as

$$e_r = \frac{X_{Comp} - X_{True}}{X_{True}} \cdot 100\%\tag{2.3}$$

2.4 Taylor Series Expansion

The Taylor series is considered as a basis of approximation in numerical analysis. If the value of a function of x is provided at x_0, then the Taylor series provides a means of evaluating the function at $x_0 + h$, where x_0 is the starting value of the independent variable and h is the difference between the starting value and the new value at which the function is to be approximated

$$f(x_0 + h) = f(x_0) + h\frac{d}{dx}f(x_0) + \frac{h^2}{2!}\frac{d^2}{dx^2}f(x_0) + \frac{h^3}{3!}\frac{d^3}{dx^3}f(x_0) + \cdots.\tag{2.4}$$

This equation can be used for generating various orders of approximations as shown below. The order of approximation is defined by the highest derivative included in the series. For example, if only terms up to the second derivative are retained in the series, the result is a second order approximation.

First order approximation:

$$f(x_0 + h) = f(x_0) + h\frac{d}{dx}f(x_0) + \cdots \qquad (2.5)$$

Second order approximation:

$$f(x_0 + h) = f(x_0) + h\frac{d}{dx}f(x_0) + \frac{h^2}{2!}\frac{d^2}{dx^2}f(x_0) + \cdots \qquad (2.6)$$

Third order approximation:

$$f(x_0 + h) = f(x_0) + h\frac{d}{dx}f(x_0) + \frac{h^2}{2!}\frac{d^2}{dx^2}f(x_0) + \frac{h^3}{3!}\frac{d^3}{dx^3}f(x_0) + \cdots \qquad (2.7)$$

It is to be noted that the significance of the higher order terms in the Taylor series increases with the nonlinearity of the function involved as well as the difference between the "starting x" value and the x value at which the function is to be approximated. Thus, the fewer the terms that are included in the series, the larger will be the error associated with the computation of the function value. If the function is linear, however, only terms up to the first derivative term need to be included.

Example 2.1. Using the Taylor series expansion for

$$f(x) = -0.15x^4 - 0.17x^3 - 0.25x^2 - 0.25x + 1.25$$

determine the zeroth, first, second, third, fourth and fifth order approximations of $f(x_0 + h)$ where $x_0 = 0$ and $h = 1, 2, 3, 4, 5$ and compare these with the exact solutions.

The following code is for $h = 1.0$. We put in the function and generate its derivatives, as follows.

Example 2.1

```
%Example 2.1
%Define values for x0, and h
x0 = 0; h = 1.0;

%Define function
f = @(x) -0.15*x^4 - 0.17*x^3 - 0.25*x^2 - 0.25*x + 1.25;
```

```
%Define derivatives
fprime = @(x) -0.60*x^3 - 0.51*x^2 - 0.50*x- 0.25;
f2prime =  @(x) -1.80*x^2 - 1.02*x - 0.50;
f3prime =  @(x) -3.60*x - 1.02;
f4prime =  @(x) -3.60;
f5prime =  @(x) 0;

%Define the terms of the Taylor polynomial at x0
term1 = f(x0);
term2 = h*fprime(x0);
term3 = h^2/2*f2prime(x0);
term4 = h^3/6*f3prime(x0);
term5 = h^4/24*f4prime(x0);
term6 = h^5/120*f5prime(x0);

%Define the approximations of different order
ftaylor0 = term1;
ftaylor1 = term1 + term2;
ftaylor2 = term1 + term2 + term3;
ftaylor3 = term1 + term2 + term3 + term4;
ftaylor4 = term1 + term2 + term3 + term4 + term5;
ftaylor5 = term1 + term2 + term3 + term4 + term5 + term6;

%Define x
x = x0 + h;

%Calculate the exact answer using the function given
Exact = f(x);

%Errors for the Taylor polynomial approximations
err0 = Exact - ftaylor0;
err1 = Exact - ftaylor1;
err2 = Exact - ftaylor2;
err3 = Exact - ftaylor3;
err4 = Exact - ftaylor4;
err5 = Exact - ftaylor5;

%Print out values for set h value
T = table(ftaylor0, ftaylor1, ftaylor2, ftaylor3, ftaylor4,
    ftaylor5)
Terr = table(err0, err1, err2, err3, err4, err5)
```

Similarly, by using $h = 2, 3, 4, 5$, the zeroth fifth order approximations for $f(2)$, $f(3)$, $f(4)$, $f(5)$ and the associated errors can be determined. These are given in Tables 2.1 and 2.2.

		zeroth order	first order	second order	third order	fourth order	fifth order	true value
	$x =$	ftaylor0(x)	ftaylor1(x)	ftaylor2(x)	ftaylor3(x)	ftaylor4(x)	ftaylor5(x)	f(x)
$h =$	0	1.25	1.25	1.25	1.25	1.25	1.25	1.25
1	1	1.25	1	0.75	0.58	0.43	0.43	0.43
2	2	1.25	0.75	-0.25	-1.61	-4.01	-4.01	-4.01
3	3	1.25	0.50	-1.75	-6.34	-18.49	-18.49	-18.49
4	4	1.25	0.25	-3.75	-14.63	-53.03	-53.03	-53.03
5	5	1.25	0	-6.25	-27.5	-121.25	-121.25	-121.25

Table 2.1: Various orders of approximation generated by Taylor series approach versus true values of $f(x)$ for $h = 1, \ldots 5$, $x = 0, \ldots 5$.

		zeroth order	first order	second order	third order	fourth order	fifth order
	$x =$	err0(x)	err1(x)	err2(x)	err3(x)	err4(x)	err5(x)
$h =$	0	0	0	0	0	0	0
1	1	-0.82	-0.57	-0.32	-0.15	0	0
2	2	-5.26	-4.76	-3.76	-2.40	0	0
3	3	-19.74	-18.99	-16.74	-12.15	0	0
4	4	-54.28	-53.28	-49.28	-38.40	0	0
5	5	-122.50	-121.25	-115.00	-93.75	0	0

Table 2.2: Errors associated with the different orders of approximation

Plots of the various Taylor series approximations of the given function and associated errors are generated below and are presented in Figs. 2.1 and 2.2. The various approximations generated by the calculations below and the associated errors are compared in the Table 2.1.

Example 2.1 (cont.)

```
%Example 2.1 (cont.)
%Define values for x0, and h
x = 0:.01:5;
length = size(x);
x0 = zeros(length);

%Define function
f = @(x) -0.15*x.^4 - 0.17*x.^3 - 0.25*x.^2 - 0.25*x + 1.25;

%Define derivatives
fprime = @(x) -0.60*x.^3 - 0.51*x.^2 - 0.50*x- 0.25;
f2prime = @(x) -1.80*x.^2 - 1.02*x - 0.50;
```

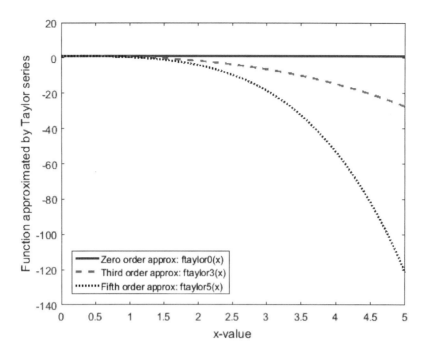

Fig. 2.1: Taylor series approximation of given function

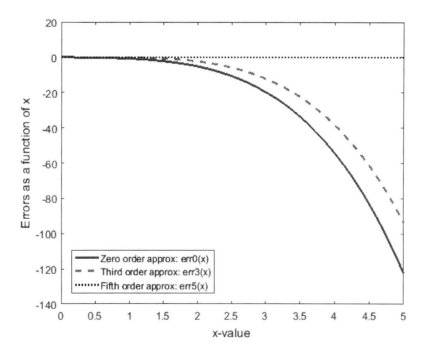

Fig. 2.2: Errors associated with the various Taylor series approximations

```
f3prime = @(x) -3.60*x - 1.02;
f4prime = @(x) -3.60;
f5prime = @(x) 0;

%Define the terms of the Taylor polynomial at x0
ftaylor0 = f(x0);
ftaylor1 = ftaylor0 + (x - x0).*fprime(x0);
ftaylor2 = ftaylor1 + (x - x0).^2/2.*f2prime(x0);
ftaylor3 = ftaylor2 + (x - x0).^3/6.*f3prime(x0);
ftaylor4 = ftaylor3 + (x - x0).^4/24.*f4prime(x0);
ftaylor5 = ftaylor4 + (x - x0).^5/120.*f5prime(x0);

%Errors generated with the various approximations
err0 = f(x) - ftaylor0;
err1 = f(x) - ftaylor1;
err2 = f(x) - ftaylor2;
err3 = f(x) - ftaylor3;
err4 = f(x) - ftaylor4;
err5 = f(x) - ftaylor5;

%Plot the Taylor approximations
figure
p1 = plot(x,ftaylor0,'blue',x,ftaylor3,'red--',x,ftaylor5,'
   black:')
xlabel('x-value')
ylabel('Function approximated by Taylor series')
legend('Zero order approx: ftaylor0(x)','Third order approx:
    ftaylor3(x)','Fifth order approx: ftaylor5(x)','Location
   ','southwest')
p1(1).LineWidth = 2;
p1(2).LineWidth = 2;
p1(3).LineWidth = 2;

%Plot the Error
figure
p2 = plot(x,err0,'blue',x,err3,'red--',x,err5,'black:')
xlabel('x-value')
ylabel('Errors as a function of x')
legend('Zero order approx: err0(x)','Third order approx:
   err3(x)','Fifth order approx: err5(x)','Location','
   southwest')
p2(1).LineWidth = 2;
p2(2).LineWidth = 2;
```

```
p2(3).LineWidth = 2;
```

Problems

2.1. Using the Taylor series expansion for $\cos(x)$, which is given by

$$f(x) = \cos(x) = 1 - \frac{x^2}{2} + \frac{x^4}{24},$$

determine the one-term, two-term and three-term approximations of $f(x_0 + h)$, where $x_0 = 0$ and $h = 0.1, 0.2, \ldots, 1.0$, and compare these with the exact solution. Generate a MATLAB script and sketch plots of the various Taylor series approximations and associated errors as function of the independent variable x.

2.2. Develop a Taylor series expansion of the following function:

$$f(x) = x^5 - 6x^4 + 3x^2 + 9.$$

Use $x = 3$ as the base and h as the increment. Generate a MATLAB script to evaluate the series for $h = 0.1, 0.2, \ldots, 1.0$, adding terms incrementally as in Problem 2.1. Compare the various Taylor series approximations obtained with true values in a table. Generate plots of the approximations and associated errors as functions of x.

2.3. Given the following function:

$$f(x) = x^3 - 3x^2 + 5x + 10,$$

determine $f(x_0 + h)$ with the help of a Taylor series expansion, where $x_0 = 2$ and $h = 0.4$. Compare the true value of $f(2.4)$ with estimates obtained by resorting to (a) one term only (b) two terms (c) three terms and (d) four terms of the series.

2.4. Given the following function:

$$f(x) = 3x^3 - 6x^2 + 15x + 25,$$

use a Taylor series expansion to determine the zeroth, first, second and third order approximations of $f(x_0 + h)$ where $x_0 = 2$ and $h = 0.5$. Compare these with the exact solution.

2.5. By developing a Taylor series expansion for

$$f(x) = e^x$$

about $x = 0$, determine the fourth-order approximation of $e^{2.5}$ and compare it with the exact solution.

2.6. By developing a Taylor series expansion for

$$f(x) = \ln(2 - x)$$

about $x = 0$, determine the fourth-order approximation of $\ln(0.5)$ and compare it with the exact solution.

2.7. By developing a Taylor series expansion for

$$f(x) = x^3 e^{-5x}$$

about $x = 1$, determine the third-order approximation of $f(1.2)$ and compare it with the exact solution.

2.8. By developing a Taylor series expansion for

$$f(x) = e^{\cos(x)}$$

about $x = 0$, determine the fourth-order approximation of $f(2\pi)$ and compare it with the exact solution.

2.9. By developing a Taylor series expansion for

$$f(x) = (x - 2)^{1/2}$$

about $x = 3$, determine the third-order approximation of $f(2.2)$, that is, $(0.2)^{1/2}$, and compare it with the exact solution.

2.10. Given the function
$$f(x) = x^2 - 5x^{0.5} + 6,$$

use a Taylor series expansion to determine the first, second, third and fourth order approximations of $f(2.5)$ by resorting to $x_0 = 2$ and $h = 0.5$. Compare these with the exact solution.

2.11. Given the function
$$f(x) = 6x^3 - 9x^2 + 25x + 40,$$

use a Taylor series expansion to determine the zeroth, first, second, and third order approximations of $f(x_0 + h)$ where $x_0 = 3$ and $h = 1$. Compare these with the exact solution.

2.12. Given the function

$$f(x) = 4x^4 - 7x^3 + 5x^2 - 6x + 90,$$

use a Taylor series expansion to determine the zeroth, first, second, third and fourth order approximations of $f(x_0 + h)$ where $x_0 = 3$ and $h = 0.5$. Compare these with the exact solution. Calculate errors and generate calculations to three decimal places.

2.13. Given the function

$$f(x) = 8x^3 - 10x^2 + 25x + 45,$$

use a Taylor series expansion to determine the zeroth, first, second, and third order approximations of $f(x_0 + h)$ where $x_0 = 2$ and $h = 1$. Compare these with the exact solution.

2.14. Given the function

$$f(x) = 1 + x + \frac{x^2}{2!} + \frac{x^3}{3!} + \frac{x^4}{4!},$$

use a Taylor series expansion to determine the zeroth, first, second, third and fourth order approximations of $f(x_0 + h)$ where $x_0 = 0$ and $h = 0.5$. Compare these with the exact solution. Generate answers correct to four decimal places.

2.15. Given the function

$$f(x) = x + \frac{x^3}{3} + \frac{2x^5}{15},$$

use a Taylor series expansion to determine the zeroth, first, second, third and fourth order approximations of $f(x_0 + h)$ where $x_0 = 0$ and $h = 0.8$. Compare these with the exact solution by computing percentage errors. Generate answers correct to four decimal places.

2.16. Given the function

$$f(x) = \sin(x),$$

use a Taylor series expansion to determine the fifth order approximation of $f(x_0 + h)$ where $x_0 = 0$ and $h = 0.2$. Compare your answer with the true value. Generate answers correct to four decimal places.

2.17. Given the function

$$f(x) = 3x^2 - 6x^{0.5} + 9,$$

use a Taylor series expansion to determine the zeroth, first, second, third and fourth order approximations of $f(x_0 + h)$ where $x_0 = 3$ and $h = 1$. Compare these with the exact solution by computing percentage errors. Generate answers correct to four decimal places.

Chapter 3
Roots Of Equations

3.1 Introduction

In many problems occurring in science and engineering, it is often necessary to find roots or zeros of equations that are nonlinear. Nonlinear equations have no closed-form solutions except in some very special cases, and thus, computer methods are indispensable in their solution. Some examples of equations whose roots may need to be found are:

$$1 + 4x - 16x^2 + 3x^3 + 3x^4 = 0, \text{ a polynomial, like a characteristic equation}$$
$$f(x) - \alpha = 0, \alpha \text{ is a number and } f(x) \text{ is a function of } x$$
$$\tan(\alpha) = \tanh(2x), \text{ a transcendental equation}$$

3.2 Methods Available

There are several methods available for finding roots of equations. Some of these are:

(1) Direct Search, which is not a very efficient technique,
(2) Bisection
(3) False Position
(4) Newton-Raphson
(5) Secant Method
(6) Bairstow's Method, which is applicable only to polynomials, and
(7) Successive Iteration or Fixed Point Iteration method.

In this chapter, however, only the Bisection, False Position, Newton-Raphson, Secant and Successive Iteration methods will be addressed along with the functions used in MATLAB to find roots.

3.3 Bisection Method

This method can be resorted to when there is only one root occurring in a given range of x. The method involves investigating a given range to seek a root and then bisecting the region successively until a root is found. Other names for this technique are Interval halving, Binary Chopping and Bolzano's Method.

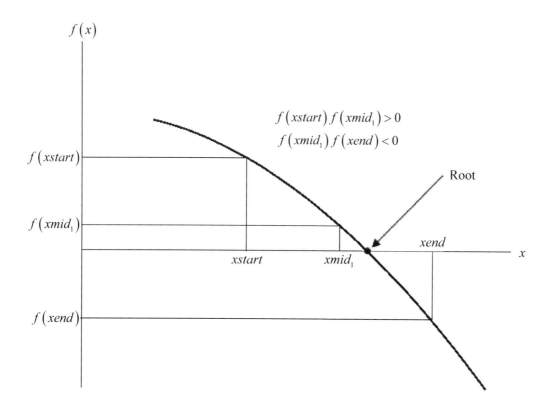

Fig. 3.1: Bisection Method

Procedure for Finding Roots

1. Choose starting and ending points $xstart$ and $xend$.
2. Compute: $f(xstart)$ and $f(xend)$.
3. Compute: $f(xstart)$ times $f(xend)$.
4. If the above product is negative, then the root lies between $xstart$ and $xend$. If this product is positive, reselect $xstart$ and $xend$.
5. If $f(xstart) * f(xend) < 0$, compute the mid-point of the $xstart$-$xend$ range. Call it "$xmid_1$" and repeat above steps, *i.e.* compute

$$f(xstart) * f(xmid_1) \text{ and } f(xmid_1) * f(xend).$$

6. If $f(xstart) * f(xmid_1) < 0$, the root lies between $xstart$ and $xmid_1$. If $f(xmid_1) * f(xend) < 0$, then the root lies between $xmid_1$ and $xend$.

7. Repeat the above procedure until convergence at a root value occurs.

Computation of Error and Convergence Criterion

A convergence criterion has to be followed in order to determine if a root has indeed been found. This is expressed in terms of the error ε or the percentage relative error ε_{rel} which are defined as

$$\varepsilon = |xmid_{i+1} - xmid_i|, \tag{3.1}$$

$$\varepsilon_{rel} = \left| \frac{xmid_{i+1} - xmid_1}{xmid_{i+1}} \right| * 100 \text{ percent}, \tag{3.2}$$

where $xmid_{i+1}$ and $xmid_i$ are the midpoints in the current and previous iterations. While, in general, the relative error should not be greater than 5%, an error of 0.01% is the largest that is tolerable for some classes of problems that require immense precision.

The true error, ε_{True}, is an indicator of the real accuracy of a solution and can be evaluated only if the true solution, x_{True}, is known. It is defined as

$$\varepsilon_{True} = \left| \frac{x_{True} - xmid_i}{x_{True}} \right| * 100. \tag{3.3}$$

Calculation of the true error clearly requires knowledge of the true solution, which, in general, will not be known to us. Therefore, the quantity ε_{rel} may have to be mostly used to determine the error associated with a solution process.

Advantages and Disadvantages of Bisection

While Bisection is a simple, robust technique for finding one root in a given interval, when the root is known to exist and it works even for non-analytic functions, its convergence process is generally slow, making it a somewhat inefficient procedure.

Sometimes, a singularity may be identified as if it were a root, since the method does not distinguish between roots and singularities, at which the function would go to infinity. Therefore, as the method proceeds, a check must be made to see if the absolute value of $[f(xend) - f(xstart)]$, in fact, converges to zero. If this quantity diverges, the method is chasing a singularity rather than a root.

When there are multiple roots, Bisection is not a desirable technique to use, since the function may not change signs at points on either side of the roots. Therefore, a graph of the function must first be drawn before proceeding to do the calculations.

Example 3.1. Obtain a root of $f(x)$ in the range of $4 < x < 20$,

$$f(x) = \frac{750.5}{x}(1 - e^{-0.1524x}) - 40.$$

Let us generate a table for x between 4 and 20 and draw a graph using MATLAB to explore where the root may lie.

$x =$	$f(x) =$
4	45.6584
8	26.1051
12	12.5031
16	2.8146
20	-4.2539

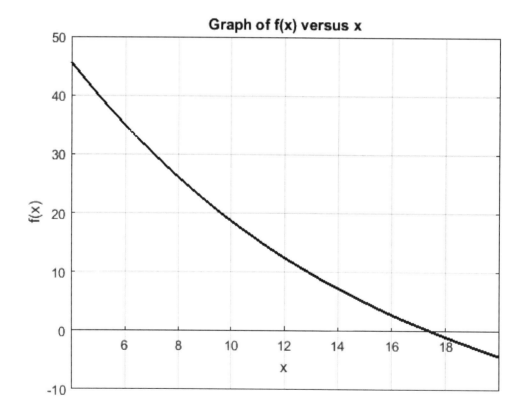

The table and graph suggest that the root lies between $xstart = 16$ and $xend = 20$. In an attempt to minimize the number of iterations needed, we will obtain a root value that is correct only to two decimal places, in this case.

Iteration #1:

$$xstart = 16, \ xend = 20, \ xmid = \frac{xstart + xend}{2} = 18;$$

$$f(xstart)f(xmid) = -2.7773, \ f(xmid)f(xend) = 4.1976$$

The root must lie between $xstart$ and $xmid$. Thus the new $xstart$ is 16 and the new $xend$ is 18.

Iteration #2:

$$xstart = 16, \ xend = 18, \ xmid = \frac{xstart + xend}{2} = 17;$$

$$f(xstart)f(xmid) = 2.366, \ f(xmid)f(xend) = -0.8295$$

The root must lie between $xmid$ and $xend$. Thus the new $xstart$ is 17 and the new $xend$ is 18.

Iteration #3:

$$xstart = 17, \ xend = 18, \ xmid = \frac{xstart + xend}{2} = 17.5;$$

$$f(xstart)f(xmid) = -0.0761, \ f(xmid)f(xend) = 0.0893$$

The root must lie between $xstart$ and $xmid$. Thus the new $xstart$ is 17 and the new $xend$ is 17.5.

Iteration #4:

$$xstart = 17, \ xend = 17.5, \ xmid = \frac{xstart + xend}{2} = 17.25;$$

$$f(xstart)f(xmid) = 0.3115, \ f(xmid)f(xend) = -0.0335$$

The root must lie between $xmid$ and $xend$. Thus the new $xstart$ is 17.25 and the new $xend$ is 17.5.

Iteration #5:

$$xstart = 17.25, \ xend = 17.5, \ xmid = \frac{xstart + xend}{2} = 17.375;$$

$$f(xstart)f(xmid) = 0.0515, \ f(xmid)f(xend) = -0.0126$$

The root must lie between $xmid$ and $xend$. Thus the new $xstart$ is 17.38 and the new $xend$ is 17.5.

Iteration #6:

$$xstart = 17.38, \; xend = 17.5, \; xmid = \frac{xstart + xend}{2} = 17.44;$$

$$f(xstart)f(xmid) = 2.5064 \times 10^{-3}, \; f(xmid)f(xend) = -1.7497 \times 10^{-3}$$

The root must lie between $xmid$ and $xend$. Thus the new $xstart$ is 17.44 and the new $xend$ is 17.5.

Iteration #7:

$$xstart = 17.44, \; xend = 17.5, \; xmid = \frac{xstart + xend}{2} = 17.47;$$

$$f(xstart)f(xmid) = -6.893 \times 10^{-4}, \; f(xmid)f(xend) = 3.2291 \times 10^{-3}$$

The root must lie between $xstart$ and $xmid$. Thus the new $xstart$ is 17.44 and the new $xend$ is 17.47.

Iteration #8:

$$xstart = 17.44, \; xend = 17.47, \; xmid = \frac{xstart + xend}{2} = 17.455;$$

$$f(xstart)f(xmid) = -1.5821 \times 10^{-4}, \; f(xmid)f(xend) = 2.9199 \times 10^{-4}$$

The root must lie between $xstart$ and $xmid$. Thus the new $xstart$ is 17.44 and the new $xend$ is 17.455.

Iteration #9:

$$xstart = 17.44, \; xend = 17.455, \; xmid = \frac{xstart + xend}{2} = 17.447;$$

$$f(xstart)f(xmid) = 1.0756 \times 10^{-4}, \; f(xmid)f(xend) = -4.5564 \times 10^{-5}$$

$$f(xstart) = 0.0193, \; f(xmid) = 5.5675 \times 10^{-3} \longleftarrow \text{ a check to see if this is small}$$

Since $f(xmid)$ is a very small quantity, it is reasonable to assume that the $xmid$ obtained in Iteration #9 is, in fact, the required root. The % error in this case is, then

$$error = \frac{17.447 - 17.455}{17.447} * 100 = -0.0459\%$$

Thus, the solution which has been obtained after 9 iterations is: $x = 17.447$.

MATLAB: BisectionMethod.m

Below is a Bisection Method MATLAB function. This function has inputs: a function f (which should be defined as an anonymous function), *xstart*, *xend*, and a tolerance value. It outputs the approximated root solution, the relative error and the number of iterations the method ran to converge to a solution within the given tolerance.

BisectionMethod.m

```
%Bisection Method
%Finds the roots of the function.
%Inputs:    f, function
%           xstart, starting point
%           xend, ending point
%           tol, tolerance of accuracy of solution
%Outputs:   r = root
%           rele = error
%           i = number of iterations


function [r, rele, i] = BisectionMethod(f,xstart,xend,tol)


format long
format compact

%Initialize e, xmidprev
e = 100;
xmidprev = 0;

%Set iteration counter
i=0;

%Check that f(xstart) and f(xend) have opposite sign.
if f(xstart)*f(xend) > 0
    error('Function has the same sign at both endpoints.')
end

%Bisection Method
%Runs while error is greater than the tolerance
while e > tol
    %Calculate the midpoint
    xmid = (xstart + xend)/2;

    %If root is xmid, solution is found, no error.
    if f(xmid) == 0
```

```
        e = 0;
        break
    end

    %Reassign xstart and xend according to method.
    if f(xstart)*f(xmid) < 0
        xend = xmid;
    else
        xstart = xmid;
    end

    %Calculate error to test against tolerance
    e = abs(xmid - xmidprev);

    %Reassign xmidprev
    xmidprev = xmid;

    %Increase counter
    i = i +1;
end

r = xmid;
rele = e/r*100;
```

Let us use our MATLAB function on Example 3.1. We will use the same function f, taking $xstart = 16$, $xend = 20$, and a tol = 0.01. Note, there will be some slight discrepancy between the solution we obtained in Example 3.1 because MATLAB will store more decimal places and round slightly differently. However, one can see that both methods produce roughly the same solution in the same number of iterations.

Example 3.1 (cont.) using BisectionMethod.m

```
f = @(x) 750.5/x.*(1 - exp(-0.1524*x)) - 40;
[x e i] = BisectionMethod(f,16,20,0.01)

x =
  17.445312500000000
e =
   0.044782803403493
i =
      9
```

3.4 The Regula Falsi or The False Position Method

The False Position method is similar to the Bisection method in that the size of the interval containing the root is reduced with every step of the iteration process until the root is found. The main difference is that while the interval size in the Bisection method is reduced by bisecting it in each step of the iteration, this reduction of interval size is achieved by a linear interpolation fitting the two end points. While the Bisection method is reliable, it is slower than the False Position method in achieving convergence.

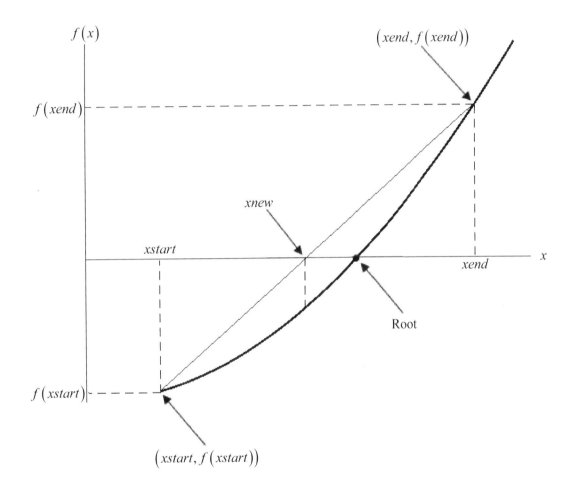

Fig. 3.2: Regula Falsi Method

The equation of a straight line connecting two points $(xstart, ystart)$ and $(xend, yend)$ is

$$y = yend + \frac{yend - ystart}{xend - xstart}(x - xend). \qquad (3.4)$$

Procedure for Finding Roots

1. Choose starting and ending points $xstart$ and $xend$ as in the Bisection Method.
2. Compute: $f(xstart)$ and $f(xend)$. Make sure that $f(xstart)$ times $f(xend)$ is still a negative product. If it is not, then there is no root between $xstart$ and $xend$.
3. The new end point $xnew$ is located by setting $y = 0$ in (3.4) and solving for x.

$$xnew = xend - \frac{xend - xstart}{yend - ystart} yend. \tag{3.5}$$

4. If $f(xstart) * f(xnew) < 0$, the root lies between $xstart$ and $xnew$. However, if $f(xnew) * f(xend) < 0$, the root lies between $xnew$ and $xend$.
5. Repeat the above procedure until convergence takes place.

A disadvantage of this method is that sometimes a root is approached from only one side and, thus, one end of the interval does not change at all in successive iterations. This is called *stagnation* of an end point. This is not desirable since it slows down the convergence process especially when the initial interval is very large or when the function is highly nonlinear. Examples 3.2 and 3.3 show the occurrence of *stagnation*.

Example 3.2. Obtain the required root for the function of Example 3.1 by the False Position method correct to four decimal places. The starting and ending points were 16 and 20 respectively.

$$f(x) = \frac{750.5}{x}(1 - e^{-0.15245x}) - 40$$

Iteration #1:

$$xstart = 16, \ xend = 20,$$
$$ystart = f(xstart) = 2.8146, \ yend = f(xend) = -4.2539;$$

$$xnew = xend - \frac{xend - xstart}{yend - ystart} yend = 17.5927;$$

$$f(xstart)f(xnew) = -0.73, \ f(xnew)f(xend) = 1.1033.$$

The root must lie between $xstart$ and $xnew$. Thus the new $xstart$ is 16 and the new $xend$ is 17.5927.

Iteration #2:

$$xstart = 16, \ xend = 17.5927,$$
$$ystart = f(xstart) = 2.8146, \ yend = f(xend) = -0.2593;$$

$$xnew = xend - \frac{xend - xstart}{yend - ystart} yend = 17.4584;$$

$$f(xstart)f(xnew) = -0.0404, \quad f(xnew)f(xend) = 3.7171 \times 10^{-3}.$$

The root must lie between $xstart$ and $xnew$. Thus the new $xstart$ is 16 and the new $xend$ is 17.4584.

Iteration #3:

$$xstart = 16, \quad xend = 17.4584,$$
$$ystart = f(xstart) = 2.8146, \quad yend = f(xend) = -0.0144;$$

$$xnew = xend - \frac{xend - xstart}{yend - ystart} yend = 17.451;$$

$$f(xstart)f(xnew) = -2.2312 \times 10^{-3}, \quad f(xnew)f(xend) = 1.143 \times 10^{-5}.$$

The root must lie between $xstart$ and $xnew$. Thus the new $xstart$ is 16 and the new $xend$ is 17.451.

Iteration #4:

$$xstart = 16, \quad xend = 17.451,$$
$$ystart = f(xstart) = 2.8146, \quad yend = f(xend) = -8.5304 \times 10^{-4};$$

$$xnew = xend - \frac{xend - xstart}{yend - ystart} yend = 17.4506;$$

$$f(xstart)f(xnew) = -1.3196 \times 10^{-4}, \quad f(xnew)f(xend) = 3.9995 \times 10^{-8}.$$

The root must lie between $xstart$ and $xnew$. Thus the new $xstart$ is 16 and the new $xend$ is 17.4506.

Iteration #5:

$$xstart = 16, \quad xend = 17.4506,$$
$$ystart = f(xstart) = 2.8146, \quad yend = f(xend) = -1.1956 \times 10^{-4};$$

$$xnew = xend - \frac{xend - xstart}{yend - ystart} yend = 17.4505;$$

$$f(xstart)f(xnew) = -1.8496 \times 10^{-5}, \quad f(xnew)f(xend) = 7.8568 \times 10^{-10}.$$

The root must lie between $xstart$ and $xnew$. Thus the new $xstart$ is 16 and the new $xend$ is 17.4505.

Iteration #6:

$$xstart = 16, \quad xend = 17.4505,$$
$$ystart = f(xstart) = 2.8146, \quad yend = f(xend) = 6.3811 \times 10^{-5};$$

$$xnew = xend - \frac{xend - xstart}{yend - ystart} yend = 17.4505;$$

$$f(xstart)f(xnew) = 9.8712 \times 10^{-6}, \; f(xnew)f(xend) = 2.238 \times 10^{-10};$$

$$f(xnew) = 3.5072 \times 10^{-6}$$

The above process indicates that in this case, the root is being approached only from the side of the original starting point and therefore stagnation has occurred. Since the $xnew$ computed in the sixth iteration is the same as the one in the fifth, and $f(xnew)$ is a very small quantity, it is reasonable to say that the $xnew$ (=17.4505) computed above is, in fact, the required root.

Example 3.3. Obtain a root of $f(x)$ by the False Position method in the range of $0 < x < 10$ correct to three decimal places.

$$f(x) = x^3 + 9x - 200$$

Iteration #1:

$$xstart = 0, \; xend = 10, \; ystart = f(xstart) = -200, \; yend = f(xend) = 890;$$

$$xnew = xend - \frac{xend - xstart}{yend - ystart} yend = 1.8349;$$

$$f(xstart)f(xnew) = 3.5462 \times 10^4, \; f(xnew)f(xend) = -1.578 \times 10^5.$$

The root must lie between $xnew$ and $xend$. Thus the new $xstart$ is 1.835 and the new $xend$ is 10.

Iteration #2:

$$xstart = 1.835, \; xend = 10,$$
$$ystart = f(xstart) = -177.3061, \; yend = f(xend) = 890;$$

$$xnew = xend - \frac{xend - xstart}{yend - ystart} yend = 3.1914;$$

$$f(xstart)f(xnew) = 2.4605 \times 10^4, \; f(xnew)f(xend) = -1.2351 \times 10^5.$$

The root must lie between $xnew$ and $xend$. Thus the new $xstart$ is 3.191 and the new $xend$ is 10.

Iteration #3:

$$xstart = 3.191, \; xend = 10,$$
$$ystart = f(xstart) = -138.7887, \; yend = f(xend) = 890;$$

$$xnew = xend - \frac{xend - xstart}{yend - ystart}yend = 4.1096;$$

$$f(xstart)f(xnew) = 1.2992 \times 10^4, \ f(xnew)f(xend) = -8.3312 \times 10^4.$$

The root must lie between *xnew* and *xend*. Thus the new *xstart* is 4.11 and the new *xend* is 10.

Iteration #4:

$$xstart = 4.11, \ xend = 10,$$
$$ystart = f(xstart) = -93.5835, \ yend = f(xend) = 890;$$

$$xnew = xend - \frac{xend - xstart}{yend - ystart}yend = 4.6704;$$

$$f(xstart)f(xnew) = 5.2493 \times 10^4, \ f(xnew)f(xend) = -4.9922 \times 10^4.$$

The root must lie between *xnew* and *xend*. Thus the new *xstart* is 4.67 and the new *xend* is 10.

Iteration #5:

$$xstart = 4.67, \ xend = 10,$$
$$ystart = f(xstart) = -56.1224, \ yend = f(xend) = 890;$$

$$xnew = xend - \frac{xend - xstart}{yend - ystart}yend = 4.9862;$$

$$f(xstart)f(xnew) = 1.7487 \times 10^3, \ f(xnew)f(xend) = -2.7732 \times 10^4.$$

The root must lie between *xnew* and *xend*. Thus the new *xstart* is 4.986 and the new *xend* is 10.

Iteration #6:

$$xstart = 4.986, \ xend = 10,$$
$$ystart = f(xstart) = -31.1731, \ yend = f(xend) = 890;$$

$$xnew = xend - \frac{xend - xstart}{yend - ystart}yend = 5.1557;$$

$$f(xstart)f(xnew) = 516.0963, \ f(xnew)f(xend) = -1.4735 \times 10^4.$$

The root must lie between *xnew* and *xend*. Thus the new *xstart* is 5.156 and the new *xend* is 10.

Iteration #7:

$$xstart = 5.156, \ xend = 10,$$
$$ystart = f(xstart) = -16.5272, \ yend = f(xend) = 890;$$

$$xnew = xend - \frac{xend - xstart}{yend - ystart} yend = 5.2443;$$

$$f(xstart)f(xnew) = 141.6022, \ f(xnew)f(xend) = -7.6254 \times 10^3.$$

The root must lie between $xnew$ and $xend$. Thus the new $xstart$ is 5.244 and the new $xend$ is 10.

Iteration #8:

$$xstart = 5.244, \ xend = 10,$$
$$ystart = f(xstart) = -8.5964, \ yend = f(xend) = 890;$$

$$xnew = xend - \frac{xend - xstart}{yend - ystart} yend = 5.2895;$$

$$f(xstart)f(xnew) = 37.8307, \ f(xnew)f(xend) = -3.9167 \times 10^3.$$

The root must lie between $xnew$ and $xend$. Thus the new $xstart$ is 5.290 and the new $xend$ is 10.

Iteration #9:

$$xstart = 5.290, \ xend = 10,$$
$$ystart = f(xstart) = -4.3541, \ yend = f(xend) = 890;$$

$$xnew = xend - \frac{xend - xstart}{yend - ystart} yend = 5.3129;$$

$$f(xstart)f(xnew) = 9.6414, \ f(xnew)f(xend) = -1.9707 \times 10^3.$$

The root must lie between $xnew$ and $xend$. Thus the new $xstart$ is 5.313 and the new $xend$ is 10.

Iteration #10:

$$xstart = 5.313, \ xend = 10,$$
$$ystart = f(xstart) = -2.2078, \ yend = f(xend) = 890;$$

$$xnew = xend - \frac{xend - xstart}{yend - ystart} yend = 5.3246;$$

$$f(xstart)f(xnew) = 2.4707, \ f(xnew)f(xend) = -995.9944.$$

The root must lie between *xnew* and *xend*. Thus the new *xstart* is 5.325 and the new *xend* is 10.

Iteration #11:

$$xstart = 5.325, \ xend = 10,$$

$$ystart = f(xstart) = -1.0813, \ yend = f(xend) = 890;$$

$$xnew = xend - \frac{xend - xstart}{yend - ystart} yend = 5.3307;$$

$$f(xstart)f(xnew) = 0.5916, \ f(xnew)f(xend) = -486.9595.$$

The root must lie between *xnew* and *xend*. Thus the new *xstart* is 5.331 and the new *xend* is 10.

Iteration #12:

$$xstart = 5.331, \ xend = 10,$$

$$ystart = f(xstart) = -0.5163, \ yend = f(xend) = 890;$$

$$xnew = xend - \frac{xend - xstart}{yend - ystart} yend = 5.3337;$$

$$f(xstart)f(xnew) = 0.1348, \ f(xnew)f(xend) = -232.3231.$$

The root must lie between *xnew* and *xend*. Thus the new *xstart* is 5.334 and the new *xend* is 10.

Iteration #13:

$$xstart = 5.334, \ xend = 10,$$

$$ystart = f(xstart) = -0.2334, \ yend = f(xend) = 890;$$

$$xnew = xend - \frac{xend - xstart}{yend - ystart} yend = 5.3352;$$

$$f(xstart)f(xnew) = 0.0275, \ f(xnew)f(xend) = -104.9753.$$

The root must lie between *xnew* and *xend*. Thus the new *xstart* is 5.335 and the new *xend* is 10.

Iteration #14:

$$xstart = 5.335, \ xend = 10,$$

$$ystart = f(xstart) = -0.139, \ yend = f(xend) = 890;$$

$$xnew = xend - \frac{xend - xstart}{yend - ystart}yend = 5.3357;$$

$$f(xstart)f(xnew) = 9.7667 \times 10^{-2}, \ f(xnew)f(xend) = -65.5217.$$

The root must lie between *xnew* and *xend*. Thus the new *xstart* is 5.336 and the new *xend* is 10.

Iteration #15:

$$xstart = 5.336, \ xend = 10,$$

$$ystart = f(xstart) = -0.0446, \ yend = f(xend) = 890;$$

$$xnew = xend - \frac{xend - xstart}{yend - ystart}yend = 5.3362;$$

$$f(xstart)f(xnew) = 1.0062 \times 10^{-3}, \ f(xnew)f(xend) = -20.0659;$$

$$f(xnew) = -0.0225.$$

The above process indicates that in this case, stagnation occurs as well, but the root is being approached only from the side of the original ending point. Since the *xnew* computed in the fifteenth iteration is about the same as the one in the fourteenth, it is reasonable to say that the *xnew* (=5.336) computed above is, in fact, the required root.

MATLAB: RegulaFalsiMethod.m

Below is a Regula Falsi Method MATLAB function. This function has inputs: a function *f* (which should be defined as an anonymous function), *xstart*, *xend*, and a tolerance value. It outputs the approximated root solution and the number of iterations the method ran to converge to a solution within the given tolerance.

RegulaFalsiMethod.m

```
%Regula Falsi Method
%Finds the roots of the function.
%Inputs:    f, function
%           xstart, starting point
%           xend, ending point
%           tol, tolerance of accuracy of solution
%Outputs:   r = root
%           i = number of iterations

function [r, i] = RegulaFalsiMethod(f,xstart,xend,tol)

format long
format compact
```

```
%Initialize res (value of f at approximation)
res = 100;

%Set iteration counter
i=0;

%Check that f(xstart) and f(xend) have opposite sign.
if f(xstart)*f(xend) > 0.0
    error('Function has same sign at both endpoints.')
end

%Regula Falsi Method
%Runs while res is greater than the tolerance
while res > tol
    xnew = xend - (xend - xstart)/(f(xend)-f(xstart))*f(xend
        );

    %If root is xnew, solution is found, no res.
    if f(xnew) == 0.0
        res = 0;
        break
    end

    %Reassign xstart and xend according to method.
    if f(xstart)*f(xnew) < 0
        xend = xnew ;
    else
        xstart = xnew;
    end

    %Calculate res
    res = abs(f(xnew));

    %Increase counter
    i = i + 1;
end

r = xnew;
```

Using a higher tolerance (10^{-6}), we can obtain similar results as given by the iterations of Example 3.2. We will use the same function f, taking $xstart = 16$ and $xend = 20$.

Example 3.2 (cont.) using RegulaFalsiMethod.m

```
f = @(x) 750.5/x.*(1 - exp(-0.1524*x)) - 40;
[x i] = RegulaFalsiMethod(f,16,20,10^(-6))

x =
   17.449103088773008
i =
       6
```

For sake of completeness, let us use our MATLAB function on Example 3.3 and observe that our program still produces the proper result even when stagnation occurs. We will use the same function f, taking $xstart = 0$, $xend = 10$, and a tol = 0.01.

Example 3.3 (cont.) using RegulaFalsiMethod.m

```
f = @(x) x.^3 + 9*x - 200;
[x i] = RegulaFalsiMethod(f,0,10,0.01)

x =
    5.336371638953779
i =
      17
```

3.5 Newton-Raphson Method

This is the most widely used iterative method for locating roots. In this method, an initial approximation of the root must be assumed, and calculations are started with a "*good initial guess*". If this initial guess is not a good one, then divergence may occur.

By starting with an approximation of the root value , x_i, and constructing a tangent to the function curve at x_i, an improved guess x_{i+1} can be determined as shown in Figure 3.3. From Figure 3.3, the slope of the function $f(x)$ at x_i can be seen to be

$$f'(x_i) = \frac{-f(x_i)}{x_{i+1} - x_i} \qquad (3.6)$$

which gives the new improved value of the guess

$$x_{i+1} = x_i - \frac{f(x_i)}{f'(x_i)} = g(x_i) \qquad (3.7)$$

where $f'(x_i)$ is the slope of the function at x_i.

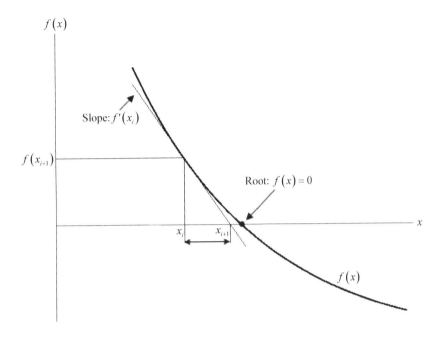

Fig. 3.3: Newton-Raphson method

Procedure for Finding Roots

1. Make a good initial guess. Call it *xold*.
2. Improve the guess using

$$xnew = xold - \frac{f(xold)}{f'(xold)} = g(xold). \qquad (3.8)$$

3. Keep improving the guess using (3.8).
4. Solution is done when a new improved value *xnew* is almost equal to the previous value *xold*.

Advantages and Disadvantages of the Method

While the Newton-Raphson method is faster than the Bisection method, is applicable to the complex domain, and can be extended to simultaneous nonlinear equations, it may not converge in some situations. The solution may oscillate about a local maximum or minimum and, if an initial estimate is chosen such that the derivative becomes zero at some point in the iteration process, then a division by zero takes place and convergence will never occur. Although convergence will occur quite rapidly if the initial estimate is sufficiently close to the root, it is possible for it to be slow when it is far from the root. Also, if the roots are *complex*, they will never be generated with *real* initial guesses.

A worthwhile feature of the Newton-Raphson method is that the numerical process will correct itself automatically for minor errors. Thus, any errors that are made in computing the *next* guess will simply generate a different point for drawing the tangent line and will not have any effect on the final answer.

Convergence Criterion for the Newton-Raphson Method

It can be mathematically shown that in order for the Newton-Raphson method to converge to a real root, the absolute value of the derivative of $g(x_i)$ of (3.7) must always be less than 1, that is,

$$|g'(x_i)| < 1.$$

This condition must be satisfied if convergence is to be attained. However, in some cases, it may not hold for the initial guess.

Example 3.4. Using the Newton-Raphson method, solve $f(x) = x^3 - 4.2x - 8.5 = 0$ for a root between 2 and 3.

Let us first draw a graph of the function in the given range.

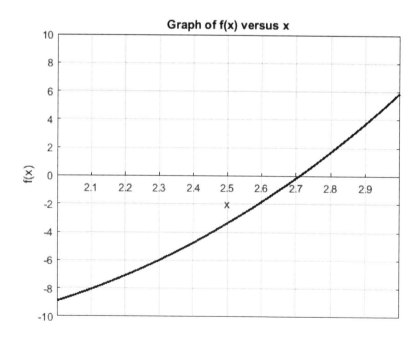

The derivative of the given function is $f'(x) = 3x^2 - 4.2$ and thus

$$f''(x) = 6x, \; g(x) = x - \frac{f(x)}{f'(x)},$$

$$g'(x) = 1 - \frac{[f'(x)]^2 - f(x)f''(x)}{[f'(x)]^2} = \frac{f(x)f''(x)}{[f'(x)]^2}$$

where $f''(x)$ is the second derivative of $f(x)$ and $g'(x)$ is the derivative of $g(x)$. Start with an initial estimate of 2.5.

Iteration #1: $xold = 2.5$, $xnew = g(xold) = 2.732$, $|g'(xnew)| = 0.0206$

Iteration #2: $xold = xnew$, $xnew = g(xold) = 2.7091$, $|g'(xnew)| = 2.1887 \times 10^{-4}$

Iteration #3: $xold = xnew$, $xnew = g(xold) = 2.7088$, $|g'(xnew)| = 2.3959 \times 10^{-8}$

Iteration #4: $xold = xnew$, $xnew = g(xold) = 2.7088$, $|g'(xnew)| = 0$

Clearly, the root is the converged value 2.7088, and convergence has been established with the absolute value of the slope of $g(x)$ being less than 1 in all the iterations.

Example 3.5. Using the Newton-Raphson method, solve $f(x) = x^3 + 7x^2 + 19x + 13 = 0$ for all roots, real, as well as complex.

Let us first draw a graph of the function.

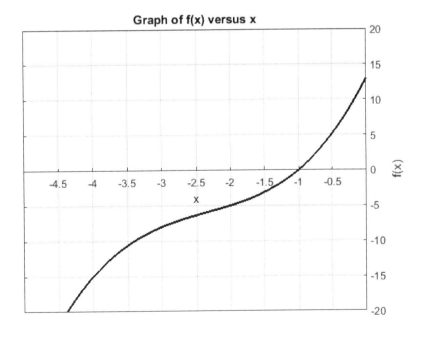

This suggests that there is a real root between 0 and -2.5. The derivative of the given function is $f'(x) = 3x^2 + 14x + 19$ with

$$f''(x) = 6x + 14, \ g(x) = x - \frac{f(x)}{f'(x)}, \ g'(x) = \frac{f(x)f''(x)}{[f'(x)]^2}$$

where $f''(x)$ is the second derivative of $f(x)$ and $g'(x)$ is the derivative of $g(x)$. Let us start with an initial estimate of -2.5 in an attempt to find the real root.

<u>Iteration #1</u>: $xold = -2.5, \ xnew = g(xold) = -0.1818, \ |g'(xnew)| = 0.0389$

<u>Iteration #2</u>: $xold = xnew, \ xnew = g(xold) = -0.7721, \ |g'(xnew)| = 0.095$

<u>Iteration #3</u>: $xold = xnew, \ xnew = g(xold) = -0.9768, \ |g'(xnew)| = 0.0164$

<u>Iteration #4</u>: $xold = xnew, \ xnew = g(xold) = -0.9997, \ |g'(xnew)| = 1.9933 \times 10^{-4}$

<u>Iteration #5</u>: $xold = xnew, \ xnew = g(xold) = -1, \ |g'(xnew)| = 2.6521 \times 10^{-8}$

<u>Iteration #6</u>: $xold = xnew, \ xnew = g(xold) = -1, \ |g'(xnew)| = 0$

From the above calculations, it is clear that the real root is the converged value of -1.

Let us now determine the complex roots by starting with an initial estimate of $-4 + i$.

<u>Iteration #1</u>: $xold = -4 + i, \ xnew = g(xold) = -2.9024 + 1.122i$

<u>Iteration #2</u>: $xold = xnew, \ xnew = g(xold) = -2.2579 + 2.5753i$

<u>Iteration #3</u>: $xold = xnew, \ xnew = g(xold) = -2.636 + 1.9589i$

<u>Iteration #4</u>: $xold = xnew, \ xnew = g(xold) = -3.0346 + 1.9196i$

<u>Iteration #5</u>: $xold = xnew, \ xnew = g(xold) = -2.9957 + 2.001i$

<u>Iteration #6</u>: $xold = xnew, \ xnew = g(xold) = -3 + 2i$

<u>Iteration #7</u>: $xold = xnew, \ xnew = g(xold) = -3 + 2i \leftarrow$ Converged

Clearly, if we had started with an initial estimate of $-4 - i$, we would have obtained the complex conjugate of the above complex root, as demonstrated below. However, there is no need to do this every time, since a complex root will always have a complex conjugate associated with it.

Iteration #1: $xold = -4 - i$, $xnew = g(xold) = -3 + 2i$

Iteration #2: $xold = xnew$, $xnew = g(xold) = -2.2579 - 2.5753i$

Iteration #3: $xold = xnew$, $xnew = g(xold) = -2.636 - 1.9589i$

Iteration #4: $xold = xnew$, $xnew = g(xold) = -3.0346 - 1.9196i$

Iteration #5: $xold = xnew$, $xnew = g(xold) = -2.9957 - 2.001i$

Iteration #6: $xold = xnew$, $xnew = g(xold) = -3 - 2i$

Iteration #7: $xold = xnew$, $xnew = g(xold) = -3 - 2i \leftarrow$ Converged

MATLAB: NewtonRaphson.m

Below is a Newton Raphson Method MATLAB function. This function has inputs: a function f (which should be defined as an anonymous function), $f1$ (the first derivative of f, also defined as an anonymous function), $xold$ (an initial guess), and a tolerance value. It outputs the approximated root solution and the number of iterations the method ran to converge to a solution within the given tolerance.

NewtonRaphsonMethod.m

```
%Newton Raphson Method
%Finds the roots of the function.
%Inputs:    f, function
%           f1, first derivative of f
%           xold, initial guess
%           tol, tolerance of accuracy of solution
%Outputs:   r = root
%           i = number of iterations
function [r, i] = NewtonRaphsonMethod(f,f1,xold,tol)

format long
format compact

%Initialize res (value of f at approximation)
res = 100;

%Set iteration counter
i=0;

%Newton Raphson Method
```

```
%Runs while res is greater than the tolerance OR until 1000
   iterations have
%been completed
while res > tol & i < 1000
    xnew = xold - f(xold)/f1(xold);

    %If root is xnew, solution is found, no res.
    if f(xnew) == 0.0
        res = 0;
        break
    end

    %Calculate res
    res = abs(f(xnew));

    %Reassign xold
    xold = xnew;

    %Increase counter
    i = i + 1;
end

r = xnew;
```

Let us use our MATLAB function on Example 3.4. We will use the same function f, f', with $xold = 2.5$, and a tol $= 10^{-6}$.

Example 3.4 (cont.) using NewtonRaphsonMethod.m

```
f = @(x) x.^3 - 4.2*x - 8.5;
f1 = @(x) 3*x.^2 - 4.2;
[r, i] = NewtonRaphsonMethod(f,f1,2.5,10^(-6))

r =
   2.708849206357658
i =
     4
```

3.6 Use of **MATLAB's** *fzero* **and** *roots* **Functions**

Use of *fzero*

The function $x = fzero(f, x0)$ returns a point x where $f(x) = 0$. The value $x0$ represents a guess value for the root.

Let us find the root of the function in Example 3.4.

Example 3.4 (cont.)

```
%Define the polynomial f(x) = x^3 - 4.2x - 8.5 as a function
    in MATLAB
f = @(x)x.^3 - 4.2*x - 8.5;

% %Initial guess
x0 = 2.5;

%Calculate the root using 'fzero'
x = fzero(f,x0)
x =
   2.708849180098042
```

Use of *roots*

The function $r = roots(p)$ returns all roots of a polynomial p, represented by its coefficients in a column vector, at the same time. It does not require an initial guess. The procedure will be clear from the following example.

Let us find the root of the function in Example 3.4.

Example 3.4 (cont.)

```
%Define the polynomial f(x) = x^3 - 4.2x - 8.5 as a vector
p = [1 0 -4.2 -8.5];

%Calculate the roots using 'roots'
r = roots(p)
r =
   2.7088 + 0.0000i
  -1.3544 + 1.1417i
  -1.3544 - 1.1417i
```

3.7 Secant Method

The Secant method is very similar to the Newton-Raphson method. The one difference is that while the derivative $f'(x)$ is evaluated analytically in the Newton-Raphson method, it is determined numerically in the Secant method.

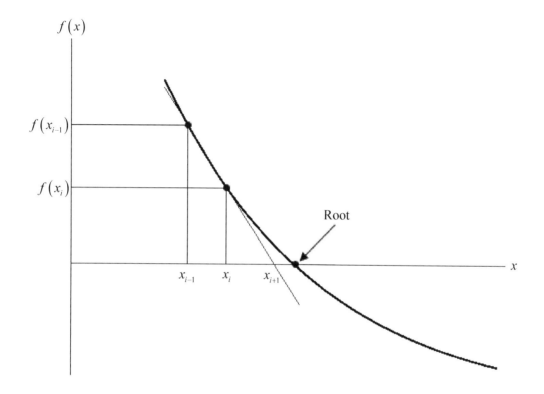

Fig. 3.4: Secant Method

From Figure 3.4, it is clear that an approximation for the slope of the given function $f(x)$ at x_i can be written as

$$f'(x_i) = \frac{-(f(x_{i-1}) - f(x_i))}{x_i - x_{i-1}}. \tag{3.9}$$

By the Newton-Raphson method, a new improved guess of the root is generated using (3.7), which is

$$x_{i+1} = x_i - \frac{f(x_i)}{f'(x_i)}. \tag{3.10}$$

Combining (3.9) and (3.10) yields the equation used in the Secant method, which is

$$x_{i+1} = x_i - \frac{f(x_i)(x_{i-1} - x_i)}{f(x_{i-1}) - f(x_i)}. \tag{3.11}$$

Note that the format of (3.11) does utilize the derivative but computes it numerically rather than analytically. However, two initial estimates x_{i-1} and x_i of the solution will be required to start the iteration process as can be seen from (3.11).

Procedure for Finding Roots

1. Make initial estimates x_0 and x_1.
2. With $i = 1$, improve the guess x_2 using (3.11), which is

$$x_{i+1} = x_i - \frac{f(x_i)(x_{i-1} - x_i)}{f(x_{i-1}) - f(x_i)}.$$

3. Continue obtaining improved estimates $x_3, x_4, \ldots$ using the above equation.
4. Solution is done when a new improved value x_{i+1} is almost equal to the previous value x_i.

Advantages and Disadvantages of the Secant Method

The Secant Method has a definite advantage when the derivative of the given function is difficult or time-consuming to evaluate analytically. Among the disadvantages are convergence to an unintended root at times, and divergence from the root if the initial guesses are bad. Also, if $f(x)$ is far from linear near the root, the iterations may start to yield points far away from the actual root.

MATLAB: SecantMethod.m

A look at the Secant Method suggests use of a recursive formula, so let us go right to the MATLAB code. Below is a Secant Method MATLAB function. This function has inputs: a function f (which should be defined as an anonymous function), $x0$ and $x1$ (initial guesses), and a tolerance value. It outputs the approximated root solution and the number of iterations the method ran to converge to a solution within the given tolerance.

SecantMethod.m

```
%Secant Method
%Finds the roots of the function.
%Inputs:    f, function
%           x0 and x1, initial guesses
%           tol, tolerance of accuracy of solution
%Outputs:   r = root
%           i = number of iterations

function [r, i] = SecantMethod(f,x0,x1,tol)

format long
```

```
format compact

%Set iteration counter
i=0;

%Secant Method
%Runs while the difference between approximations is greater
    than the
%tolerance OR until 1000 iterations have
%been completed
while abs(x1 - x0) > tol & i < 1000
    x = x1 - f(x1)*(x1-x0)/(f(x1) - f(x0))
    %Note, by not adding a semicolon after this line, the
        program will
    %print out the approximation at each step, hence we can
        see the
    %progress towards convergence.

    x0 = x1;
    x1 = x;

    %Increase counter
    i = i + 1;
end

r = x;
```

Example 3.6. Obtain a real root of $f(x) = 1.15x^3 + 1.2x^2 - 3.5x - 3.12$ between 0 and 10 by the Secant Method.

We first draw a graph of the given function to see approximately where a real root lies in the range given.

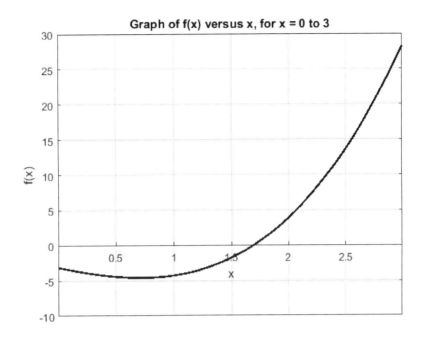

From the plot, it appears like the root lies between 1 and 2. We will, therefore, choose x_0 to be 1 and x_1 to be 2. We will choose a tolerance of 0.001.

```
f = @(x) 1.15*x.^3 + 1.2*x.^2 - 3.5*x - 3.12;
[r, i] = SecantMethod(f,1,2,0.001)

x =
   1.523926380368098
x =
   1.662739103765339
x =
   1.699646956582786
x =
   1.695347471102793
x =
   1.695441021038149
r =
   1.695441021038149
i =
     5
```

For comparison, let us solve the problem by Newton Raphson and compare answers.

```
f = @(x) 1.15*x.^3 + 1.2*x.^2 - 3.5*x - 3.12;
f1 = @(x) 3.45*x.^2 + 2.4*x - 3.5;
[r, i] = NewtonRaphsonMethod(f,f1,2,0.001)


r =
     1.695442702971454
i =
       3
```

Let us verify the above root using the *roots* function.

```
f = [1.15 1.2 -3.5 -3.12];
r = roots(f)


r =
     1.695441285720710
    -1.894074921748306
    -0.844844624841969
```

Example 3.7. Obtain all roots, real as well as complex, of the function $f(x) = x^3 + 7x^3 + 19x + 13$ of Example 3.5 by the Secant method.
We choose x_0 to be 1 and x_1 to be 2. We will choose a tolerance of 0.001.

```
f = @(x) x.^3 + 7*x.^2 + 19*x + 13;
[r, i] = SecantMethod(f,1,2,10^(-6))


x =
     0.149936170212766
x =
    -0.267833331366602
x =
    -0.728497001901068
x =
    -0.922433313460394
x =
    -0.990356012208628
x =
    -0.999634088500069
x =
    -0.999998239991578
x =
```

```
  -0.999999999678026
x =
  -1.000000000000000
r =
  -1.000000000000000
i =
      9
```

To find the complex roots, let us use the initial estimate of $x_0 = -4 + i$ and $x_1 = -4 + 2i$. Note, in MATLAB, the imaginary number $i = \sqrt{-1}$ is entered as 1i.

```
[r, i] = SecantMethod(f,-4+1i,-4+2*1i,.001)

x =
 -3.211618257261411 + 1.456431535269710i
x =
 -2.929181579299343 + 1.735276483693400i
x =
 -2.913631672724691 + 2.076644300429516i
x =
 -3.016722650591315 + 1.989867847889195i
x =
 -3.000934526735285 + 2.000830100567605i
x =
 -3.000008300910662 + 1.999989153547146i
x =
 -3.000000002567719 + 1.999999990812831i
r =
 -3.000000002567719 + 1.999999990812831i
i =
      7
```

Convergence has occurred with a complex root determined as $-3 + 2i$. Clearly, the other complex root will be the complex conjugate $-3 - 2i$.

Let us verify the above root using the *roots* function.

```
f = [1 7 19 13];
r = roots(f)

r =
 -2.99999999999999 + 1.999999999999999i
 -2.99999999999999 - 1.999999999999999i
 -1.000000000000000 + 0.000000000000000i
```

3.8 Method of Successive Substitution

This method encompasses all iteration schemes for finding roots of nonlinear functions. Applications of this technique can be found in the use of the Newton-Raphson method and the Secant method. Another name for this method is Fixed Point Iteration. In this method, the equation $f(x) = 0$ is written in the form $x = g(x)$. Thus, if x_1 is an assumed initial approximation to the root, then a successive approximation can be generated using

$$x_{i+1} = g(x_i). \tag{3.12}$$

Iterations continue until convergence to a root is indicated.

Advantages and Disadvantages of the Iteration Method

While the method provides a simple computational technique for finding roots of equations, offers flexibility in the selection of the function $g(x)$, and is easy to program, it is still possible for the solution to diverge with improper choices of the function. To ensure convergence of the iteration, the function selected must be such that the absolute value of its slope is always less than unity. Otherwise, divergence will occur.

Example 3.8. The function $y(x) = x^2 - 3x + e^x - 4$ has two roots, one positive and the other negative. Determine the negative root by the method of successive substitution.

Rewrite the given equation as follows:

$$y(x) = x^2 - 3x + e^x - 4 \implies g(x) = \frac{x^2 + e^x - 4}{3} = x \implies g'(x) = \frac{1}{3}(2x + e^x).$$

Let the initial guess be 0. Using the above recursive relationship, we find revised values of x until convergence.

Iteration #1: $x = 0$, $g(x) = -1$

Iteration #2: $x = g(x) = -1$, $g(x) = -0.8774$, $|g'(x)| = 0.544$

Iteration #3: $x = g(x) = -0.8774$, $g(x) = -0.9381$, $|g'(x)| = 0.4463$

Iteration #4: $x = g(x) = -0.9381$, $g(x) = -0.9095$, $|g'(x)| = 0.495$

Iteration #5: $x = g(x) = -0.9095$, $g(x) = -0.9233$, $|g'(x)| = 0.4721$

Iteration #6: $x = g(x) = -0.9233$, $g(x) = -0.9167$, $|g'(x)| = 0.4832$

<u>Iteration #7:</u> $x = g(x) = -0.9167$, $g(x) = -0.9199$, $|g'(x)| = 0.4779$

<u>Iteration #8:</u> $x = g(x) = -0.9199$, $g(x) = -0.9184$, $|g'(x)| = 0.4804$

<u>Iteration #9:</u> $x = g(x) = -0.9184$, $g(x) = -0.9191$, $|g'(x)| = 0.4792$

<u>Iteration #10:</u> $x = g(x) = -0.9191$, $g(x) = -0.9188$, $|g'(x)| = 0.4798$

<u>Iteration #11:</u> $x = g(x) = -0.9188$, $g(x) = -0.9189$, $|g'(x)| = 0.4795$

Note that convergence has taken place at $x = -0.919$ and the absolute value of the slope of the function selected is less than unity throughout the iteration process.

MATLAB: IterationMethod.m

Below is a Iteration Method MATLAB function. This function has inputs: a function g (obtained by rewriting the function $f(x)$ in the form $g(x) = x$, which should be defined as an anonymous function), $x0$ (an initial guess), and a tolerance value. It outputs the approximated root $x = g(x)$ for each iteration, then the final approximated solution and the number of iterations the method ran to converge to that solution within the given tolerance.

IterationMethod.m

```
%Iteration Method
%Finds the roots of the function.
%Inputs:    g, function derived from f(x) such that g(x) = x
       .
%           x, initial guess
%           tol, tolerance of accuracy of solution
%Outputs:   r = root
%           i = number of iterations

function [r, i] = IterationMethod(g,x0,tol)

format long
format compact

%Set iteration counter
i=0;

%Initiate xprev so loop will start
xprev = x0 + 100;

%Iteration Method
```

```
%Runs while the difference between approximations is greater
    than the
%tolerance OR until 1000 iterations have
%been completed
while abs(x0 - xprev) > tol & i < 1000
    x = g(x0)
    xprev = x0;
    x0 = x;


    %Increase counter
    i = i + 1;
end


r = x;
```

Let us use our MATLAB function on Example 3.8. We will use the same function g, with $x0 = 0$, and a tol = .001.

Example 3.8 (cont.) using IterationMethod.m

```
g = @(x) 1/3*(x.^2 + exp(x) - 4);
[r,i] = IterationMethod(g,0,.001)


x =
    -1
x =
  -0.877373519609519
x =
  -0.938113981433386
x =
  -0.909525631983027
x =
  -0.923349303606043
x =
  -0.916746516980061
x =
  -0.919919365368529
x =
  -0.918399061467942
x =
  -0.919128535782010
r =
  -0.919128535782010
i =
```

9

3.9 Multiple Roots and Difficulties in Computation

When a given function makes contact with the x-axis and has a slope of zero, multiple roots can occur as indicated in Figure 3.5. These roots are difficult to compute by the methods discussed in this chapter for the following reasons.

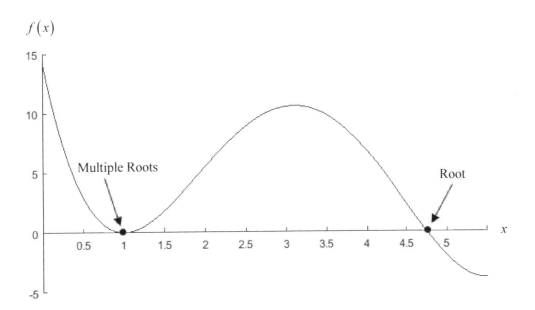

Fig. 3.5: Case of Multiple Roots

1. In the case of the Bisection method, the function does not change sign at the root.
2. In the case of the Newton-Raphson and Secant methods, the derivative at the multiple root is zero.

Because the Newton-Raphson and Secant methods in their original forms are methods that resort to linear convergence, they cannot be employed to generate multiple roots. The following modification to the original Newton-Raphson equation has been suggested [1].

$$x_{i+1} = x_i - m \frac{f(x_i)}{f'(x_i)}, \qquad (3.13)$$

where m is the multiplicity of the root (for example, $m = 2$ for a double root). However, this may not be a very practical route since it assumes prior knowledge about the multiplicity of a root.

Another approach also suggested [1] involves defining a new function $u(x)$

$$u(x) = \frac{f(x)}{f'(x)}, \tag{3.14}$$

which has the same roots as the original given function $f(x)$, and then resorting to the following alternative form of the Newton-Raphson formula

$$x_{i+1} = x_i - \frac{u(x_i)}{u'(x_i)}, \tag{3.15}$$

where $u'(x)$ represents the derivative of the new function $u(x)$. Substitution of (3.14) into the Newton-Raphson equation, which is now (3.15), yields the desired formula

$$x_{i+1} = x_i - \frac{f(x_i)f'(x_i)}{[f'(x_i)]^2 - f(x_i)f''(x_i)} \tag{3.16}$$

where f' and f'' represent first and second derivatives, respectively.

The modified formula for the Secant Method that will be suitable for the generation of multiple roots can be obtained by simply substituting $u(x)$ for $f(x)$ in the Secant method formula giving

$$x_{i+1} = x_i - \frac{u(x_i)(x_{i-1} - x_i)}{u(x_{i-1}) - u(x_i)}. \tag{3.17}$$

Example 3.9. The function $f(x) = x^3 - 4x^2 + 5x - 2 = (x-1)(x-1)(x-2)$ has a double root at 1 and a single root at 2, which we will verify using (3.16).

The first and second derivatives of the given function are $f'(x) = 3x^2 - 8x + 5$ and $f'' = 6x - 8$.

In order to determine the multiple root by the modified form of the Newton-Raphson formula, let us employ (3.16) and start with an initial estimate of 0.25.

<u>Iteration #1:</u> $xold = 0.25$, $xnew = xold - \frac{f(xold)f'(xold)}{[f'(xold)]^2 - f(xold)f''(xold)} = 1.0841$

<u>Iteration #2:</u> $xold = xnew$, $xnew = xold - \frac{f(xold)f'(xold)}{[f'(xold)]^2 - f(xold)f''(xold)} = 1.0042$

<u>Iteration #3:</u> $xold = xnew$, $xnew = xold - \frac{f(xold)f'(xold)}{[f'(xold)]^2 - f(xold)f''(xold)} = 1$

<u>Iteration #4:</u> $xold = xnew$, $xnew = xold - \frac{f(xold)f'(xold)}{[f'(xold)]^2 - f(xold)f''(xold)} = 1$

It is clear that the multiple root is the converged value of 1. To determine the single root, the above approach can still be employed, but with a different starting estimate, as shown below.

Iteration #1: $xold = 2.50$, $xnew = xold - \dfrac{f(xold)f'(xold)}{[f'(xold)]^2 - f(xold)f''(xold)} = 1.8182$

Iteration #2: $xold = xnew$, $xnew = xold - \dfrac{f(xold)f'(xold)}{[f'(xold)]^2 - f(xold)f''(xold)} = 1.9101$

Iteration #3: $xold = xnew$, $xnew = xold - \dfrac{f(xold)f'(xold)}{[f'(xold)]^2 - f(xold)f''(xold)} = 1.9809$

Iteration #4: $xold = xnew$, $xnew = xold - \dfrac{f(xold)f'(xold)}{[f'(xold)]^2 - f(xold)f''(xold)} = 1.9992$

Iteration #5: $xold = xnew$, $xnew = xold - \dfrac{f(xold)f'(xold)}{[f'(xold)]^2 - f(xold)f''(xold)} = 2$

Thus, the single root is the converged value of 2.

The following steps will now demonstrate the application of the modified Secant Method formula, which is (3.17), to the determination of the multiple root at 1. Let $u(x) = \frac{f(x)}{f'(x)}$. Taking $x_0 = 0.25$ and $x_1 = 0.26$, we proceed as follows.

Iteration #1: $x_2 = x_1 - \dfrac{u(x_1)(x_0 - x_1)}{u(x_0) - u(x_1)} = 1.0835$

Iteration #2: $x_3 = x_2 - \dfrac{u(x_2)(x_1 - x_2)}{u(x_1) - u(x_2)} = 0.9802$

Iteration #3: $x_4 = x_3 - \dfrac{u(x_3)(x_2 - x_3)}{u(x_2) - u(x_3)} = 0.9991$

Iteration #4: $x_5 = x_4 - \dfrac{u(x_4)(x_3 - x_4)}{u(x_3) - u(x_4)} = 1 \leftarrow$ Convergence at the double root $x = 1$

Application of the *roots* function confirms the correctness of the above analysis.

```
f = [1 -4 5 -2];
r = roots(f)

r =
   2.000000000000000 + 0.000000000000000i
   1.000000000000000 + 0.000000028326346i
   1.000000000000000 - 0.000000028326346i
```

3.10 Solution of Systems of Nonlinear Equations

The methods discussed so far deal with finding the roots of functions of only a single variable. In certain situations, it may be necessary to solve nonlinear equations in two or more variables. In these cases, iteration can be resorted to as presented in the following example.

Example 3.10. Solve: $1.1x^2 + 1.2xy = 10.5$, $y + 3.2xy^2 = 58.2$.

Let us put the given equations in the form

$$x = \frac{10.5 - 1.1x^2}{1.2y}, \ y = 58.2 - 3.2xy^2$$

and make the following initial guesses:

$$x = 1, \ y = 3.$$

Then,

$$x = \frac{10.5 - 1.1x^2}{1.2y} = 2.6111 \text{ and } y = 58.2 - 3.2xy^2 = -17.$$

A second iteration gives

$$x = \frac{10.5 - 1.1x^2}{1.2y} = -0.1471 \text{ and } y = 58.2 - 3.2xy^2 = 194.214.$$

Notice that the approach resorted to is diverging and will not yield a solution. Thus, the computations must be repeated with equations set up in a different format as shown below.

<u>Iteration #1:</u> $x = 1$, $y = 3$, $x = \sqrt{\frac{10.5-1.2xy}{1.1}} = 2.5045$,
$y = \sqrt{\frac{58.2-y}{3.2x}} = 2.6244$

<u>Iteration #2:</u> $x = 2.5045$, $y = 2.6244$, $x = \sqrt{\frac{10.5-1.2xy}{1.1}} = 1.5411$,
$y = \sqrt{\frac{58.2-y}{3.2x}} = 3.357$

<u>Iteration #3:</u> $x = 1.5411$, $y = 3.357$, $x = \sqrt{\frac{10.5-1.2xy}{1.1}} = 1.9753$,
$y = \sqrt{\frac{58.2-y}{3.2x}} = 2.9456$

<u>Iteration #4:</u> $x = 1.9753$, $y = 2.9456$, $x = \sqrt{\frac{10.5-1.2xy}{1.1}} = 1.7883$,
$y = \sqrt{\frac{58.2-y}{3.2x}} = 3.1073$

<u>Iteration #5:</u> $x = 1.7883$, $y = 3.1073$, $x = \sqrt{\frac{10.5-1.2xy}{1.1}} = 1.8664$,
$y = \sqrt{\frac{58.2-y}{3.2x}} = 3.0372$

<u>Iteration #6</u>: $x = 1.8664$, $y = 3.0372$, $x = \sqrt{\frac{10.5-1.2xy}{1.1}} = 1.8335$,
$y = \sqrt{\frac{58.2-y}{3.2x}} = 3.0663$

<u>Iteration #7</u>: $x = 1.8335$, $y = 3.0663$, $x = \sqrt{\frac{10.5-1.2xy}{1.1}} = 1.8473$,
$y = \sqrt{\frac{58.2-y}{3.2x}} = 3.054$

<u>Iteration #8</u>: $x = 1.8473$, $y = 3.054$, $x = \sqrt{\frac{10.5-1.2xy}{1.1}} = 1.8415$,
$y = \sqrt{\frac{58.2-y}{3.2x}} = 3.0591$

<u>Iteration #9</u>: $x = 1.8415$, $y = 3.0591$, $x = \sqrt{\frac{10.5-1.2xy}{1.1}} = 1.8439$,
$y = \sqrt{\frac{58.2-y}{3.2x}} = 3.057$

<u>Iteration #10</u>: $x = 1.8439$, $y = 3.057$, $x = \sqrt{\frac{10.5-1.2xy}{1.1}} = 1.8429$,
$y = \sqrt{\frac{58.2-y}{3.2x}} = 3.0579$

<u>Iteration #11</u>: $x = 1.8429$, $y = 3.0579$, $x = \sqrt{\frac{10.5-1.2xy}{1.1}} = 1.8433$, $y = \sqrt{\frac{58.2-y}{3.2x}} = 3.0575$

Notice that after ten iterations convergence has taken place yielding the solution as: $x = 1.843$ and $y = 3.058$. This example illustrates a very serious disadvantage associated with the successive substitution method which is the dependence of convergence on the format in which the equations are put and utilized in the iteration process. Also, even in situations where a converged solution can be attained, initial estimates that are fairly close to the true solution must be resorted to, because, otherwise, divergence may occur and a solution may never be obtained. The results of the iterative process are summarized in the table.

Iteration #	x	y
0	1.0	3.0
1	2.505	2.624
2	1.541	3.357
3	1.975	2.946
4	1.788	3.107
5	1.866	3.037
6	1.833	6.066
7	1.847	3.054
8	1.841	3.059
9	1.844	3.057
10	1.843	3.058
11	1.843	3.058

3.11 Solving Systems of Equations Using MATLAB's *fsolve* Function

MATLAB allows you to solve a nonlinear system of equations, of the form $F(x) = 0$, for x, a vector. The function requires a system of functions that are equated to 0 and a vector of initial guesses. The procedure will be clear from the following example.

Example 3.11. Using the *fsolve* function, solve

$$1.5x^2 + 2y^2 = 6.5, \; x + y = 2.75.$$

We will use the initial guesses: $x = 1$ and $y = 1$.

We first enter the equations to be solved as a single anonymous function in the form of a column vector. Notice that we use $x(1)$ for x $x(2)$ for y. Then, we use *fsolve*, calling our function and entering our initial guess, entered as a vector.

```
>> F = @(x) [1.5*x(1).^2 + 2*x(2).^2 - 6.5; x(1) + x(2) -
   2.75];
>> x = fsolve(F,[1,1])

Equation solved.

fsolve completed because the vector of function values is
   near zero
as measured by the default value of the function tolerance,
   and
the problem appears regular as measured by the gradient.

<stopping criteria details>

x =
    1.5000    1.25009
```

3.12 Applications in Root-Finding

The following are examples of situations where roots of nonlinear equations need to be evaluated.

3.12.1 Maximum Design Load for a Column

A steel pipe with an outside diameter of 10.70 inches and a wall thickness of 0.375 inches is to serve as a pin-ended column that is 22 feet long. It supports an eccentric load at an eccentricity of $e = 1.5$ inches from the column center-line. The maximum load that the column can carry with a factor of safety of 2.75 is to be determined. The modulus of elasticity E for steel is 30×10^6 psi and its yield strength, σ_{yld}, is 40,000 psi.

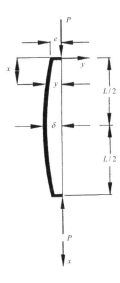

Fig. 3.6: Eccentrically Loaded Column

The equation for the stress level σ_{max} resulting from the application of the maximum load P_{max} is [2, 10]

$$\sigma_{max} = \frac{P_{max}}{A}\left(1 + \frac{ec}{K^2}sec\left(\sqrt{\frac{P_{max}}{AE}}\frac{L}{2K}\right)\right), \tag{3.18}$$

where A is the column cross-sectional area, e is the eccentricity at which the load is applied, as shown in Figure 3.6, c is the distance of the outermost fiber in the cross-section from the neutral axis, K is the radius of gyration, L is the column length and E is the modulus of elasticity. This relationship between σ_{max} and P_{max} is not linear and there is no proportionality between the applied load and the stress that is produced. Thus, it must be solved iteratively using trial and error. This is accomplished easily with MATLAB and the *fzero* function, as demonstrated below.

```
%Example 3.12.1 Maximum Design Load for a Column

sigyld = 40000;     %sigma_yld (psi)
```

```
E = 30*10^6;            %(psi)
FS = 2.75;
do = 10.70;             %(inches)
t = 0.375;              %(inches)
di = do - 2*t           %(inches)
e = 1.5;
L = 264;
c = do/2

I = pi/64*(do^4 - di^4) %(inches^4)
A = pi/4*(do^2 - di^2)   %(inches^2)

K = sqrt(I/A)            %(inches)

%With a factor of safety of 2.75, the maximum stress level that the column
%can have is:
sigmax = sigyld/FS %(psi)

%The corresponding maximum allowable load may be determined from (3.18).
g = @(Pmax)sqrt(Pmax/(E*A))*L/(2*K);
f = @(Pmax)sigmax - Pmax/A*(1 + e*c/K^2*sec(g(Pmax)));

%Guess
Pmax0 = 125000;         %(lbs)

%Use fsolve
x = fzero(f,Pmax0)

di =
   9.949999999999999
c =
   5.350000000000000
I =
    1.623057257480638e+02
A =
  12.163854055617978
K =
   3.652845637307988
sigmax =
    1.454545454545455e+04
x =
```

```
1.022062466435904e+05
```

Hence the maximum allowable load a column can carry is 1.0221×10^5.

3.12.2 Natural Frequency of Vibration of a Uniform Beam

For a uniform beam that is clamped at one end and free at the other, as shown in Figure 3.7, the natural frequencies of vibration [12] are given by the equation

$$1 + \cos(\beta')\cosh(\beta') = 0, \tag{3.19}$$

where

$$\beta' = \beta L \tag{3.20}$$

and

$$\beta = \left(\frac{\rho\omega^2}{EI}\right)^{1/4} \tag{3.21}$$

in which ρ is the mass per unit length of the beam, EI is the flexural rigidity or bending stiffness about the neutral axis, and ω refers to the natural frequencies in rad/sec.

Fig. 3.7: A Fixed-Free Beam

For a beam with a length of 20 feet, an EI value of 16×10^6 lb-in^2, and a weight per unit length of 0.03 lb/in, the natural frequencies may be determined as shown below.

```
%Example 3.12.2 Natural Frequencies of Vibration of a
   Uniform Beam

rhowt = 0.03;        %(lb/in)
rho = rhowt*12/32.2

EI = 16*10^6/144     %(lb-ft^2)
```

```
L = 20;                      %(ft)

%Define the function
f = @(betaprime)1 + cos(betaprime)*cosh(betaprime);

%Guess
betaprime0 = 1;

%Use fsolve
x = fzero(f,betaprime0)

beta = x/L

omega = sqrt(EI*beta^4/rho)

rho =
   0.011180124223602
EI =
    1.111111111111111e+05
x =
   1.875104068711961
beta =
   0.093755203435598
omega =
  27.710616741756805
```

We can rerun the program with a different initial guess to obtain a different root.

```
%Guess
betaprime0 = 5;

%Use fsolve
x = fzero(f,betaprime0)

beta = x/L

omega = sqrt(EI*beta^4/rho)

rho =
   0.011180124223602
EI =
    1.111111111111111e+05
x =
```

```
    4.694091132974175
beta =
    0.234704556648709
omega =
      1.736594707987196e+02
```

Similarly by making appropriate guesses, higher natural frequencies can be determined using the *fzero* function. Some of these are listed below.

Third natural frequency:	486.3	rad/sec
Fourth natural frequency:	952.8	rad/sec
Fifth natural frequency:	1575.1	rad/sec
Sixth natural frequency:	2353	rad/sec
Seventh natural frequency:	3286	rad/sec

3.12.3 Solving the Characteristic Equation in Control Systems Engineering

A characteristic equation is an algebraic equation that is formulated from the differential equation or equations of a control system [7]. Its solution, which often requires evaluation of the roots of a polynomial of degree higher than two, is crucial in determining system stability and assessing system transient response in terms of its time constant, natural frequencies, damping qualities, etc. An application involving the use of MATLAB's *roots* function in determining the roots of a characteristic polynomial of a control system is presented below.

For the unity-feedback system shown in Figure 3.8, the characteristic polynomial is

$$s^3 + 12s^2 + 20s + K = 0,$$

where K is a variable system parameter that can be selected based on the performance requirements that may be prescribed. For varying values of this parameter, the roots of the characteristic polynomial can be evaluated as shown below, and the system transient response and stability studied, following which, an appropriate range for K may be recommended.

For $K = 1$:

```
p = [1 12 20 1];
r = roots(p)


r =
  -10.0125
   -1.9359
   -0.0516
```

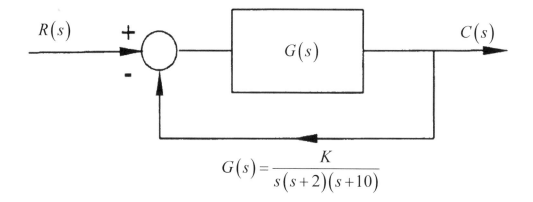

Fig. 3.8: Feedback Control System Block Diagram

Negative real roots indicate a stable system.

For $K = 10$:

```
p = [1 12 20 10];
r = roots(p)


r =
 -10.1216 + 0.0000i
  -0.9392 + 0.3255i
  -0.9392 - 0.3255i
```

Negative real parts of roots indicate a stable system.

For $K = 100$:

```
p = [1 12 20 100];
r = roots(p)


r =
 -11.0084 + 0.0000i
  -0.4958 + 2.9729i
  -0.4958 - 2.9729i
```

Negative real parts of roots indicate a stable system.

For $K = 400$:

```
p = [1 12 20 400];
r = roots(p)
```

```
r =
  -12.8628 + 0.0000i
    0.4314 + 5.5598i
    0.4314 - 5.5598i
```

Positive real parts of roots indicate an unstable system.

3.12.4 Horizontal Tension in a Uniform Cable

Flexible cables are often used in suspension bridges, transmission lines, telephone lines, mooring lines and many other applications. A cable hanging under its own weight takes the shape of a catenary in which the deflection y along the span is given by the following relationship [4]

$$y = \frac{H}{w}\left(\cosh\left(\frac{wx}{H}\right) - 1\right), \tag{3.22}$$

where x is the horizontal distance along the span as shown in Figure 3.9, H is the horizontal component of tension in the cable and w is the weight per unit length of the cable.

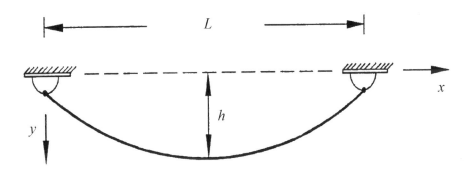

Fig. 3.9: Catenary Cable

The constant H is obtained by using the boundary condition that $y = h$ at $x = L/2$, which gives

$$h = \frac{H}{w}\left(\cosh\left(\frac{wL}{2H}\right) - 1\right). \tag{3.23}$$

Thus, the root of the following equation must be evaluated by using a method such as the Secant Method

$$h = g(H), \tag{3.24}$$

where

$$g(H) = \frac{H}{w}\left(\cosh\left(\frac{wL}{2H}\right) - 1\right). \tag{3.25}$$

For a cable with a span of $L = 22$ meters, a weight per unit length of $w = 5.5$ N/m and a maximum sag of $h = 6.5$ meters,

$$h = 6.5, \ w = 5.5, \ L = 22.$$

The intersection of the plot of $g(H)$ with $h = 6.5$ in Figure 3.10 suggests that $f(H)$ has a root at about $H = 50$ Newtons.

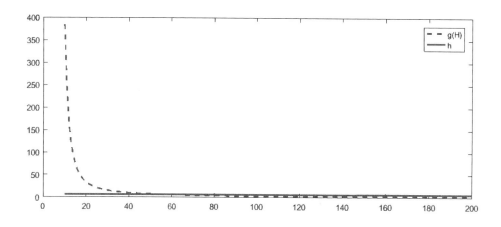

Fig. 3.10: Plot of $g(H)$

The use of the Secant Method, using the function given in Section 3.7 is shown below.

```
h = 6.5;
w = 5.5;
L = 22;
f = @(H)h - H/w.*(cosh(w*L/(2*H))-1);
[r,i] = SecantMethod(f,25,35,10^(-5))

x =
  41.184582430720575
x =
  49.010946896830369
x =
  53.826095355935706
x =
  55.905255067697958
```

```
x =
   56.287847432725556
x =
   56.310020586847820
x =
   56.310221715695654
x =
   56.310221815662366
r =
   56.310221815662366
i =
      8
```

MATLAB's *fzero* function can also be used to determine the root of $f(H)$.

```
h = 6.5;
w = 5.5;
L = 22;
f = @(H)h-H/w.*(cosh(w*L/(2*H))-1);
x = fzero(f,35)

x =
   56.310221815662807
```

By solving $f(H) = 0$, the horizontal tension in the cable has been found as $H = 56.31$N.

Problems

3.1. Generate a MATLAB script to obtain a root of the following polynomial lying in the range 1 to 3 by the Bisection Method using *BisectionMethod.m*

$$f(x) = x^3 - 3.45x^2 + 3.35x - 0.934.$$

Using MATLAB, draw a graph of the polynomial for the given range of x. Label it and give it a title. Verify your answer by using the *fzero* function. Also obtain all the roots of the polynomial with the *roots* function.

3.2. Estimate a root of the polynomial

$$x^3 - 3.5x^2 + 3.28x - 0.924$$

between $x = 2$ and $x = 3$ using the Bisection Method. Generate an answer that is good to three decimal places.

3.3. Estimate a root of the polynomial

$$x^3 - 6.1x^2 + 11.26x - 6.336$$

between $x = 1.5$ and $x = 2$ using the Bisection Method.

3.4. Generate a MATLAB script to obtain all roots of the following polynomial lying in the range -5.5 to 4.0 by the Newton-Raphson Method using *NewtonRahphson.m*.

$$f(x) = 1.1x^3 + 1.15x^2 - 17.1x + 15.2$$

Using MATLAB, draw a graph of the polynomial for the given range of x. Label it and give it a title. Verify your answers by using the *fzero* function. Also obtain all the roots of the polynomial with the *roots* function.

3.5. Generate a MATLAB script to obtain all roots of the following polynomial lying in the range -2.5 to 1.5 by the Newton-Raphson Method using *NewtonRaphson.m*.

$$f(x) = x^3 + 4.25x^2 - 4.05$$

Using MATLAB, draw a graph of the polynomial for the given range of x. Label it and give it a title. Verify your answers by using the *fzero* function. Also obtain all the roots of the polynomial with the *roots* function.

3.6. Estimate a root of the polynomial

$$x^3 - 2x^2 - 5x + 6$$

between $x = 2$ and $x = 4$ using the Newton-Raphson Method.

3.7. Using the Newton-Raphson method, estimate a real root of the function

$$f(x) = e^{-x} - x^3$$

between $x = 0$ and $x = 1$. Obtain an answer that is good to at least three decimal places.

3.8. Using the Newton-Raphson method, estimate a real root of the function

$$f(x) = x^3 - 5\cos(x) - 1$$

between $x = 1$ and $x = 2$. Obtain an answer that is good to at least three decimal places.

3.9. Using the Newton-Raphson method, estimate a real root of the function

$$f(x) = \cos(x) - x$$

between $x = 0$ and $x = 4$. Obtain an answer that is good to at least three decimal places.

3.10. Using the Newton-Raphson method, estimate a real root of the function

$$f(x) = e^{-x} - x^2$$

between $x = 0$ and $x = 1$. Obtain an answer that is correct to four decimal places.

3.11. Generate a MATLAB script to obtain all roots of the following polynomial lying in the range 0 to 1.0 by the Secant Method using *SecantMethod.m*.

$$f(x) = x^3 - 1.72x^2 + 0.85x - 0.110$$

Using MATLAB, draw a graph of the polynomial for the given range of x. Label it and give it a title. Verify your answers by using the *fzero* function. Also obtain all the roots of the polynomial with the *roots* function.

3.12. Generate a MATLAB script to obtain all roots of the following polynomial lying in the range 0 to 1.0 by the Secant Method using *SecantMethod.m*.

$$f(x) = x^4 - 3.05x^3 + 2.75x^2 + 0.43x - 0.45$$

Using MATLAB, draw a graph of the polynomial for the given range of x. Label it and give it a title. Verify your answers by using the *fzero* function. Also obtain all the roots of the polynomial with the *roots* function.

3.13. Using the Secant Method, estimate a root of the polynomial

$$x^3 + x^2 - 17x + 15$$

between $x = 1.5$ and $x = 4$. Start with initial estimates of 1.5 and 4.0.

3.14. Using the Secant Method, estimate a root of the polynomial

$$x^4 - 2x^3 - 15x^2 - 4x + 20$$

between $x = 2$ and $x = 6$. Start with initial estimates of 4.0 and 4.5.

3.15. Using the Secant Method, estimate a root of the function

$$f(x) = x^2 - \sin(x) - 1$$

between $x = 1$ and $x = 2$.

3.16. Using the Secant Method, estimate a root of the polynomial

$$f(x) = 5x^4 - 2x^3 - 25x^2 - 6x + 45$$

between $x = 1$ and $x = 2$. Generate an answer that is correct to four decimal places.

3.17. Using the Secant Method, estimate a root of the function

$$f(x) = 2\cos(x) - e^x$$

between $x = 0$ and $x = 1$. Generate an answer that is correct to three decimal places.

3.18. Using the Secant Method, estimate a root of the function

$$f(x) = e^{-x} - x^2$$

between $x = 0$ and $x = 1$. Generate an answer that is correct to three decimal places.

3.19. Using the Secant Method, estimate a root of the polynomial

$$f(x) = x^4 - 5x^3 - 40x^2 - 12x + 24$$

between $x = 0$ and $x = 2$. Generate an answer that is correct to three decimal places.

3.20. Generate a MATLAB script to obtain a root of the following polynomial lying in the range -10 to 10 by the method of Successive Substitution using *IterationMethod.m*.

$$f(x) = x^3 + 0.25x^2 - 0.75x - 0.350$$

Using MATLAB, draw a graph of the polynomial for the given range of x. Label it and give it a title. Notice what this plot suggests in terms of the interval where the roots may lie. Then, draw a second graph for a narrower range (-0.60 to 1.40). Start with an initial estimate of 0.9. Verify your answer by using the *fzero* function. Also obtain all the roots of the polynomial with the *roots* function.

3.21. Generate a MATLAB script to to obtain a root of the following polynomial lying in the range -5 to 25 by the method of Successive Substitution using *IterationMethod.m*.

$$f(x) = x^3 - 17.45x^2 - 82.89x - 84.50$$

Using MATLAB, draw a graph of the polynomial for the given range of x. Label it and give it a title. Start with a reasonable initial estimate. Verify your answer by using the *fzero* function. Also obtain all the roots of the polynomial with the *roots* function.

3.22. Obtain the solution of the following system of nonlinear equations by iteration.

$$e^x - 1.1y = 0 \text{ and } 1.1xy - e^{1.05x} = 0$$

Start with an initial estimate of $y = 2.2$.

3.23. Using the *fsolve* function of MATLAB, obtain the solution to the following system of equations.

$$3.25x - 1.01y + 2.1z = -3.72$$
$$2.12x + 3.15y - 2.2z = -18.25$$
$$-x + 2.22y + 4.15z = -6$$

3.24. The dynamic response of an underdamped second-order system, which is a common mathematical model in control system analysis, to a unit step function is given by [7]

$$c(t) = 1 - \frac{1}{\sqrt{1-\zeta^2}} e^{-\zeta\omega_n t} \cos\left(\omega_n \sqrt{1-\zeta^2}\, t - \phi\right),$$

where ζ is the system damping ratio, ω_n is the undamped natural frequency, and ϕ is

$$\phi = \arctan\left(\frac{\zeta}{\sqrt{1-\zeta^2}}\right).$$

A precise analytical relationship between the *damping ratio* and the *rise time*, which is the time required for the response to go from 10% of the final value to 90% (that is, from 0.1 to 0.9 in this case), cannot be determined. However, using MATLAB's *fzero* function, the *normalized rise time* which is ω_n times the *rise time*, can be found for a specified damping ratio ζ by solving for the values of $\omega_n t$ that yield $c(t) = 0.9$ and $c(t) = 0.1$. Subtracting these two values yields the *normalized rise time* for the value of ζ considered. Using a range of *damping ratios* from $0.1, 0.2, 0.3, \ldots, 0.9$, generate a MATLAB script to construct a table and plot depicting *normalized rise time* as a function of the *damping ratio*.

3.25. The frequency equation for the free undamped longitudinal vibration of a slender bar of length L and mass m with one end fixed and with the other end carrying a mass M is given by [13]

$$\beta \tan(\beta) = \alpha$$

where

$$\beta = \omega \frac{L}{c_0}, \quad c_0 = \sqrt{\frac{E}{\rho}}, \quad \alpha = \frac{m}{M},$$

in which E is Young's modulus for the material of the bar, ρ is the mass per unit volume and ω is the natural frequency.

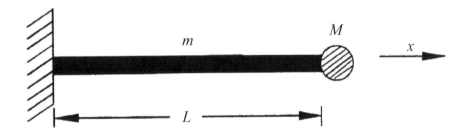

For a steel bar with mass ratio $\alpha = 0.70$, $E = 30 \times 10^6$ psi, $L = 98$ in., and $\rho = 7.35 \times 10^{-4}$ lb-sec^2/in^4, determine the first three natural frequencies with the help of a suitable MATLAB script.

3.26. For a uniform beam of length L with one end fixed and the other simply supported, the natural frequencies of transverse vibration are given by the relationship [13]

$$\tan(kL) = \tanh(kL),$$

where

$$k^2 = \omega\sqrt{\frac{\rho A}{EI}},$$

in which ω is the natural frequency, ρ is the mass density of the beam material, A is the area of cross section of the beam, E is Young's modulus, and I is the moment of inertia of the beam cross section.

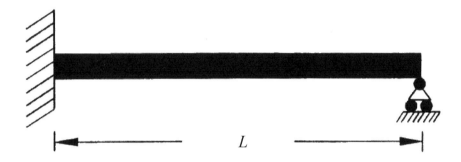

Generate a MATLAB script to determine the first three natural frequencies of a 36 in. long steel beam whose area of cross section A is 12.50 in^2, moment of inertia I is 12.75 in^4, and $\rho = 7.35 \times 10^{-4}$ lb-sec^2/in^4. E for steel is 30×10^6 psi.

Chapter 4
Matrices and Linear Algebra

4.1 Basic Matrix Operations

Basic matrix operations are addition, subtraction and multiplication. Determination of the inverse of a matrix is linked with the concepts of transpose, minor, cofactor and adjoint.

Addition and Subtraction:

Two matrices with the same number of rows and columns can be added by adding the corresponding elements. Similarly, subtraction is done by subtracting the corresponding elements.

Multiplication:

If the product of two matrices A and B is C, the element C_{ij} of C is obtained by multiplying the elements of the ith row of A by the elements of the jth column of B in accordance with

$$C_{ij} = \sum_k (a_{ik} b_{kj}) \qquad (4.1)$$

Transpose:
 The transpose of a matrix is one in which the rows and the columns are interchanged.

Minor:

The minor M_{ij} of the element a_{ij} is the determinant obtained by deleting the ith row and the jth column from the given determinant.

$$\text{If } A = \begin{pmatrix} 2 & 3 & 4 \\ 5 & 7 & 9 \\ 1 & 6 & 8 \end{pmatrix} \text{ then, } M_{12} = \left| \begin{pmatrix} 5 & 9 \\ 1 & 8 \end{pmatrix} \right|, \text{ that is, } M_{12} = 31.$$

Cofactor:
 The cofactor C_{ij} of the element a_{ij} is given by:

$$C_{ij} = (-1)^{i+j} M_{ij}.$$ (4.2)

For the above case, $C_{12} = (-1)^3(31)$, that is, $C_{12} = -31$.

Adjoint Matrix:

The adjoint of a square matrix is the transpose of the matrix of its cofactors.

Inverse of a Matrix:

The inverse A^{-1} of a matrix A must satisfy the relationship

$$AA^{-1} = I,$$ (4.3)

where I is the Identity or the Unit matrix which is a matrix with "1" along the diagonal and zero elsewhere. The inverse A^{-1} is calculated as follows

$$A^{-1} = \frac{adj(A)}{|A|},$$ (4.4)

where $adj(A)$ is the adjoint of A and $|A|$ is the determinant of the given matrix, which must be non-zero for the inverse to exist.

Example 4.1. Determine the inverse of the following matrix A:

$$A = \begin{pmatrix} 1 & 2 & 3 \\ 1 & 3 & 2 \\ 1 & 0 & 4 \end{pmatrix}.$$

The determinant of this matrix is $|A| = -1$.

The minors of A are

$$M_{11} = \left| \begin{pmatrix} 3 & 2 \\ 0 & 4 \end{pmatrix} \right|, \ M_{12} = \left| \begin{pmatrix} 1 & 2 \\ 1 & 4 \end{pmatrix} \right|, \ M_{13} = \left| \begin{pmatrix} 1 & 3 \\ 1 & 0 \end{pmatrix} \right|,$$

$$M_{21} = \left| \begin{pmatrix} 2 & 3 \\ 0 & 4 \end{pmatrix} \right|, \ M_{22} = \left| \begin{pmatrix} 1 & 3 \\ 1 & 4 \end{pmatrix} \right|, \ M_{23} = \left| \begin{pmatrix} 1 & 2 \\ 1 & 0 \end{pmatrix} \right|,$$

$$M_{31} = \left| \begin{pmatrix} 2 & 3 \\ 3 & 2 \end{pmatrix} \right|, \ M_{32} = \left| \begin{pmatrix} 1 & 3 \\ 1 & 2 \end{pmatrix} \right|, \ M_{33} = \left| \begin{pmatrix} 1 & 2 \\ 1 & 3 \end{pmatrix} \right|.$$

That is,

$$M_{11} = 12, \ M_{12} = 2, \ M_{13} = -3,$$
$$M_{21} = 8, \ M_{22} = 1, \ M_{23} = -2,$$
$$M_{31} = -5, \ M_{32} = -1, \ M_{33} = 1.$$

Multiplying the minors by $(1)^{i+j}$ will yield the cofactor matrix C as:

$$C = \begin{pmatrix} 12 & -2 & -3 \\ -8 & 1 & 2 \\ -5 & 1 & 1 \end{pmatrix}.$$

The adjoint matrix is the transpose of the cofactor matrix, and the inverse of the matrix A will now be the adjoint matrix divided by the determinant of A.

$$A^{-1} = \frac{adj(A)}{|A|}$$

or

$$A^{-1} = \frac{\begin{pmatrix} 12 & -8 & 5 \\ -2 & 1 & 1 \\ -3 & 2 & 1 \end{pmatrix}}{-1} = \begin{pmatrix} -12 & 8 & -5 \\ 2 & -1 & -1 \\ 3 & -2 & -1 \end{pmatrix}.$$

The correctness of the result can now be verified as follows. Multiplying A by its inverse obtained above gives

$$\begin{pmatrix} 1 & 2 & 3 \\ 1 & 3 & 2 \\ 1 & 0 & 4 \end{pmatrix}\begin{pmatrix} -12 & -8 & 5 \\ 2 & -1 & -1 \\ 3 & -2 & -1 \end{pmatrix} = \begin{pmatrix} 1 & 0 & 0 \\ 0 & 1 & 0 \\ 0 & 0 & 1 \end{pmatrix}.$$

4.2 Use of MATLAB in Performing Matrix Operations

We enter matrices by hand, separating rows by semi-colons. How to perform matrix operations will be clear in the following examples.

Given the two matrices A and B:

$$A = \begin{pmatrix} 1 & 0 & 2 \\ 1 & 3 & 2 \\ 7 & 8 & 9 \end{pmatrix} \text{ and } B = \begin{pmatrix} 3 & 2 & 1 \\ 1 & 2 & 3 \\ 1 & 5 & 9 \end{pmatrix}$$

```
A = [1 0 2; 1 3 2; 7 8 9]

A =

        1        0        2
        1        3        2
        7        8        9

B = [3 2 1; 1 2 3; 1 5 9]
```

```
B =
       3        2        1
       1        2        3
       1        5        9
```

Addition:

```
A + B

ans =
       4        2        3
       2        5        5
       8       13       18
```

Subtraction:

```
A - B

ans =
      -2       -2        1
       0        1       -1
       6        3        0
```

Multiplication:

```
A*B

ans =
       5       12       19
       8       18       28
      38       75      112


B*A

ans =
      12       14       19
      24       30       33
      69       87       93
```

Note: The order in which matrices are multiplied is important. $AB \neq BA$.

Scalar Subtraction:

```
A - 5

ans =
      -4       -5       -3
```

```
      -4      -2      -3
       2       3       4
```

Scalar Multiplication:

```
A*5

ans =
       5       0      10
       5      15      10
      35      40      45
```

Matrix Inverse:

```
A^(-1)

ans =
   -0.7333    -1.0667     0.4000
   -0.3333     0.3333     0.0000
    0.8667     0.5333    -0.2000
```

Determinant of *A*:

```
det(A)

ans =
  -15.0000
```

Transpose of *A*:

```
A'

ans =
       1       1       7
       0       3       8
       2       2       9
```

4.3 Solution of Linear Algebraic Equations By Using the Inverse

For a system of linear algebraic equations that can be written in matrix form as

$$Ax = b \qquad (4.5)$$

where the matrix A and the column vector b contains known constants, the inverse of the matrix A can be utilized in the determination of the solution vector x as follows

$$x = A^{-1}b \tag{4.6}$$

Example 4.2. Solve:

$$2x + 4y + z = -11$$
$$-x + 3y - 2z = -16$$
$$2x - 3y + 5z = 21$$

Putting the given equations in the form $Ax = b$, where

$$A = \begin{pmatrix} 2 & 4 & 1 \\ -1 & 3 & -2 \\ 2 & -3 & 5 \end{pmatrix} \text{ and } b = \begin{pmatrix} -11 \\ -16 \\ 21 \end{pmatrix},$$

the inverse of A can be easily obtained as

$$A^{-1} = \begin{pmatrix} 0.474 & -1.211 & -0.579 \\ 0.053 & 0.421 & 0.158 \\ -0.158 & 0.737 & 0.526 \end{pmatrix}$$

and A multiplied by A^{-1} will yield the identity matrix as shown

$$AA^{-1} = \begin{pmatrix} 1 & 0 & 0 \\ 0 & 1 & 0 \\ 0 & 0 & 1 \end{pmatrix}.$$

The solution can then be generated by performing the matrix operation

$$x = A^{-1}b$$

yielding

$$x = \begin{pmatrix} 2 \\ -4 \\ 1 \end{pmatrix}.$$

4.4 Solution of Linear Algebraic Equations by Cramer's Rule

As an alternative to the above procedure, the solution x to the matrix equation (4.5)

$$Ax = b$$

can be computed using Cramer's rule as follows.

Letting

$$A = \begin{pmatrix} A_{11} & A_{12} & A_{13} \\ A_{21} & A_{22} & A_{23} \\ A_{31} & A_{32} & A_{33} \end{pmatrix} \text{ and } b = \begin{pmatrix} b_1 \\ b_2 \\ b_3 \end{pmatrix},$$

the solution x can be computed using

$$x_1 = \frac{\left| \begin{pmatrix} b_1 & A_{12} & A_{13} \\ b_2 & A_{22} & A_{23} \\ b_3 & A_{32} & A_{33} \end{pmatrix} \right|}{\left| \begin{pmatrix} A_{11} & A_{12} & A_{13} \\ A_{21} & A_{22} & A_{23} \\ A_{31} & A_{32} & A_{33} \end{pmatrix} \right|}, \quad x_2 = \frac{\left| \begin{pmatrix} A_{11} & b_1 & A_{13} \\ A_{21} & b_2 & A_{23} \\ A_{31} & b_3 & A_{33} \end{pmatrix} \right|}{\left| \begin{pmatrix} A_{11} & A_{12} & A_{13} \\ A_{21} & A_{22} & A_{23} \\ A_{31} & A_{32} & A_{33} \end{pmatrix} \right|}, \quad x_3 = \frac{\left| \begin{pmatrix} A_{11} & A_{12} & b_1 \\ A_{21} & A_{22} & b_2 \\ A_{31} & A_{32} & b_3 \end{pmatrix} \right|}{\left| \begin{pmatrix} A_{11} & A_{12} & A_{13} \\ A_{21} & A_{22} & A_{23} \\ A_{31} & A_{32} & A_{33} \end{pmatrix} \right|}.$$

For Example 4.2,

$$A = \begin{pmatrix} 2 & 4 & 1 \\ -1 & 3 & -2 \\ 2 & -3 & 5 \end{pmatrix}, \; b = \begin{pmatrix} -11 \\ -16 \\ 21 \end{pmatrix}, \; D = |A| = 19.$$

Hence

$$x = \frac{\left| \begin{pmatrix} b_1 & A_{12} & A_{13} \\ b_2 & A_{22} & A_{23} \\ b_3 & A_{32} & A_{33} \end{pmatrix} \right|}{D} = 2, \; y = \frac{\left| \begin{pmatrix} A_{11} & b_1 & A_{13} \\ A_{21} & b_2 & A_{23} \\ A_{31} & b_3 & A_{33} \end{pmatrix} \right|}{D} = -4, \; z = \frac{\left| \begin{pmatrix} A_{11} & A_{12} & b_1 \\ A_{21} & A_{22} & b_2 \\ A_{31} & A_{32} & b_3 \end{pmatrix} \right|}{D} = 1.$$

4.5 Solution of Linear Algebraic Equations Using the "\" Command

The "\" command in MATLAB can be used to solve a system of linear algebraic equations.

Given $Ax = b$, the command $x = A \backslash b$ will return the solution vector x, provided A is not singular. For Example 4.2,

```
A = [2 4 1; -1 3 -2; 2 -3 5];
b = [-11; -16; 21];
x = A\b


x =
    2.0000
   -4.0000
    1.0000
```

Example 4.3. Application of Matrices to Electrical Circuit Analysis

Formulate a set of linear equations that represent the relationship between voltage, current and resistances for the circuit shown in Figure 4.1. Solve the simultaneous equations generated using (1) the inverse (2) Cramer's Rule and (3) MATLAB's "\" command.

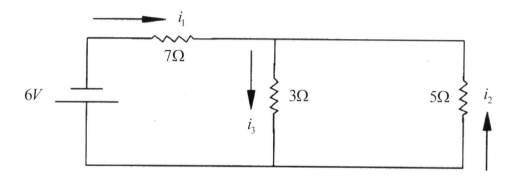

Fig. 4.1: Electrical circuit example

The governing equations are:

$$i_1 + i_1 = i_3$$
$$7i_1 + 3i_3 = 6$$
$$7i_1 - 5i_2 = 6$$

These must be put in the form $Ax = b$ and solved for x.

```
A = [1 1 -1; 7 0 3; 7 -5 0];
b = [0; 6; 6];
```

(1) Using the inverse:

```
x = A^(-1)*b
x =
      0.6761
     -0.2535
      0.4225
```

(2) Using Cramer's Rule

```
L = [b A(:,2) A(:,3)]

L =
      0      1     -1
      6      0      3
      6     -5      0

M = [A(:,1) b A(:,3)]

M =
      1      0     -1
      7      6      3
      7      6      0

N = [A(:,1) A(:,2) b]

N =
      1      1      0
      7      0      6
      7     -5      6

i1 = det(L)/det(A)

i1 =
    0.6761

i2 = det(M)/det(A)

i2 =
   -0.2535

i3 = det(N)/det(A)

i3 =
    0.4225
```

(3) Using MATLAB's "\" command

```
  x = A\b

x =
    0.6761
   -0.2535
```

```
     0.4225
```

We see from all three methods, we obtain currents:

$$i_1 = 0.6761, \ i_2 = -0.2535, \ i_3 = 0.4225.$$

4.6 The Eigenvalue Problem

Eigenvalue problems occur in a variety of physical situations. Some examples of eigenvalue problems are given below.

1. Determination of natural frequencies and mode shapes of oscillating systems.
2. Computation of principal stresses and principal directions.
3. Computation of principal moments of inertia and principal axes.
4. Buckling of structures.
5. Oscillations of electrical networks.

The eigenvalue problem can be mathematically stated as

$$Ax = \lambda x \tag{4.7}$$

where A is a known square matrix, x is a column vector of unknowns, and λ is an unknown scalar quantity. The solution of the eigenvalue problem involves the determination of vectors x and associated constants λ satisfying equation (4.7). These vectors x are termed eigenvectors. With each eigenvector is associated a constant λ which is called an eigenvalue.

(4.7) can be written in the form

$$(A - \lambda I)x = 0. \tag{4.8}$$

A trivial solution to the above is

$$x = 0$$

which is not of interest to us. The condition for the existence of a non-trivial solution is

$$\det(A - \lambda I) = 0. \tag{4.9}$$

Expansion of the above determinant produces a polynomial in λ. For instance, if A is a 3×3 matrix, then (4.9) would give a cubic in λ. This polynomial is called the characteristic polynomial and its roots are called *eigenvalues*. Associated with each eigenvalue is a solution vector x called the *eigenvector*.

It can be shown that the adjoint of matrix $(A - \lambda_i I)$ contains columns, each of which is the ith eigenvector $x^{(i)}$ associated with the eigenvalue λ_i multiplied by an arbitrary constant. Thus, to determine an eigenvector corresponding to an eigenvalue λ_i, compute the adjoint of $(A - \lambda_i I)$ and choose any column of it as the eigenvector.

Example 4.4. Compute the eigenvalues and eigenvectors of $A = \begin{pmatrix} 17 & -6 \\ 45 & -16 \end{pmatrix}$.

The $A - \lambda I$ matrix can be written as:

$$A - \lambda I = \begin{pmatrix} 17 - \lambda & -6 \\ 45 & -16 - \lambda \end{pmatrix}.$$

A non-trivial solution is obtained by setting the determinant of $A - \lambda I$ equal to zero

$$\left| \begin{pmatrix} 17 - \lambda & -6 \\ 45 & -16 - \lambda \end{pmatrix} \right| = 0$$

which gives $\lambda^2 - \lambda - 2 = 0$, or, $\lambda_1 = 2$, $\lambda_2 = -1$. The adjoint of the matrix $A - \lambda I$, in this case, is

$$\begin{pmatrix} -16 - \lambda & 6 \\ -45 & 17 - \lambda \end{pmatrix}.$$

For $\lambda_1 = 2$, the corresponding eigenvector is the first or second column of the above adjoint matrix with $\lambda = \lambda_1$ which gives

$$x^{(1)} = \begin{pmatrix} -18 \\ -45 \end{pmatrix} \text{ or } \begin{pmatrix} 2 \\ 5 \end{pmatrix} \text{ or } \begin{pmatrix} 0.4 \\ 1 \end{pmatrix}$$

as the first eigenvector.

Similarly, the second eigenvector is obtained by putting $\lambda = \lambda_2$ in any one column of the adjoint matrix which gives

$$x^{(2)} = \begin{pmatrix} -15 \\ -45 \end{pmatrix} \text{ or } \begin{pmatrix} 1 \\ 3 \end{pmatrix} \text{ or } \begin{pmatrix} 0.333 \\ 1 \end{pmatrix}.$$

4.7 Solving the Eigenvalue Problem with MATLAB

The MATLAB function *[V, D] = eig(A)* returns a diagonal matrix *D* whose diagonal elements are the eigenvalues of *A* and a matrix *V* whose columns are the corresponding right eigenvectors of *A*, such that $AV = VD$.

```
A = [1 1 1; 1 2 2; 1 0 3]

A =

     1     1     1
     1     2     2
     1     0     3
```

```
[V,D] = eig(A)

V =
    -0.4332    -0.9226    -0.5348
    -0.7547     0.1265    -0.7460
    -0.4926     0.3644     0.3969



D =
     3.8794          0          0
          0     0.4679          0
          0          0     1.6527
```

Note, if only the eigenvalues of a matrix are needed the same command can be used, set equal to a scalar instead of a matrix.

```
A = [1 1 1; 1 2 2; 1 0 3]

A =
     1     1     1
     1     2     2
     1     0     3

e = eig(A)

e =
     3.8794
     0.4679
     1.6527
```

From Example 4.4, the eigenvalues and eigenvectors obtained by MATLAB are as follows:

```
A = [17 -6; 45 -16];
[V, D] = eig(A)

V =
     0.3714     0.3162
     0.9285     0.9487

D =
     2.0000          0
          0    -1.0000
```

4.8 Application of the Eigenvalue Problem to Vibration Engineering

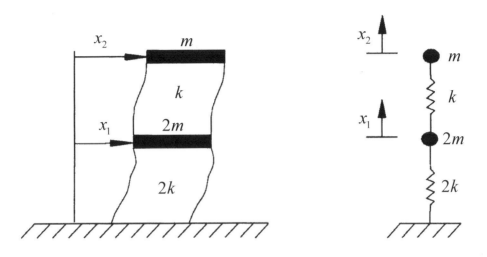

Fig. 4.2: Mathematical model of two-story building

Consider the vibration problem of a two-story building which is mathematically modeled as the two degree of freedom system shown in Figure 4.2, in which the building is represented by lumped masses m and $2m$ and springs k and $2k$.

After drawing suitable free body diagrams of the two masses m and $2m$, the governing differential equations of motion can be seen to be

$$2m\frac{d^2x_1}{dt^2} + 3kx_1 - kx_2 = 0,$$
$$m\frac{d^2x_2}{dt^2} + k(x_2 - x_1) = 0. \tag{4.10}$$

Expressing the above equations in matrix form as:

$$M\ddot{x} + Kx = 0, \tag{4.11}$$

where M is the mass or inertia matrix, and K is the stiffness matrix, and assuming that

$$x = A\sin(\omega t), \tag{4.12}$$

we obtain a set of linear homogeneous algebraic equations that can be written in matrix form as

$$(K - \omega^2 M)A = 0. \tag{4.13}$$

For a non-trivial solution, the determinant $|K - \omega^2 M|$ must be zero. The problem can also be posed slightly differently in the familiar form

$$|A - \lambda I| = 0, \tag{4.14}$$

where the λ's ($\lambda = \omega^2$) are the eigenvalues of the matrix A, which, in this case is

$$A = M^{-1}K. \tag{4.15}$$

To find the natural frequencies and mode shapes in this case, we need to determine the eigenvalues and eigenvectors of the matrix A. The square roots of the eigenvalues will then give the natural frequencies and the corresponding eigenvectors will be the mode shapes.

Let $m = 1$ and $k = 1$ in this problem, for convenience. Then, the mass and stiffness matrices

$$M = \begin{pmatrix} 2m & 0 \\ 0 & m \end{pmatrix}, \quad K = \begin{pmatrix} 3k & -k \\ -k & k \end{pmatrix}$$

give

$$M = \begin{pmatrix} 2 & 0 \\ 0 & 1 \end{pmatrix}, \quad K = \begin{pmatrix} 3 & -1 \\ -1 & 1 \end{pmatrix}.$$

The $[A]$ matrix, which is called the dynamic matrix in the language of vibrations is,

$$A = M^{-1}K$$

which gives

$$A = \begin{pmatrix} 1.5 & -0.5 \\ -1 & 1 \end{pmatrix}.$$

The eigenvalues of A are obtained from setting the determinant of $A - \lambda I$ equal to zero, as follows

$$|A - \lambda I| = 0.$$

This yields

$$(1.5 - \lambda)(1 - \lambda) - 0.5 = 0 \text{ or } \lambda_1 = 0.5 \text{ and } \lambda_2 = 2.$$

The adjoint of the matrix $A - \lambda I$ is

$$\begin{pmatrix} 1 - \lambda & 0.5 \\ 1 & 1.5 - \lambda \end{pmatrix}.$$

In *Vibration Engineering*, eigenvectors are termed as natural modes or mode shapes, and these are simply the configurations that the system takes when vibrating at a natural frequency. Because the system considered here is a two-degree-of-freedom system, there will be two natural frequencies and correspondingly two modes. While the natural frequencies are simply the square roots of the eigenvalues, the associated eigenvectors or mode shapes can be determined by putting $\lambda = \lambda_1$ (for the first mode) and $\lambda = \lambda_2$ (for the second mode) in either column of the adjoint of $A - \lambda I$.

This procedure generates the following mode shapes

$$FirstMode = \begin{pmatrix} 0.5 \\ 1 \end{pmatrix} \text{ and } SecondMode = \begin{pmatrix} 1 \\ 1 \end{pmatrix}.$$

The determination of eigenvalues and eigenvectors using MATLAB is done as follows:

```
A = [1.5 -0.5; -1 1];
lambda = eig(A)

lambda =
    2.0000
    0.5000

omega = sqrt(lambda)

omega =
    1.4142
    0.7071
```

In Vibration Engineering, the lowest natural frequency is always considered as the first or fundamental natural frequency. In this case, the natural frequencies are

$$\omega_2 = 0.707 \leftarrow \text{First natural frequency in rads/sec,}$$

$$\omega_1 = 1.414 \leftarrow \text{Second natural frequency in rads/sec.}$$

The eigenvectors or mode shapes can be determined, using MATLAB as follows:

```
[V,D] = eig(A)

V =
    0.7071    0.4472
   -0.7071    0.8944

D =
    2.0000         0
         0    0.5000
```

Here V is the *modal matrix* in Vibrations language. A close inspection of the analysis will show that it is not possible to obtain unique values for the eigenvector components. Therefore, it is traditional to select a value of unity for one of the components of an eigenvector and compute the other one accordingly. This is called normalization and should be clear from the calculation shown below.

The *first natural mode*, corresponding to the *first natural frequency* is:

```
FirstMode = V(:,2)/V(2,2)

FirstMode =
     0.5000
     1.0000
```

while the *second natural mode*, corresponding to the *second natural frequency* is:

```
SecondMode = V(:,1)/V(2,1)

SecondMode =
     -1
      1
```

These *mode shapes* are sketched in Figure 4.3.

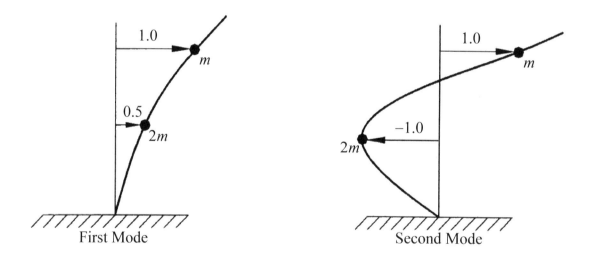

Fig. 4.3: Mode shapes of the two-story building

Example 4.5. Investigate the free vibration of a three-story building mathematically modeled as the three-degree-of-freedom system shown in Figure 4.4.

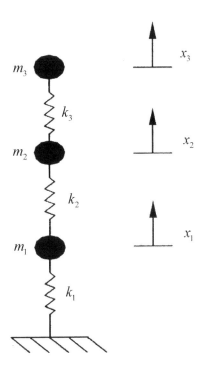

Fig. 4.4: Mathematical model of a three-story building

The equations of motion of the mathematical model resorted to can be shown to be

$$m_1 \frac{d^2 x_1}{dt^2} + k_1 x_1 - k_2(x_2 - x_1) = 0,$$

$$m_2 \frac{d^2 x_2}{dt^2} + k_2(x_2 - x_1) - k_3(x_3 - x_2) = 0,$$

$$m_3 \frac{d^2 x_3}{dt^2} + k_3(x_3 - x_2) = 0. \tag{4.16}$$

These can be put in the following matrix format

$$M \frac{d^2 \boldsymbol{x}}{dt^2} + K \boldsymbol{x} = \boldsymbol{0} \tag{4.17}$$

where

$$M = \begin{pmatrix} m_1 & 0 & 0 \\ 0 & m_2 & 0 \\ 0 & 0 & m_3 \end{pmatrix} \text{ and } K = \begin{pmatrix} k_1 + k_2 & -k_2 & 0 \\ -k_2 & k_2 + k_3 & -k_3 \\ 0 & -k_3 & k_3 \end{pmatrix}. \tag{4.18}$$

Letting $m_1 = 2 \times 10^6$ kg, $m_2 = 14 \times 10^5$ kg, $m_3 = 7 \times 10^5$ kg; and $k_1 = 12 \times 10^8$ N/m, $k_2 = 8 \times 10^8$ N/m, $k_3 = 4 \times 10^8$ N/m, the A matrix can be computed, using MATLAB, as follows:

```
m1  =  2*10^6;
m2  =  14*10^5;
m3  =  7*10^5;
k1  =  12*10^8;
k2  =  8*10^8;
k3  =  4*10^8;
M  =  [m1 0 0;  0 m2 0;  0 0 m3]


M  =

      2000000                0                0
            0          1400000                0
            0                0           700000


K  =  [k1+k2 -k2 0;  -k2 k2+k3 -k3;  0 -k3 k3]


K  =
   1.0e+09  *


    2.0000    -0.8000              0
   -0.8000     1.2000        -0.4000
         0    -0.4000         0.4000


A  =  M^(-1)*K


A  =
   1.0e+03  *


    1.0000    -0.4000              0
   -0.5714     0.8571        -0.2857
         0    -0.5714         0.5714
```

The eigenvalues and the eigenvectors are:

```
[V,D]  =  eig(A)


V  =
   -0.5661    -0.4666     0.2667
    0.7011    -0.2786     0.5520
   -0.4336     0.8395     0.7900



D  =
   1.0e+03  *
```

```
     1.4953             0             0
         0        0.7611             0
         0             0        0.1721
```

Note that MATLAB has found the highest eigenvalue first. The natural frequencies in Hz and the corresponding eigenvectors are computed below.

```
e = eig(A)

e =
   1.0e+03  *

   1.4953
   0.7611
   0.1721

f = sqrt(e)/(2*pi)

f =
   6.1544
   4.3908
   2.0882
```

The *normalized* eigenvectors or *mode shapes* can be determined as shown below:

```
VNorm = [V(:,1)/V(1,1) V(:,2)/V(1,2) V(:,3)/V(1,3)]

VNorm =
    1.0000    1.0000    1.0000
   -1.2383    0.5972    2.0696
    0.7659   -1.7993    2.9619
```

where the columns of *V Norm* represent mode number 3, 2, and 1, respectively.

Figure 4.5 shows the natural modes of the building as it vibrates at its natural frequencies.

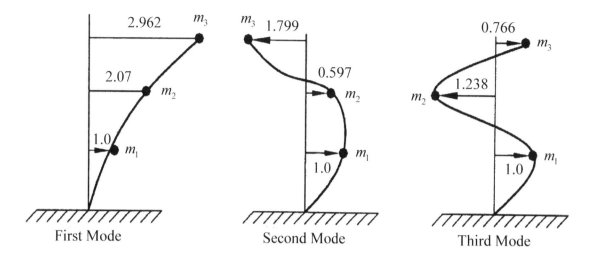

Fig. 4.5: Mode shapes of a three-story building

4.9 Application of the Eigenvalue Problem to Stress Analysis - Determination of Principal Stresses and Principal Directions

If σ is the state of stress at a point in a material given by the stress components σ_{xx}, σ_{yy}, σ_{zz}, σ_{xy}, σ_{yz} and σ_{zx}, the principal stresses are the eigenvalues λ of the stress matrix and the principal directions, which are the x, y and z components of the unit vectors along the normals to the principal planes, are the eigenvectors $\boldsymbol{\eta}$ of the stress matrix. Thus, the eigenvalue problem in this case is stated as

$$(\sigma - \lambda I)\boldsymbol{\eta} = \mathbf{0}, \qquad (4.19)$$

where the eigenvalues λ and the eigenvectors $\boldsymbol{\eta}$ are to be determined.

Example 4.6. The two-dimensional state of stress in a mechanical element, which is shown in Figure 4.6 is given by the components:

$$\sigma_{xx} = 80 \text{ MPa}, \sigma_{yy} = 0 \text{ MPa, and } \sigma_{xy} = 50 \text{ MPa}.$$

Determine the principal stresses and their associated directions.

Because the stress matrix is symmetrical, σ_{yx} must be equal to σ_{xy}. Thus, the matrix of stresses is

$$\sigma = \begin{pmatrix} 80 & 50 \\ 50 & 0 \end{pmatrix} \text{ (MPa)}$$

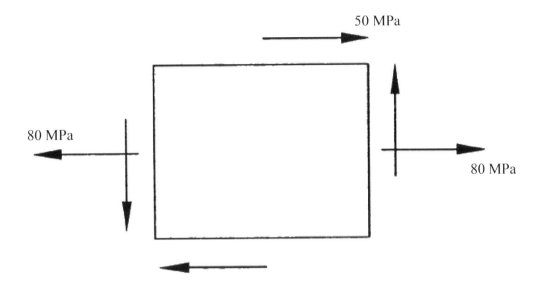

Fig. 4.6: Two-dimension state of stress

The principal stresses are the eigenvalues of the given stress matrix while the principal directions are the associated eigenvectors. These are:

```
sigma = [80 50; 50 0];
[V, D] = eig(sigma)

V =
     0.4332    -0.9013
    -0.9013    -0.4332

D =
   -24.0312          0
          0   104.0312
```

The principal direction associated with the maximum principal stress (104.031 MPa) can be found in the form of a unit vector along the normal to the principal plane. Its x and y components are computed below. Figure 4.7 shows the principal stresses on the element and the associated principal directions.

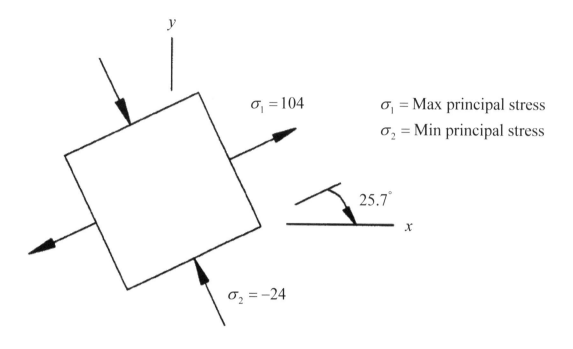

Fig. 4.7: Principal stresses and principal directions for two-dimensional stress example

```
prindir = V(:,2)

prindir =
   -0.9013
   -0.4332
```

Example 4.7. The three-dimensional state of stress in a mechanical element, which is shown in Figure 4.8, is given by:

$$\sigma_{xx} = 1000 \text{ psi}, \ \sigma_{yy} = -1000 \text{ psi}, \ \sigma_{xy} = 500 \text{ psi},$$
$$\sigma_{yz} = -200 \text{ psi}, \ \sigma_{zx} = 100 \text{ psi}, \ \sigma_{zz} = 250 \text{ psi}.$$

Determine the principal stresses and their associated directions.

The stress matrix can be written as

$$\sigma = \begin{pmatrix} 1000 & 500 & 100 \\ 500 & -1000 & -200 \\ 100 & -200 & 250 \end{pmatrix} \text{ (psi)}.$$

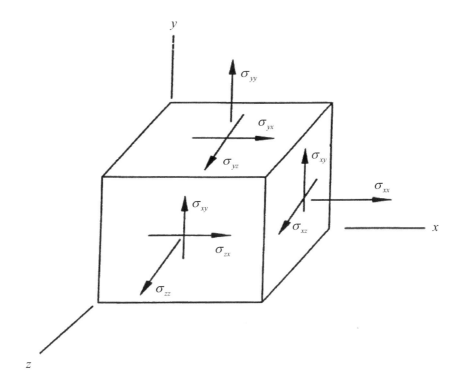

Fig. 4.8: Three-dimensional state of stress

The principal stresses and principal directions can be determined using MATLAB as shown below:

```
sigma = [1000 500 100; 500 -1000 -200; 100 -200 250];
[V, D] = eig(sigma)

V =
    -0.2304    -0.0236     0.9728
     0.9609    -0.1633     0.2236
     0.1535     0.9863     0.0603

D =
    1.0e+03 *

    -1.1518         0         0
          0    0.2807         0
          0         0    1.1211
```

If only the principal direction associated with one of the principal stresses, say 280.7 psi, is required, it can be found as follows.

```
prindir2 = V(:,2)

prindir2 =
   -0.0236
   -0.1633
    0.9863
```

These are the x and y components of the unit vector along the normal to the principal plane associated with the principal stress, 280.7 psi.

The principal stresses and their directions are shown in Figure 4.9. Note the orthogonality of the principal stress directions with respect to one another.

```
acos(V(:,3))*180/pi

ans =
   13.3924
   77.0780
   86.5412
```

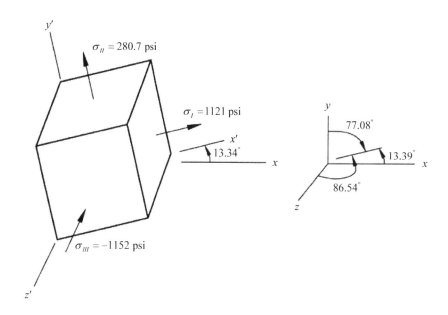

Fig. 4.9: Principal stresses and principal directions for three-dimensional state of stress

4.10 Repeated Roots in the Determinantal Equation

When equal roots are encountered in the determinantal equation, the associated eigenvectors are not unique and thus a linear combination of these eigenvectors may also be considered as eigenvectors. The following examples will illustrate this situation.

Example 4.8. For the given matrix A,

$$A = \begin{pmatrix} 0 & -1 & 1 \\ -1 & 0 & 1 \\ 1 & 1 & 0 \end{pmatrix}$$

the eigenvalues and eigenvectors are found using MATLAB as follows:

```
A = [0 -1 1; -1 0 1; 1 1 0];
[V,D] = eig(A)

V =
   -0.5774    -0.3938     0.7152
   -0.5774     0.8163    -0.0166
    0.5774     0.4225     0.6987

D =
   -2.0000          0          0
         0     1.0000          0
         0          0     1.0000
```

It is clear that the first and third eigenvectors corresponding to the repeated root $\lambda = 1$ are arbitrary, since they are both different, while the one corresponding to $\lambda = -2$ is

$$\begin{pmatrix} -1 \\ -1 \\ 1 \end{pmatrix}.$$

Example 4.9. The following problem is, clearly, a case of repeated roots with a double root at $\lambda = 1$. Consider

$$A = \begin{pmatrix} 1 & 1 & 0 \\ 0 & 1 & 1 \\ 0 & 0 & -1 \end{pmatrix}.$$

```
A = [1 1 0; 0 1 1; 0 0 -1];
[V,D] = eig(A)
```

```
V =

    1.0000       1.0000      -0.2182
         0       0.0000      -0.4364
         0            0       0.8729


D =

    1       0       0
    0       1       0
    0       0      -1
```

Note that the first and second eigenvectors corresponding to the repeated (double) root at $\lambda = 1$ are, in fact, arbitrary since they have two components that are zero, while the one corresponding to $\lambda = -1$ is the third one which is

$$\begin{pmatrix} -1 \\ -2 \\ 4 \end{pmatrix}.$$

Example 4.10. For the given matrix A,

$$A = \begin{pmatrix} -14 & 1 & 0 \\ 0 & 2 & 0 \\ 1 & 0 & 2 \end{pmatrix}$$

the eigenvalues and eigenvectors are found using MATLAB as follows:

```
A = [-14 1 0; 0 2 0; 1 0 2];
[V,D] = eig(A)

V =

         0       0.9981       0.0000
         0            0       0.0000
    1.0000      -0.0624      -1.0000


D =

    2       0       0
    0     -14       0
    0       0       2
```

This is, again, a case of repeated roots in which the first and third eigenvectors corresponding to the repeated roots are arbitrary. Thus, there is no unique eigenvector corresponding to the repeated root.

4.11 Solution of Nonlinear Simultaneous Equations

There are no direct methods available for solving nonlinear simultaneous equations as in the case of linear algebraic equations. In general, iterative procedures must be resorted to, requiring initial guesses as a starting point. The following procedure utilizes an adaptation of the Taylor series approach in obtaining a solution to a set of nonlinear equations.

Consider the following two nonlinear equations:

$$f(x, y) = 0; \ g(x, y) = 0 \tag{4.20}$$

which have the exact solution $x = x_r$ and $y = y_r$.

If $x = x_i$ and $y = y_i$ are approximate solutions, a Taylor series approximation about (x_i, y_i) gives

$$f(x_r, y_r) = f(x_i, y_i) + h\frac{\partial f}{\partial x}(x_i, y_i) + j\frac{\partial f}{\partial y}(x_i, y_i) + \cdots = 0 \tag{4.21}$$

and

$$g(x_r, y_r) = f(x_i, y_i) + h\frac{\partial g}{\partial x}(x_i, y_i) + j\frac{\partial g}{\partial y}(x_i, y_i) + \cdots = 0, \tag{4.22}$$

where

$$x_r = x_i + h \text{ and } y_r = y_i + j. \tag{4.23}$$

If only linear terms are retained in the Taylor series, two linear equations are generated in the two unknowns h and j, where h and j are approximations to $(x_r - x_i)$ and $(y_r - y_i)$. Defining a, b, c and d as the partial derivatives in 4.21 and 4.22, p as $f(x_i, y_i)$ and q as $g(x_i, y_i)$, these equations become

$$ah + bj = -p \text{ and } ch + dj = -q. \tag{4.24}$$

When these two simultaneous equations are solved for h and j, we generate new improved values for x and y, say x_{i+1} and y_{i+1}, where $x_{i+1} = x_i + h$ and $y_{i+1} = y_i + j$. These new improved values replace the old values x_i and y_i in the next step in an effort to obtain still better solutions. This procedure is repeated until convergence occurs. The following example will clarify the procedure.

Example 4.11. Determine the solution to: $f(x, y) = x^2 + 3y^2 - 54 = 0, g(x, y) = -4x^2 + 3xy - 2y + 15 = 0$.

<u>Iteration #1:</u>

$$f(x, y) = x^2 + 3y^2 - 54, \ g(x, y) = -4x^3 + 3xy - 2y + 15$$
$$\frac{\partial f}{\partial x} = 2x, \ \frac{\partial f}{\partial y} = 6y, \ \frac{\partial g}{\partial x} = -8x + 3y, \ \frac{\partial g}{\partial y} = 3x - 2.$$

Then

$$x_{old} = 1.5, \ y_{old} = 2.0 \leftarrow \text{ Assumed starting values of solution}$$

$$p = f(x_{old}, y_{old}) = -39.75, \ q = g(x_{old}, y_{old}) = 11,$$

$$a = \frac{\partial f}{\partial x}(x_{old}, y_{old}) = 3, \ b = \frac{\partial f}{\partial y}(x_{old}, y_{old}) = 12,$$

$$c = \frac{\partial g}{\partial x}(x_{old}, y_{old}) = -6, \ d = \frac{\partial g}{\partial y}(x_{old}, y_{old}) = 2.5.$$

Now solve the equations obtained from the linear Taylor series approximations, namely

$$ah + bj = -p \text{ and } ch + dj = -q$$

in the form $AH = P$ using the "\" command as follows:

```
A = [3 12; -6 2.5];
P = [39.75; -11];
H = A\P
H =
   2.910377358490566
   2.584905660377359
```

Then, $h = H_1 = 2.91$ and $j = H_2 = 2.585$.

$$x_{new} = x_{old} + h = 4.41, \ y_{new} = y_{old} + j = 4.585.$$

Iteration #2:

$$x_{old} = x_{new}, \ y_{old} = y_{new}$$

$$p = f(x_{old}, y_{old}) = 28.516, \ q = g(x_{old}, y_{old}) = -11.312,$$

$$a = \frac{\partial f}{\partial x}(x_{old}, y_{old}) = 8.821, \ b = \frac{\partial f}{\partial y}(x_{old}, y_{old}) = 27.509,$$

$$c = \frac{\partial g}{\partial x}(x_{old}, y_{old}) = -21.528, \ d = \frac{\partial g}{\partial y}(x_{old}, y_{old}) = 11.231.$$

```
A = [8.821 27.509; -21.528 11.231];
P = [-28.516; 11.312];
H = A\P
H =
  -0.913440008395527
  -0.743703721907123
```

Then, $h = H_1 = -0.9134$ and $j = H_2 = -0.7437$.

$$x_{new} = x_{old} + h = 3.4966, \quad y_{new} = y_{old} + j = 3.8413.$$

Following the same procedure as above, new improved values for x and y can be generated in iterations 3, 4 and 5 as

Iteration #3: $h = -0.1166$, $j = -0.0728$, $\Rightarrow x_{new} = 3.3804$, $y_{new} = 3.7684$.

Iteration #4: $h = -2.1741 \times 10^{-3}$, $j = -6.5547 \times 10^{-4}$, $\Rightarrow x_{new} = 3.3782$, $y_{new} = 3.7677$.

Iteration #5: $h = -0.9101 \times 10^{-6}$, $j = -0.0086 \times 10^{-6}$, $\Rightarrow x_{new} = 3.3782$, $y_{new} = 3.7677$.

Checking to see if a solution has indeed been achieved, we see that $f(x_{new}, y_{new}) = -1.9492 \times 10^{-7}$ and $g(x_{new}, y_{new}) = -7.0146 \times 10^{-8}$. Thus, it is clear that convergence has occurred in the fourth iteration because the values of the functions $f(x, y)$ and $g(x, y)$ are zero and the answers x_{new} and y_{new} obtained in the fifth iteration are exactly the same as in the fourth. The solution is: $x = 3.3782$ and $y = 3.7677$. These answers may now be verified by using the *fsolve* command. We enter the equations to be solved as a column vector function. Then, using *fsolve*, calling our function and entering our initial guess, $x = 1$ and $y = 1$, we obtain:

```
>> F = @(x) [x(1)^2+3*x(2)^2-54; -4*x(1)^2+3*x(1)*x(2)-2*x
   (2)+15];
>> x = fsolve(F,[1.5 2])

Equation solved.

fsolve completed because the vector of function values is
   near zero
as measured by the default value of the function tolerance,
   and
the problem appears regular as measured by the gradient.

<stopping criteria details>

x =
    3.3782    3.7677
```

Problems

4.1. Given the matrix
$$\begin{pmatrix} -2 & -1 & -5 \\ 1 & 1 & 4 \\ 0 & 3 & 3 \end{pmatrix}$$

find its inverse or else show that it is singular. Do calculations on a calculator. Also check your answers with MATLAB.

4.2. Given the matrix
$$\begin{pmatrix} 0 & 0 & -1 \\ 1 & 12 & 0 \\ 1 & -2 & 4 \end{pmatrix}$$

find its inverse or else show that it is singular. Do calculations on a calculator. Also check your answers with MATLAB.

4.3. Solve the following by Cramer's rule:

(a) $x + y = 4; 2x - y = 2$
(b) $5x - 3y = 37; -2x + 7y = -38$

4.4. Solve the following system of equations

$$8x - y - z = 4; \ x + 2y - 3z = 0; \ 2x - y + 4z = 5.$$

Do this problem on a calculator. Check your answers with (1) MATLAB, using the inverse and (2) MATLAB's "\" command.

4.5. Solve the following system of equations

$$x + y + z = 6; \ 2x - y + 3z = 9; \ x + 2y - z = 2.$$

Do this problem on a calculator. Check your answers with (1) MATLAB, using the inverse and (2) MATLAB's "\" command.

4.6. Solve the following system of equations

$$x + y + 3z = 96; \ 2x - y + 7z = 6; \ x + 2y - 5z = 2.$$

Do this problem on a calculator. Check your answers with (1) MATLAB, using the inverse and (2) MATLAB's "\" command.

4.7. Solve the following by Cramer's Rule:

$$x + y - 3z = 0; \ y - 4z = 0; \ x - y - z = 5.$$

Do this problem on a calculator. Check your answers with (1) MATLAB, using the inverse and (2) MATLAB's "\" command.

4.8. Find the eigenvalues of the matrix

$$\begin{pmatrix} 1 & 3 \\ 2 & 1 \end{pmatrix}.$$

Corresponding to each eigenvalue, find an eigenvector. Do this problem on a calculator. Check your answers with MATLAB, using the *eig(A)* function.

4.9. Find the eigenvalues of the matrix

$$\begin{pmatrix} -5 & 0 \\ 1 & 2 \end{pmatrix}.$$

Corresponding to each eigenvalue, find an eigenvector. Do this problem on a calculator. Check your answers with MATLAB, using the *eig(A)* function.

4.10. Determine the eigenvalues and eigenvectors of the following matrices.

(a)

$$\begin{pmatrix} 3 & 4 \\ 4 & 3 \end{pmatrix}$$

(b)

$$\begin{pmatrix} 5 & 0 \\ 0 & 5 \end{pmatrix}$$

(c)

$$\begin{pmatrix} 6 & 0 \\ 0 & 6 \end{pmatrix}$$

(d)

$$\begin{pmatrix} 4 & 2 \\ 5 & 1 \end{pmatrix}$$

(e)

$$\begin{pmatrix} 10 & 0 \\ 0 & 10 \end{pmatrix}$$

(f)

$$\begin{pmatrix} 6 & 2 \\ 8 & 1 \end{pmatrix}$$

4.11. The differential equations of motion of the spring-mass system shown in Figure 4.10 are:

$$m\frac{d^2x_1}{dt^2} + (2kx_1 - kx_2) = 0 \text{ and } 2m\frac{d^2x_2}{dt^2} + (2kx_2 - kx_1) = 0.$$

Obtain the natural frequencies (eigenvalues) and mode shapes (eigenvectors) of the system for $m = 1$ lb-sec^2/ft and $k = 1$ lb/ft.

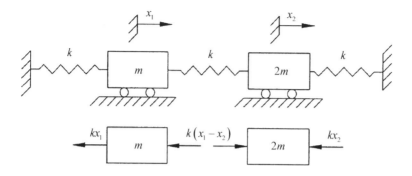

Fig. 4.10

4.12. The two-dimensional state of stress in psi at a point on a machine element is prescribed as:

$$\sigma = \begin{pmatrix} 12 & 4 \\ 4 & 6 \end{pmatrix}$$

Obtain the eigenvalues (principal stresses) and their associated directions (eigenvectors).

4.13. For the two pendulums shown in Figure 4.11 which are coupled by means of a spring k, the governing differential equations are

$$mL^2 \frac{d^2\theta_1}{dt^2} = -mgL\theta_1 - ka^2(\theta_1 - \theta_2)$$

and

$$mL^2 \frac{d^2\theta_2}{dt^2} = -mgL\theta_2 - ka^2(\theta_2 - \theta_1).$$

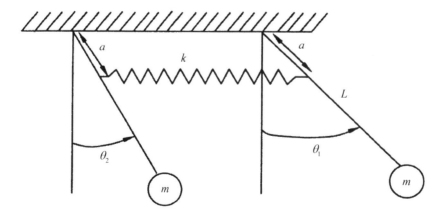

Fig. 4.11

Determine the natural frequencies (eigenvalues) and mode shapes (eigenvectors) of the system for $m = 1$ lb-sec^2/ft, $L = 1$ft, $g = 32.2$ ft/sec^2, $k = 1$ lb/ft and $a = 0.5$ ft.

4.14. The spring-mass system shown in Figure 4.12 has the following mass and stiffness characteristics:

$$M = \begin{pmatrix} 2m & 0 & 0 \\ 0 & m & 0 \\ 0 & 0 & 2m \end{pmatrix} \text{ and } K = \begin{pmatrix} 4k & -k & 0 \\ -k & 2k & -k \\ 0 & -k & 4k \end{pmatrix}$$

Use MATLAB to determine its natural frequencies (eigenvalues) and mode shapes (eigenvectors) if $m = 1$ kg and $k = 1$ N/m.

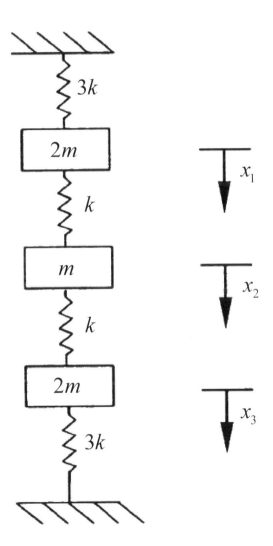

Fig. 4.12

4.15. Determine the roots of the nonlinear simultaneous equations

$$f(x, y) = x^2 + y^2 - 4.5 = 0 \text{ and } g(x, y) = x^3 - 1.5y = 0$$

using the Taylor series approach. Check your answer using the MATLAB function *fsolve*.

4.16. Determine the roots of the nonlinear simultaneous equations

$$f(x, y) = x^3 + y^3 - 5.5 = 0 \text{ and } g(x, y) = x^4 - 3y^2 = 0$$

using the Taylor series approach. Check your answer using the MATLAB function *fsolve*.

4.17. A two-degree-of-freedom mathematical model of an automobile suspension system is shown in Figure 4.13. With the system modeled as a rigid bar of mass m and mass moment of inertia I connected to springs, the governing differential equations are:

$$\frac{W}{g}\frac{d^2x}{dt^2} + 4000 + 2000\theta = 0 \text{ and } I\frac{d^2\theta}{dt^2} + 2000 + 65000\theta = 0,$$

where x represents the linear up and down (bounce) motion and θ represents the angular motion (pitch) of the system. Determine the natural frequencies (eigenvalues) and mode shapes (eigenvectors) if $W = 3000$ lbs, $I = 300$ lb-ft-sec^2, and $g =$ acceleration due to gravity $= 32.2$ ft/sec^2.

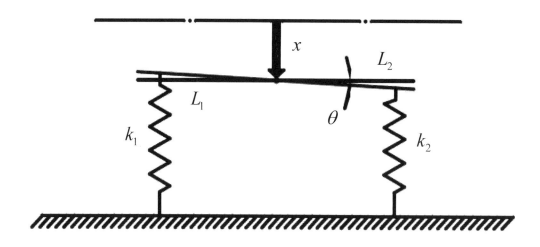

Fig. 4.13

4.18. The governing differential equations of motion of the double pendulum shown in terms of angular displacements $\theta_1(t)$ and $\theta_2(t)$ in Figure 4.14 are

$$L\frac{d^2\theta_1}{dt^2} + 2g\theta_1 - g\theta_2 = 0 \text{ and } L\frac{d^2\theta_2}{dt^2} + 2g\theta_2 - 2g\theta_1 = 0,$$

where g is the acceleration due to gravity = 32.2 ft/sec^2 and L is the length of each pendulum. Using matrix methods, determine the natural frequencies (eigenvalues) and mode-shapes (eigenvectors) of the system for $L = 1$ ft.

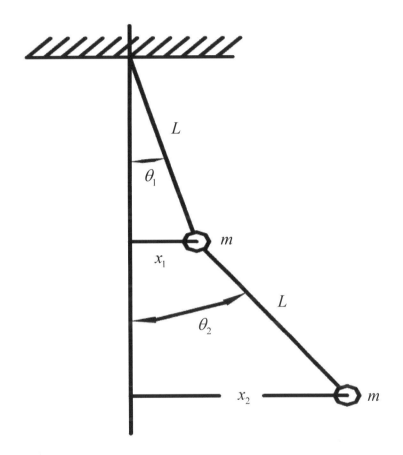

Fig. 4.14

4.19. An automobile is math-modeled as the two-degree-of-freedom system shown above in Figure 4.13. Its up and down linear motion (bounce) is represented by the coordinate $x(t)$ while its angular motion (pitch) is represented by the coordinate $\theta(t)$. The governing differential equations of motion are:

$$m\frac{d^2x}{dt^2} + [(k_1 + k_2)x - (k_1L_1 - k_2L_2)\theta] = 0$$

and

$$J_0 \frac{d^2\theta}{dt^2} + [(k_1 L_1 - k_2 L_2)x + (k_1 L_1^2 + k_2 L_2^2)\theta] = 0.$$

Determine the natural frequencies (eigenvalues) and mode-shapes (eigenvectors) of an automobile with the following data:

$$m = 100 \text{ lb-sec}^2/\text{ft}, \ J_0 = 1600 \text{ lb-ft-sec}^2,$$
$$L_1 = 5.5 \text{ ft}, \ L_2 = 4.5 \text{ ft}, k_1 = 2600 \text{ lbs/ft}, \ k_2 = 2400 \text{ lbs/ft}.$$

4.20. A rigid rod of negligible mass and length $2L$ is pivoted at the middle point and is constrained to move in the vertical plane by springs and masses shown in Figure 4.15. The governing differential equations of motion of the system are given as:

$$m\frac{d^2x}{dt^2} + 2kx + kL\theta = 0 \text{ and } 4mL^2\frac{d^2\theta}{dt^2} + kLx + 2kL^2\theta = 0.$$

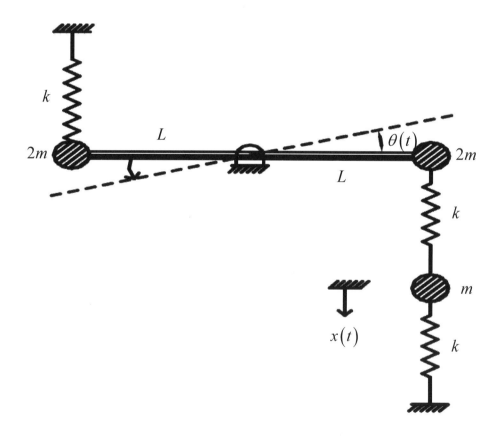

Fig. 4.15

Determine the natural frequencies (eigenvalues) and mode-shapes (eigenvectors) of the system for $m = 1$ kg, $L = 1$ meter, and $k = 1$ N/m.

4.21. The governing differential equations of motion of the double pendulum shown in Figure 4.14 in terms of coordinates $x_1(t)$ and $x_2(t)$ are

$$L\frac{d^2x_1}{dt^2} + 3gx_1 - gx_2 = 0 \text{ and } L\frac{d^2x_2}{dt^2} + gx_2 - gx_1 = 0,$$

where g is the acceleration due to gravity $= 32.2$ ft/sec^2 and L is the length of each pendulum. Determine the natural frequencies (eigenvalues) and mode-shapes (eigenvectors) of the system for $L = 1$ ft.

4.22. Determine the roots of the nonlinear simultaneous equations

$$f(x, y) = x^2 + 2xy - 64 = 0 \text{ and } g(x, y) = 3x^2 + 6y^2 - 264 = 0$$

using the Taylor series approach. Obtain answers that are correct to two decimal places. Use starting values $x_{old} = 3$ and $y_{old} = 5$. Check your answer using MATLAB's *fsolve* command.

Chapter 5
Numerical Interpolation

In any field where measured or statistical data is involved, a need to interpolate between given data points is bound to exist. Because measured or available data is typically not provided in the form of an analytically determined function, the process known as interpolation must be resorted to in order to obtain function values at points other than the given data points. This process involves the generation of a curve that must pass through the given data points and its use in determining the function value at any intermediate point on this curve. As will be seen in the sections following, a polynomial fitting n data points will be of order $n-1$, that is one less than the number of data points given. Thus, four data points will generate a cubic while three data points will give a quadratic and so on.

5.1 Linear Interpolation

Given two data points (x_k, y_k) and (x_{k+1}, y_{k+1}), as shown in the figure below, the connection between the coordinates of a point (x, y) lying between the data points can be expressed by the linear relationship

$$y = \frac{y_k(x_k - x_{k+1}) - y_{k+1}(x - x_k)}{x_k - x_{k+1}}. \tag{5.1}$$

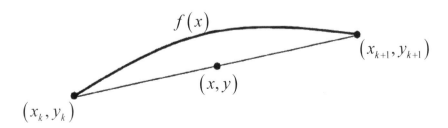

5.2 The Method of Undetermined Coefficients

Given the data points (x_k, y_k), $k = 0, \ldots, n$, it is required to find an interpolating polynomial $P_n(x)$ such that the following constraint equations are satisfied

$$
P_n(x_0) = y_0,
$$
$$
P_n(x_1) = y_1,
$$
$$
\vdots
$$
$$
P_n(x_n) = y_n. \tag{5.2}
$$

Assuming the interpolating polynomial $P_n(x)$ is of the form

$$
P_n(x) = a_0 + a_1 x + a_2 x^2 + \cdots + a_n x^n, \tag{5.3}
$$

Equations (5.2) yield the following matrix equation

$$
\begin{pmatrix}
1 & x_0 & x_0^2 & \cdots & x_0^n \\
1 & x_1 & x_1^2 & \cdots & x_1^n \\
\vdots & \vdots & \vdots & \vdots & \vdots \\
1 & x_n & x_n^2 & \cdots & x_n^n
\end{pmatrix}
\begin{pmatrix}
a_0 \\
a_1 \\
\vdots \\
a_n
\end{pmatrix}
=
\begin{pmatrix}
y_0 \\
y_1 \\
\vdots \\
y_n
\end{pmatrix}. \tag{5.4}
$$

Once the equations represented by the matrix equation (5.4) are solved for the n unknowns $a_0, a_1, \ldots, a_n$, the interpolating polynomial $P_n(x)$ satisfying the constraint equations is completely determined. In general, the higher the order of the interpolating polynomial, the more accurate would be the results of the interpolation process.

Example 5.1. Determine the polynomial $f(x)$ that passes thru (0,2), (1,2.25) and (2,5.82), and compute $f(0.5)$ and $f(1.5)$.

The given data is input as follows.

$$
x = \begin{pmatrix} 0 \\ 1 \\ 2 \end{pmatrix} \text{ and } y = \begin{pmatrix} 2 \\ 2.25 \\ 5.82 \end{pmatrix}.
$$

The order of the polynomial fitting 3 data points is 2 and the form, thus, is

$$
f(x) = a + bx + cx^2.
$$

Therefore, the matrix equation that needs to be solved for the coefficients a, b and c is

$$
\begin{pmatrix}
1 & 0 & 0^2 \\
1 & 1 & 1^2 \\
1 & 2 & 2^2
\end{pmatrix}
\begin{pmatrix}
a \\
b \\
c
\end{pmatrix}
=
\begin{pmatrix}
2 \\
2.25 \\
5.82
\end{pmatrix}.
$$

Using Cramer's rule, the solution to the above equation can be written as:

$$a = \frac{|m1|}{|D|} = 2, \; b = \frac{|m2|}{|D|} = -1.41, \; \text{and} \; c = \frac{|m3|}{|D|} = 1.66,$$

where

$$m1 = \begin{pmatrix} 2 & 0 & 0 \\ 2.25 & 1 & 1 \\ 5.82 & 2 & 4 \end{pmatrix}, \; m2 = \begin{pmatrix} 1 & 2 & 0 \\ 1 & 2.25 & 1 \\ 1 & 5.82 & 4 \end{pmatrix},$$

$$m3 = \begin{pmatrix} 1 & 0 & 2 \\ 1 & 1 & 2.25 \\ 1 & 2 & 5.82 \end{pmatrix}, \; \text{and} \; D = \begin{pmatrix} 1 & 0 & 0 \\ 1 & 1 & 1 \\ 1 & 2 & 4 \end{pmatrix}.$$

Thus, the interpolating polynomial generated is

$$f(x) = 2 - 1.41x + 1.66x^2.$$

It is plotted in Figure 5.1, which gives

$$f(0.5) = 1.71 \text{ and } f(1.5) = 3.62.$$

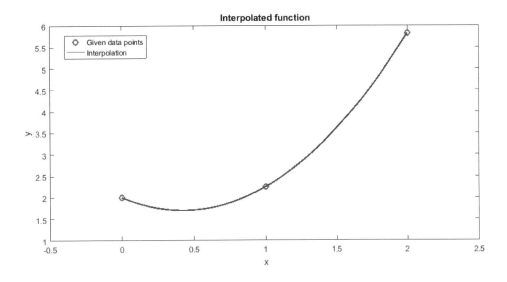

Fig. 5.1: Interpolated function using undetermined coefficient method

5.3 The Gregory-Newton Interpolating Polynomial

The form of the nth order Gregory-Newton interpolating polynomial is

$$f(x) = a_1 + a_2(x - x_1) + a_3(x - x_1)(x - x_2)$$
$$+ a_4(x - x_1)(x - x_2)(x - x_3) + \cdots$$
$$+ a_n(x - x_1)(x - x_2) \cdots (x - x_{n-1})$$
$$+ a_{n+1}(x - x_1)(x - x_2) \cdots (x - x_n) \quad (5.5)$$

where the a's are unknown coefficients that can be determined as was done in the method of undetermined coefficients. That is,

$$f(x_k) = y_k \text{ for } k = 1, \ldots, n+1 \quad (5.6)$$

where the x_k and y_k are the given data points that the interpolating polynomial must pass through.

To obtain a second order polynomial, put $x = x_1$, $x = x_2$ and $x = x_3$ in (5.5) yielding

$$a_1 = y_1$$
$$a_2 = \frac{y_2 - a_1}{x_2 - x_1}$$
$$a_3 = \frac{y_3 - a_1 - a_2(x_3 - x_1)}{(x_3 - x_1)(x_3 - x_2)}. \quad (5.7)$$

The interpolating polynomial is then determined as

$$f(x) = a_1 + a_2(x - x_1) + a_3(x - x_1)(x - x_2) \quad (5.8)$$

which is a second order polynomial passing through the three data points (x_1, y_1), (x_2, y_2) and (x_3, y_3).

For obtaining a third order polynomial, a fourth data point will be needed, and a fourth order polynomial will require the use of a fourth as well as a fifth data point. In general, determining an nth order polynomial will require $n + 1$ data points to be prescribed. Thus, the coefficients a_4, a_5 and a_6 can be determined using

$$a_4 = \frac{y_4 - a_1 - a_2(x_4 - x_1) - a_3(x_4 - x_1)(x_4 - x_2)}{(x_4 - x_1)(x_4 - x_2)(x_4 - x_3)}, \quad (5.9)$$

$$a_5 = \frac{\begin{bmatrix} y_5 - a_1 - a_2(x_5 - x_1) \\ - a_3(x_5 - x_1)(x_5 - x_2) \\ - a_4(x_5 - x_1)(x_5 - x_2)(x_5 - x_3) \end{bmatrix}}{(x_5 - x_1)(x_5 - x_2)(x_5 - x_3)(x_5 - x_4)}, \quad (5.10)$$

and

$$a_6 = \frac{\begin{bmatrix} y_6 - a_1 - a_2(x_6 - x_1) - a_3(x_6 - x_1)(x_6 - x_2) \\ - a_4(x_6 - x_1)(x_6 - x_2)(x_6 - x_3) \\ - a_5(x_6 - x_1)(x_6 - x_2)(x_6 - x_3)(x_6 - x_4) \end{bmatrix}}{(x_6 - x_1)(x_6 - x_2)(x_6 - x_3)(x_6 - x_4)(x_6 - x_5)}. \quad (5.11)$$

Example 5.2. Given three data points: (100, 975), (200, 1575), (400, 2054); determine the Gregory-Newton Polynomial $f(x)$ and evaluate $f(251)$.

The form of this polynomial would be:

$$y = f(x) = a_1 + a_2(x - x_1) + a_3(x - x_1)(x - x_2)$$

with

$$a_1 = y_1, a_2 = \frac{y_2 - y_1}{x_2 - x_1}, \text{ and } a_3 = \frac{y_3 - a_1 - a_2(x_3 - x_1)}{(x_3 - x_1)(x_3 - x_2)}.$$

The data is put in vector form as follows:

$$x = \begin{pmatrix} 100 \\ 200 \\ 400 \end{pmatrix} \text{ and } y = \begin{pmatrix} 975 \\ 1575 \\ 2054 \end{pmatrix}$$

and the coefficients a_1, a_2 and a_3 are computed as:

$$a_1 = 975, a_2 = 6, \text{ and } a_3 = -0.012.$$

Thus, the interpolating polynomial generated is:

$$f(x) = 975 + 6(x - 100) - 0.012(x - 100)(x - 200)$$

which is plotted in Figure 5.2, giving

$$f(251) = 1.788 \times 10^3.$$

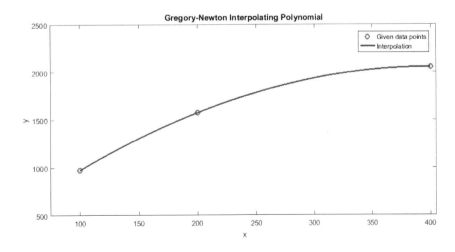

Fig. 5.2: Interpolated function obtained using Gregory-Newton polynomial method

Example 5.3. Given

$$\begin{array}{c|cccccc} x & 0 & 100 & 200 & 300 & 400 & 500 \\ \hline y & 104.2 & 97.3 & 48.1 & 23.7 & 8.6 & 5.2 \end{array}$$

Determine a fifth order Gregory-Newton interpolating polynomial $f(x)$ and evaluate $f(150)$, $f(350)$, and $f(450)$.

Because six data points are given, the interpolating polynomial in this case will be of fifth order, and will have the following form

$$\begin{aligned} f(x) = a_1 &+ a_2(x - x_1) + a_3(x - x_1)(x - x_2) \\ &+ a_4(x - x_1)(x - x_2)(x - x_3) + a_5(x - x_1)(x - x_2)(x - x_3)(x - x_4) \\ &+ a_6(x - x_1)(x - x_2)(x - x_3)(x - x_4)(x - x_5), \end{aligned}$$

where $a_1, a_2, \ldots$ are computed as shown below.

$$a_1 = y_1 = 104.2,$$

$$a_2 = \frac{y_2 - y_1}{x_2 - x_1} = -0.069,$$

$$a_3 = \frac{y_3 - a_1 - a_2(x_3 - x_1)}{(x_3 - x_1)(x_3 - x_2)} = -2.115 \times 10^{-3},$$

$$a_4 = \frac{y_4 - a_1 - a_2(x_4 - x_1) - a_3(x_4 - x_1)(x_4 - x_2)}{(x_4 - x_1)(x_4 - x_2)(x_4 - x_3)} = 1.118 \times 10^{-5},$$

$$a_5 = \frac{\left[\begin{array}{l} y_5 - a_1 - a_2(x_5 - x_1) - a_3(x_5 - x_1)(x_5 - x_2) \\ - a_4(x_5 - x_1)(x_5 - x_2)(x_5 - x_3) \end{array}\right]}{(x_5 - x_1)(x_5 - x_2)(x_5 - x_3)(x_5 - x_4)}$$
$$= -3.442 \times 10^{-8},$$

and

$$a_6 = \frac{\left[\begin{array}{l} y_6 - a_1 - a_2(x_6 - x_1) - a_3(x_6 - x_1)(x_6 - x_2) \\ - a_4(x_6 - x_1)(x_6 - x_2)(x_6 - x_3) \\ - a_5(x_6 - x_1)(x_6 - x_2)(x_6 - x_3)(x_6 - x_4) \end{array}\right]}{(x_6 - x_1)(x_6 - x_2)(x_6 - x_3)(x_6 - x_4)(x_6 - x_5)} = 8.375 \times 10^{-11},$$

which are inserted into the interpolating polynomial yielding

$$f(150) = 70.68, \quad f(350) = 16.435, \quad f(450) = 1.84.$$

The interpolated curve $f(x)$ is shown in Figure 5.3 along with the given data points (x, y).

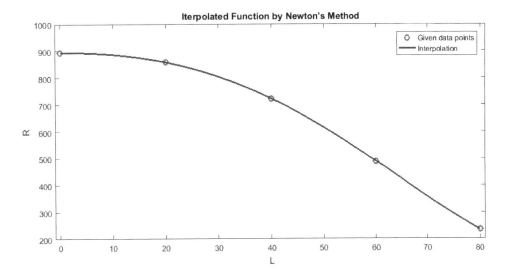

Fig. 5.3: Fifth-order Gregory-Newton interpolating polynomial

5.4 Interpolating Using Finite Differences

A finite difference table can furnish a way of developing an interpolating polynomial so long as the known values of the independent variable are equally spaced. For an increment Δx in the independent variable x, the first finite difference of the dependent variable $y = f(x)$ is

$$\Delta f = f(x + \Delta x) - f(x). \tag{5.12}$$

The second finite difference is

$$\Delta^2 f = \Delta(\Delta f) = [f(x + 2\Delta x) - f(x + \Delta x)] - [f(x + \Delta x) - f(x)]. \tag{5.13}$$

Similarly, the $(n - 1)$th finite difference will be

$$\Delta^n f = \Delta[\Delta^{n-1} f]. \tag{5.14}$$

The finite differences as derived above are arranged in a table as shown in Table 5.1 which can be used to generate an interpolating polynomial, as will be demonstrated later.

An alternate representation of the above is shown in Table 5.2, in which the independent variable goes from x_0 to x_3 and successive finite differences up to the fourth are generated.

5.5 Newton's Method Utilizing Finite Differences

Let (x_0, y_0), (x_1, y_1), (x_2, y_2) and (x_3, y_3) be four given data points for which a third degree Newton interpolating polynomial utilizing finite differences has to be determined. Assume the interpolating polynomial to be

x	$f(x)$	Δf	$\Delta^2 f$	$\Delta^3 f$	$\cdots$ $\Delta^n f$
x	$f(x)$				
		$\Delta f(x)$			
$x+\Delta x$	$f(x+\Delta x)$		$\Delta^2 f(x)$		
		$\Delta f(x+\Delta x)$		$\Delta^3 f(x)$	
$x+2\Delta x$	$f(x+2\Delta x)$		$\Delta^2 f(x+\Delta x)$		
		$\Delta f(x+2\Delta x)$			
$x+3\Delta x$	$f(x+3\Delta x)$				

Table 5.1: Table of Finite Differences

x_i	y_i	Δy_i	$\Delta^2 y_i$	$\Delta^3 y_i$
x_0	y_0			
		$\Delta y_0 = y_1 - y_0$		
x_1	y_1		$\Delta^2 y_0 = \Delta y_1 - \Delta y_0$	
		$\Delta y_1 = y_2 - y_1$		$\Delta^3 y_0 = \Delta^2 y_1 - \Delta^2 y_0$
x_2	y_2		$\Delta^2 y_1 = \Delta y_2 - \Delta y_1$	
		$\Delta y_2 = y_3 - y_2$		
x_3	y_3			

Table 5.2: Alternate form of the finite-difference table

$$f(x) = C_0 + C_1(x - x_0) + C_2(x - x_0)(x - x_1) + C_3(x - x_0)(x - x_1)(x - x_2) \qquad (5.15)$$

where the C's are undetermined coefficients that must be computed using the following constraint equations that the polynomial must satisfy

$$y_0 = f(x_0), \quad y_1 = f(x_1), \quad y_2 = f(x_2), \quad y_3 = f(x_3), \qquad (5.16)$$

which yield

$$y_0 = C_0 \qquad (5.17)$$
$$y_1 = C_0 + C_1(x_1 - x_0)$$
$$y_2 = C_0 + C_1(x_2 - x_0) + C_2(x_2 - x_0)(x_2 - x_1)$$
$$y_3 = C_0 + C_1(x_3 - x_0) + C_2(x_3 - x_0)(x_3 - x_1)$$
$$+ C_3(x_3 - x_0)(x_3 - x_1)(x_3 - x_2).$$

Using the finite differences

$$x_1 - x_0 = \Delta x, \quad x_2 - x_0 = 2\Delta x, \quad x_3 - x_0 = 3\Delta x, \qquad (5.18)$$

the undetermined coefficients are obtained as

$$C_0 = y_0, \quad C_1 = \frac{\Delta y_0}{\Delta x}, \quad C_2 = \frac{\Delta^2 y_0}{2!\Delta x^2}, \quad C_3 = \frac{\Delta^3 y_0}{3!\Delta x^3}. \qquad (5.19)$$

Defining

$$x - x_0 = n\Delta x, \tag{5.20}$$
$$x - x_1 = (n-1)\Delta x,$$
$$x - x_2 = (n-2)\Delta x,$$

where

$$n = \frac{x - x_0}{\Delta x}, \tag{5.21}$$

the interpolating polynomial of equation (5.15) can now be written as

$$f(x) = f(x_0) + n\Delta f(x_0) + \frac{n(n-1)}{2!}\Delta^2 f(x_0)$$
$$+ \frac{n(n-1)(n-2)}{3!}\Delta^3 f(x_0). \tag{5.22}$$

From the above process, it can be seen that the form of an mth order interpolating polynomial will be

$$f(x) = f(x_0) + n\Delta f(x_0) + \frac{n(n-1)}{2!}\Delta^2 f(x_0) + \frac{n(n-1)(n-2)}{3!}\Delta^3 f(x_0)$$
$$+ \cdots + \frac{n(n-1)\cdots(n-m+1)}{m!}\Delta^m f(x_0). \tag{5.23}$$

Example 5.4. The following data is given on the radiation flux R in gram-calories per square centimeter per day for a certain month in a given year as a function of latitude L (deg N).

L	0	20	40	60	80
R	895	858	722	489	235

Generate the finite difference table and obtain an interpolating polynomial using Newton's method. Estimate the flux R at a latitude of 45 degrees.

The following finite difference table can be generated using the given data.

L	R	ΔR	$\Delta^2 R$	$\Delta^3 R$	$\Delta^4 R$
0	895				
		-37			
20	858		-99		
		-136		2	
40	722		-97		74
		-233		76	
60	489		-21		
		-254			
80	235				

The interpolating polynomial can now be written as:

$$R(L) = R(L_0) + n\Delta R(L_0) + \frac{1}{2}n(n-1)\Delta^2 R(L_0)$$
$$+ \frac{1}{6}n(n-1)(n-2)\Delta^3 R(L_0)$$
$$+ \frac{1}{24}n(n-1)(n-2)(n-3)\Delta^4 R(L_0)$$

where

$$R(L_0) = 895; \quad \Delta R(L_0) = -37; \quad \Delta^2 R(L_0) = -99; \quad \Delta^3 R(L_0) = 2;$$
$$\Delta^4 R(L_0) = 74; \quad n = \frac{L - L_0}{\Delta L} = \frac{L - 0}{20} = \frac{L}{20}.$$

The interpolating polynomial is plotted in Figure 5.4.

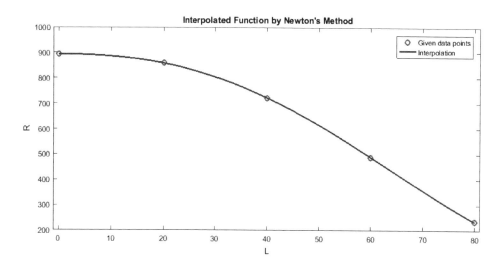

Fig. 5.4: The Newton interpolating polynomial

The interpolation yields $R(45) = 671.14$.

5.6 The Lagrange Interpolating Polynomial

In many practical problems, data measurements are recorded at unequal spacings or intervals. In such situations, the Lagrangian interpolation method offers a viable means of deducing an interpolating polynomial connecting the dependent variable with the independent variable at intervals that are not necessarily constant.

By this method, given a data sample

$$(x_1, y_1), (x_2, y_2), \ldots, (x_n, y_n)$$

an interpolating polynomial can be generated using

$$f(x) = \sum_{i=1}^{n} w_i(x) y_i \tag{5.24}$$

where

$$w_i(x) = \frac{\prod_{j=1}^{n} (x - x_j)}{\prod_{j=1}^{n} (x_i - x_j)}, \, j \neq i. \tag{5.25}$$

For example, if three data points are prescribed, $n = 3$ and the interpolating polynomial will be

$$f(x) = \sum_{i=1}^{3} w_i(x) y_i$$

with

$$w_1(x) = \frac{(x - x_2)(x - x_3)}{(x_1 - x_2)(x_1 - x_3)}, \tag{5.26}$$

$$w_2(x) = \frac{(x - x_1)(x - x_3)}{(x_2 - x_1)(x_2 - x_3)},$$

$$w_3(x) = \frac{(x - x_1)(x - x_2)}{(x_3 - x_1)(x_3 - x_2)}.$$

Example 5.5. Given the following data

x	96	207	375	450
y	932	850	767	1235

determine the Lagrange Interpolating Polynomial $f(x)$ that passes through the above points. Determine $f(102)$, $f(322)$, and $f(415)$.

The given data is

$$x_1 = 96, \quad x_2 = 207, \quad x_3 = 375, \quad x_4 = 450,$$
$$y_1 = 932, \quad y_2 = 850, \quad y_3 = 767, \quad y_4 = 1235.$$

The Lagrange interpolating polynomial, in this case, will be a cubic of the following form

$$f(x) = w_1(x) y_1 + w_2(x) y_2 + w_3(x) y_3 + w_4(x) y_4$$

where

$$w_1(x) = \frac{(x-x_2)(x-x_3)(x-x_4)}{(x_1-x_2)(x_1-x_3)(x_1-x_4)},$$

$$w_2(x) = \frac{(x-x_1)(x-x_3)(x-x_4)}{(x_2-x_1)(x_2-x_3)(x_2-x_4)},$$

$$w_3(x) = \frac{(x-x_1)(x-x_2)(x-x_4)}{(x_3-x_1)(x_3-x_2)(x_3-x_4)},$$

$$w_4(x) = \frac{(x-x_1)(x-x_2)(x-x_3)}{(x_4-x_1)(x_4-x_2)(x_4-x_3)}.$$

The interpolating polynomial is shown in Figure 5.5.

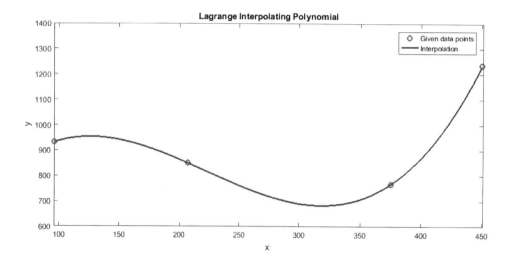

Fig. 5.5: The Lagrange interpolating polynomial

The polynomial yields

$$f(102) = 940.053, \quad f(322) = 683.419, \quad f(415) = 955.728.$$

5.7 Interpolating Using Linear, Quadratic and Cubic Splines

For n data points that are provided, the highest-order interpolating polynomial that can be generated will be of order $(n-1)$. Although, in general, the accuracy of the interpolation process increases with the order of the polynomial, there are situations when the accuracy can, in fact, decrease with the polynomial order. This can happen when the measured data reflects abrupt changes in the dependent variable values for steady changes in the independent variable. In these cases, accuracy can be improved by resorting to lower order polynomials, commonly referred to as splines. Splines normally used are linear, quadratic, and cubic.

Linear Splines: A linear spline results from connecting adjacent data points with straight lines. Given n data points (x_1, y_1), (x_2, y_2), (x_3, y_3), ..., (x_n, y_n), the interpolation function for x between x_1 and x_2 is

$$f(x) = y_1 + \frac{x - x_1}{x_2 - x_1}(y_2 - y_1). \tag{5.27}$$

Similarly, for x between x_2 and x_3 the interpolation function will be

$$f(x) = y_2 + \frac{x - x_2}{x_3 - x_2}(y_3 - y_2). \tag{5.28}$$

It follows, then, that for x between x_{n-1} and x_n

$$f(x) = y_{n-1} + \frac{x - x_{n-1}}{x_n - x_{n-1}}(y_n - y_{n-1}). \tag{5.29}$$

The resulting linear spline, however, must satisfy the following constraint equations

$$f(x_i) = f_{i+1}(x_i) \text{ for } i = 1, 2, \ldots, n-1. \tag{5.30}$$

Quadratic Splines: Quadratic splines are of the form: $ax^2 + bx + c$ The conditions to be satisfied are:

(1) The spline must pass through the given data points.
(2) The spline is to be continuous at the interior data points.
(3) The second derivative of the spline between the first two data points is to be zero.

Cubic Splines: Cubic splines have the form: $ax^3 + bx^2 + cx + d$ and must satisfy the following conditions:

(1) The spline function must pass through the given data points.
(2) The first derivatives of the spline must be continuous.
(3) The second derivatives of the spline must also be continuous.
(4) The second derivative must be zero at the first and second data points.

5.8 Interpolating with MATLAB

Interpolation in MATLAB allows you to either connect the data points with straight lines (linear interpolation) or with sections of a cubic polynomial (cubic spline interpolation). These interpolation functions return a curve passing through the points you specify.

Linear Interpolation: This is done using the *interp1* function as shown below.

interp1(vx,vy,xx): Uses the data vectors *vx* and *vy* to return a linearly interpolated value of y corresponding to x. The quantities *vx* and *vy* must be specified as vectors and *vx* must contain real values in ascending order. Vector *xx* is the domain values used to plot the interpolation.

Cubic Spline Interpolation: Cubic spline interpolation enables you to pass a curve through a set of points such that the first and second derivatives of the curve are continuous at each point. MATLAB does this by taking four adjacent points and constructing a cubic polynomial that passes through these points. These cubics are then connected together to make up the interpolated curve.

In order to fit a cubic spline curve through a set of points, the procedure shown below must be followed:

1. Create the vectors vx and vy containing the x and y coordinates of the points of interest through which you want to go. The elements of vx must be put in ascending order.
2. Generate the vector $vs = spline(vx, vy)$. This vector vs is a vector of intermediate results to be used with *ppval*.
3. To evaluate the spline at a point or a vector $x1$, do the following: $ppval(vs, x1)$.

   Note: Steps 2 and 3 can be combined by doing: $spline(vx, vy, x1)$.

There are other options for cubic splines in MATLAB. We will discuss two of those options below.

One can use the same *spline* command as above, but impose clamped boundary conditions - that is, end slopes of 0 are prescribed. To do this, we do the following: $vs = spline(vx, [0 \, vy \, 0])$.

Another option is to use a a piecewise Cubic Hermite interpolating polynomial (PCHIP). To do this, we generate the vector $vs = pchip(vx, vy)$. This vector vs is a vector of intermediate results and works in a manner similar to spline.

For Example 5.1, the vx and vy vectors are:

$$vx = \begin{pmatrix} 0 \\ 1 \\ 2 \end{pmatrix} \text{ and } vy = \begin{pmatrix} 2 \\ 2.25 \\ 5.82 \end{pmatrix}.$$

As shown below, the *interp1* function is used to do a linear interpolation. The resulting linear spline function is drawn in Figure 5.6 and the values of the interpolated function at $x = 0.5$ and 1.5 are calculated.

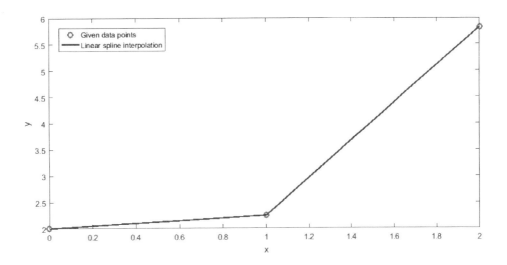

Fig. 5.6: Interpolated function obtained with *interp1*

```
vx = [0 1 2];
vy = [2 2.25 5.82];
x = 0:0.1:2;
y = interp1(vx,vy,x);

p = plot(vx,vy,'redo',x,y,'blue');
xlabel('x')
ylabel('y')
legend('Given data points','Linear spline interpolation')
p(1).LineWidth = 2;
p(2).LineWidth = 2;
interp1(vx,vy,0.5)
ans =
    2.1250
interp1(vx,vy,1.5)
ans =
    4.0350
```

The *spline* function, along with clamped boundary conditions, or the *pchip* function, can be utilized as follows to generate cubic splines. Figure 5.7 shows a comparison of the various splines generated using MATLAB.

```
vx = [0 1 2];
vy = [2 2.25 5.82];
x = 0:0.1:2;
y = interp1(vx,vy,x);
```

```
vs1 = spline(vx,vy,x);
vs2 = spline(vx,[0 vy 0],x);
vs3 = pchip(vx,vy,x);

p = plot(vx,vy,'redo',x,y,'blue',x,vs1,'magenta',x,vs2,'
   green',x,vs3,'cyan')
title('Comparison of MATLAB Splines')
xlabel('x')
ylabel('y')
legend('Given data points','Linear spline interpolation','
   Cubic spline interpolation','Cubic spline w/clamped
   boundaries','Cubic Hermite interpolation')
p(1).LineWidth = 2;
p(2).LineWidth = 2;
p(3).LineWidth = 2;
p(4).LineWidth = 2;
p(5).LineWidth = 2;
```

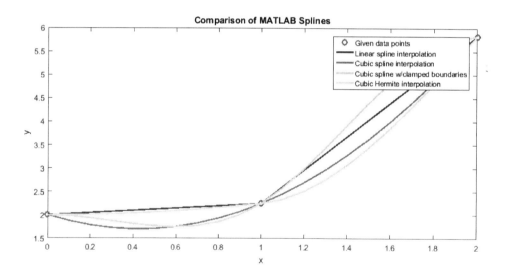

Fig. 5.7: Comparison of spline functions obtained with MATLAB

Values of the interpolated cubic splines at $x = 0.5$ and 1.5 are:

```
spline(vx,vy,0.5)

ans =
    1.7100
```

```
spline(vx,vy,1.5)

ans =
    3.6200

spline(vx,[0 vy 0],0.5)

ans =
    1.7669

spline(vx,[0 vy 0],1.5)

ans =
    4.3931

pchip(vx,vy,0.5)

ans =
    2.0666

pchip(vx,vy,1.5)

ans =
    3.4397
```

For the problem of Example 5.2, interpolations using the MATLAB *interp1* and *spline* functions yield the following. The results are sketched in Figure 5.8.

```
vx = [100 200 400];
vy = [975 1575 2054];
x = 100:1:400;
y = interp1(vx,vy,x);
vs = spline(vx,vy,x);

p = plot(vx,vy,'redo',x,y,'blue--',x,vs,'magenta')
title('Interpolation with MATLAB')
xlabel('x')
ylabel('y')
legend('Given data points','Linear spline interpolation','
    Cubic spline interpolation')
p(1).LineWidth = 2;
p(2).LineWidth = 2;
p(3).LineWidth = 2;
```

```
interp1(vx,vy,251)

ans =
    1.6971e+03

spline(vx,vy,251)

ans =
    1.7885e+03
```

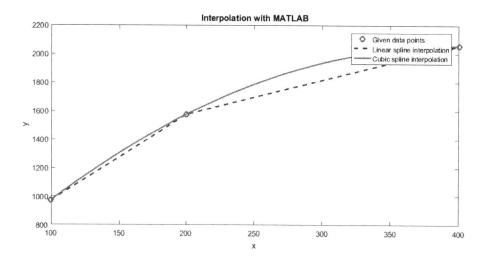

Fig. 5.8: Interpolation with MATLAB

For the problem of Example 5.3, interpolation using the MATLAB spline functions is shown below.

```
vx = [0 100 200 300 400 500];
vy = [104.2 97.3 48.1 23.7 8.6 5.2];
x = 0:1:500;
y = interp1(vx,vy,x);

p = plot(vx,vy,'redo',x,y,'blue')
xlabel('x')
ylabel('y')
legend('Given data points','Linear spline interpolation')
p(1).LineWidth = 2;
p(2).LineWidth = 2;
```

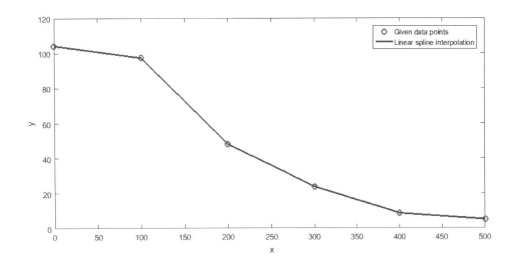

Fig. 5.9: Linear interpolation for Example 5.3

Linear interpolation values at $x = 150$, $x = 350$ and $x = 450$ are:

```
interp1(vx,vy,150)

ans =
    72.7000

interp1(vx,vy,350)

ans =
    16.1500

interp1(vx,vy,450)

ans =
    6.9000
```

The Gregory Newton polynomial for this problem was derived earlier. Figure 5.10 shows a comparison of the MATLAB spline functions with the Gregory-Newton interpolation $f(x)$.

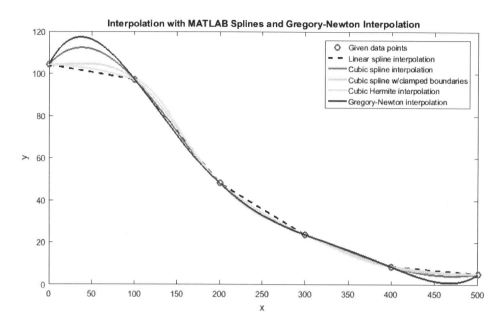

Fig. 5.10: Comparison of MATLAB Splines with the Gregory-Newton Interpolating Polynomial

The MATLAB interpolated values at $x = 150$, 350 and 450 are shown below.

```
spline(vx,vy,150)

ans =
    72.3425

spline(vx,vy,350)

ans =
    15.4800

spline(vx,vy,450)

ans =
    4.6450

spline(vx,[0 vy 0],150)

ans =
    74.2061
```

```
spline(vx,[0 vy 0],350)

ans =
    15.3291

spline(vx,[0 vy 0],450)

ans =
    5.6767

pchip(vx,vy,150)

ans =
    75.2649

pchip(vx,vy,350)

ans =
    14.5119

pchip(vx,vy,450)

ans =
    6.2062
```

In the following, MATLAB splines for the problem of Example 5.5 are generated and compared with the Lagrange interpolating polynomial obtained earlier.

```
vx = [96 207 375 450];
vy = [932 850 767 1235];
x = 96:10:450;
y = interp1(vx,vy,x);

vs1 = spline(vx,vy,x);
vs2 = spline(vx,[0 vy 0],x);
vs3 = pchip(vx,vy,x);

w1 = ((x - vx(2)).*(x - vx(3)).*(x - vx(4)))./((vx(1) - vx
    (2))*(vx(1) - vx(3))*(vx(1) - vx(4)));
w2 = ((x - vx(1)).*(x - vx(3)).*(x - vx(4)))./((vx(2) - vx
    (1))*(vx(2) - vx(3))*(vx(2) - vx(4)));
```

```
w3 = ((x - vx(1)).*(x - vx(2)).*(x - vx(4)))./((vx(3) - vx
    (1))*(vx(3) - vx(2))*(vx(3) -vx(4)));
w4 = ((x - vx(1)).*(x - vx(2)).*(x - vx(3)))./((vx(4) - vx
    (1))*(vx(4) - vx(2))*(vx(4) -vx(3)));
f = w1*vy(1) + w2*vy(2) + w3*vy(3) + w4*vy(4);


p = plot(vx,vy,'redo',x,y,'black--',x,vs1,'magenta--^',x,vs2
    ,'green',x,vs3,'cyan',x,f,'blue')
axis([96 451 600 1300])
title('Lagrange Polynomial and MATLAB Interpolations
    Compared')
xlabel('x')
ylabel('y')
legend('Given data points','Linear spline interpolation','
    Cubic spline interpolation','Cubic spline w/clamped
    boundaries','Cubic Hermite interpolation','Lagrange
    polynomial interpolation')
p(1).LineWidth = 2;
p(2).LineWidth = 2;
p(3).LineWidth = 2;
p(4).LineWidth = 2;
p(5).LineWidth = 2;
p(6).LineWidth = 2;
```

The various interpolations resorted to give the following interpolated function values f or $x = 102, 322$ and 415.

x	Lagrange	Linear	Spline	Spline w/Clamped BC	Hermite
102	940.0528	927.5676	940.0527	932.0047	927.0024
322	683.4194	793.1845	683.4194	596.8077	779.7000
415	955.7285	1.0166×10^3	955.7285	1.0818×10^3	941.5509

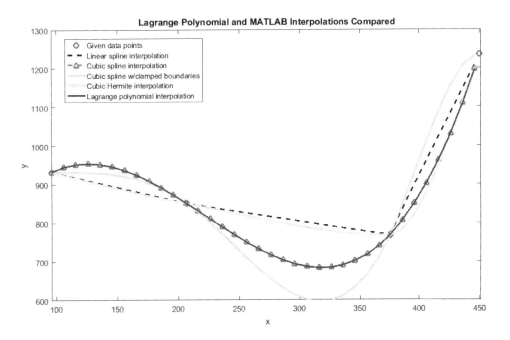

Fig. 5.11: Comparison of MATLAB splines with Lagrangian Interpolation

5.9 Applications in Numerical Interpolation

In the examples that follow, data from various practical areas such as design of machinery, noise control and vibration analysis, is utilized in interpolation procedures to generate function values at points other than the given data points.

5.9.1 Stress-Strain Data for Titanium

The stress versus strain data given in the table below is obtained from a tensile test of annealed A-40 titanium [10]. A cubic spline can be developed using MATLAB as follows and the stresses interpolated for any values of strain in the range provided.

Strain ε (in/in)	Stress σ (kpsi)
0	0
0.00030	5
0.00060	10
0.00090	15
0.00120	20
0.00175	25
0.00220	30
0.00285	34.9
0.00349	39.9
0.00469	44.9
0.00698	49.9
0.01610	60.9
0.04807	73.3
0.07676	78.2
0.14364	86.2
0.26677	94.5
0.34470	98.7
0.72202	118.2

The cubic spline interpolation generated together with the given data points is presented in Figure 5.12. Notice that the spline generated passes through all the given data points as is expected of an interpolating polynomial.

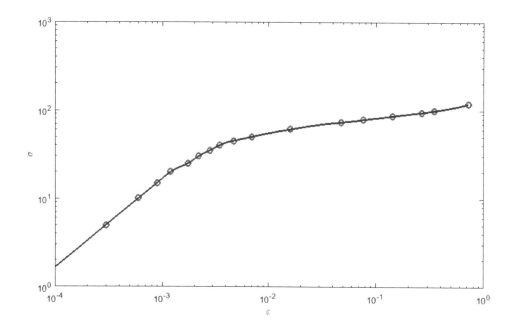

Fig. 5.12: MATLAB cubic spline for given stress-strain data

```
veps = [0 0.0003 0.0006 0.0009 0.0012 0.00175 0.0022 0.00285
     0.00349 0.00469 0.00698 0.0161 0.04807 0.07676 0.14364
   0.26677 0.3447 0.72202];
vsig = [0 5 10 15 20 25 30 34.9 39.9 44.9 49.9 60.9 73.3
   78.2 86.2 94.5 98.7 118.2];
eps = 0:.0001:0.722;
vs = spline(veps,vsig,eps);

p = loglog(veps,vsig,'redo',eps,vs,'blue')
l = xlabel('$\varepsilon$')
ylabel('\sigma')
p(1).LineWidth = 2;
p(2).LineWidth = 2;
set(l,'interpreter','latex')

sig1 = spline(veps,vsig,0.004)
sig2 = spline(veps,vsig,0.65)

sig1 =
  42.698878321403861

sig2 =
   1.145027382179784e+02
```

5.9.2 Notch Sensitivity of Aluminum

The fatigue stress concentration factor K_f is used with the nominal stress σ_0 to compute the maximum resulting stress σ_{max} at a discontinuity in a machine part via the following relationship [10].

$$\sigma_{max} = K_f \sigma_0. \tag{5.31}$$

The fatigue stress concentration factor K_f, which is, in fact, just a reduced value of the geometrical stress concentration factor K_t, is a function of the sensitivity of the material of which the part is made to notches (known as notch sensitivity q). These quantities are connected by the following relationship.

$$K_f = 1 + q(K_t - 1). \tag{5.32}$$

Notch sensitivity charts which are graphs of notch sensitivity versus notch radius are available for metals and alloys subjected to reversed bending or reversed axial loads. The data given below provides notch sensitivity (q) versus notch radius (r) information for an aluminum alloy and can be used to generate an interpolation from which notch sensitivity values at points other than the given data points can be readily obtained.

$$
\begin{array}{c|ccccccc}
r \text{ (in)} & 0.015 & 0.04 & 0.06 & 0.10 & 0.12 & 0.14 & 0.16 \\
q & 0.25 & 0.55 & 0.65 & 0.75 & 0.775 & 0.80 & 0.825
\end{array}
$$

Since seven data points are given, the interpolating polynomial that can be generated will be of order 6, having the form

$$f(r) = a + br + cr^2 + dr^3 + er^4 + fr^5 + gr^6.$$

Resorting to the method of undetermined coefficients results in the following matrix equation

$$MC = A,$$

where

$$
M = \begin{pmatrix}
1 & 0.015 & 0.015^2 & 0.015^3 & 0.015^4 & 0.015^5 & 0.015^6 \\
1 & 0.04 & 0.04^2 & 0.04^3 & 0.04^4 & 0.04^5 & 0.04^6 \\
1 & 0.06 & 0.06^2 & 0.06^3 & 0.06^4 & 0.06^5 & 0.06^6 \\
1 & 0.10 & 0.10^2 & 0.10^3 & 0.10^4 & 0.10^5 & 0.10^6 \\
1 & 0.12 & 0.12^2 & 0.12^3 & 0.12^4 & 0.12^5 & 0.12^6 \\
1 & 0.14 & 0.14^2 & 0.14^3 & 0.14^4 & 0.14^5 & 0.14^6 \\
1 & 0.16 & 0.16^2 & 0.16^3 & 0.16^4 & 0.16^5 & 0.16^6
\end{pmatrix},
$$

$$
C = \begin{pmatrix} a \\ b \\ c \\ d \\ e \\ f \\ g \end{pmatrix}, \quad
A = \begin{pmatrix} 0.25 \\ 0.55 \\ 0.65 \\ 0.75 \\ 0.775 \\ 0.80 \\ 0.825 \end{pmatrix}
$$

The coefficients in the column vector C can be obtained using the MATLAB command "\".

```
M = [1 0.015 0.015^2 0.015^3 0.015^4 0.015^5 0.015^6;
     1 0.04 0.04^2 0.04^3 0.04^4 0.04^5 0.04^6;
     1 0.06 0.06^2 0.06^3 0.06^4 0.06^5 0.06^6;
     1 0.10 0.10^2 0.10^3 0.10^4 0.10^5 0.10^6;
     1 0.12 0.12^2 0.12^3 0.12^4 0.12^5 0.12^6;
     1 0.14 0.14^2 0.14^3 0.14^4 0.14^5 0.14^6;
     1 0.16 0.16^2 0.16^3 0.16^4 0.16^5 0.16^6];
A = [0.25 0.55 0.65 0.75 0.775 0.80 0.825]';

C = M\A

C =
```

```
   1.0e+05 *

 -0.000001874638269
  0.000404623749155
 -0.009224310391775
  0.127036569848125
 -1.009880338628485
  4.227547939667974
 -7.168648110573889
```

Thus, the interpolating polynomial $f(x)$ is completely determined with

```
r = 0.015:0.01:0.16;

f = C(1) + C(2)*r + C(3)*r^2 + C(4)*r^3 + C(5)*r^4 + C(6)*r
    ^5 + C(7)*r^6;
```

MATLAB cubic spline interpolation can also be employed as shown below and the resulting plot compared with the results of the undetermined coefficients method and with the given data points. This is done in Figure 5.13.

```
vr = [0.015 0.04 0.06 0.10 0.12 0.14 0.16];
vq = [0.25 0.55 0.65 0.75 0.775 0.80 0.825];

vs = spline(vr,vq,r);

p = plot(vr,vq,'redo',r,f,'blue',r,vs,'green--*')
title('MATLAB Interpolation/Notch Sensitivity')
xlabel('r')
ylabel('q')
legend('Given data points','Interpolation by undetermined
   coefficient method','MATLAB cubic spline interpolation')
p(1).LineWidth = 2;
p(2).LineWidth = 2;
```

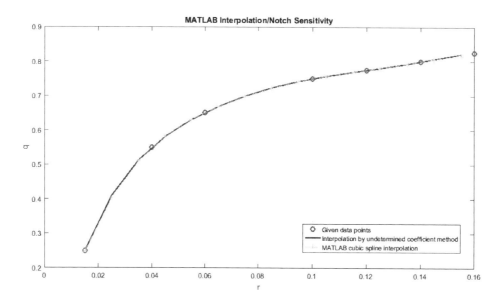

Fig. 5.13: Interpolation of notch sensitivity data

5.9.3 Speech Interference Level

In the field of Noise and Vibration Control, it often becomes necessary to determine the effect of steady background noise on speech communication in a given setting. The preferred speech interference level ($PSIL$) was established in an effort to study this effect under the constraint that speech sounds would not be allowed to be reflected back to the listener [6]. For effective communication at a given voice level, the maximum distance that there can be between the speaker and the listener is a function of the preferred speech interference level existing at the location. The following data which is provided for communication at the level of a normal male voice can be utilized in an interpolation scheme to determine the maximum $PSIL$ permitted for a given distance between the speaker and the listener.

Dist (ft)	0	2	4	6	8	10	12
$PSIL$ (dB)	83	62.5	56	52.5	50	47.5	46.5

Because there are 7 data points prescribed, the interpolating polynomial to be generated will be of order 6 and if a Gregory-Newton interpolating polynomial is to be determined, it will have the form

$$f(x) = a_1 + a_2(x - x_1) + a_3(x - x_1)(x - x_2)$$
$$+ a_4(x - x_1)(x - x_2)(x - x_3) + a_5(x - x_1)(x - x_2)(x - x_3)(x - x_4)$$
$$+ a_6(x - x_1)(x - x_2)(x - x_3)(x - x_4)(x - x_5)$$
$$+ a_7(x - x_1)(x - x_2)(x - x_3)(x - x_4)(x - x_5)(x - x_6),$$

where the *a*'s are unknown coefficients to be determined.

```
x = [0 2 4 6 8 10 12];
y = [83 62.5 56 52.5 50 47.5 46.5];

a1 = y(1)
a2 = (y(2) - y(1))/(x(2) - x(1))
a3 = (y(3) - a1 - a2*(x(3) - x(1)))/((x(3) - x(1))*(x(3) - x
   (2)))
a4 = (y(4) - a1 - a2*(x(4) - x(1)) - a3*(x(4) - x(1))*(x(4)
   - x(2)))/((x(4) - x(1))*(x(4) - x(2))*(x(4) - x(3)))
a5 = (y(5) - a1 - a2*(x(5) - x(1)) - a3*(x(5)-x(1))*(x(5) -
   x(2)) - a4*(x(5) - x(1))*(x(5) - x(2))*(x(5) - x(3)))/((x
   (5) - x(1))*(x(5) - x(2))*(x(5) - x(3))*(x(5) - x(4)))
a6 = (y(6) - a1 - a2*(x(6) - x(1)) - a3*(x(6) - x(1))*(x(6)
   - x(2)) - a4*(x(6) - x(1))*(x(6) - x(2))*(x(6) - x(3)) -
   a5*(x(6) - x(1))*(x(6) - x(2))*(x(6) - x(3))*(x(6) - x(4)
   ))/((x(6) - x(1))*(x(6) - x(2))*(x(6) - x(3))*(x(6) - x
   (4))*(x(6) - x(5)))
a7 = (y(7) - a1 - a2*(x(7) - x(1)) - a3*(x(7) - x(1))*(x(7)
   - x(2)) - a4*(x(7) - x(1))*(x(7) - x(2))*(x(7) - x(3)) -
   a5*(x(7) - x(1))*(x(7) - x(2))*(x(7) - x(3))*(x(7) - x(4)
   )- a6*(x(7) - x(1))*(x(7) - x(2))*(x(7) - x(3))*(x(7) - x
   (4))*(x(7) - x(5)))/((x(7) - x(1))*(x(7) - x(2))*(x(7) -
   x(3))*(x(7) - x(4))*(x(7) - x(5))*(x(7) - x(6)))

a1 =
    83


a2 =
 -10.250000000000000


a3 =
   1.750000000000000


a4 =
  -0.229166666666667
```

```
a5 =
   0.023437500000000


a6 =
  -0.002083333333333


a7 =
    2.061631944444444e-04
```

The interpolating polynomial obtained by the Gregory-Newton method can now be obtained using MATLAB:

```
x1 = 0:.01:12;

f = a1 + a2*(x1 - x(1)) + a3*(x1 - x(1)).*(x1 - x(2)) + a4*(
    x1 - x(1)).*(x1 - x(2)).*(x1 - x(3)) + a5*(x1 - x(1)).*(
    x1 - x(2)).*(x1 - x(3)).*(x1 - x(4)) + a6*(x1 - x(1)).*(
    x1 - x(2)).*(x1 - x(3)).*(x1 - x(4)).*(x1 - x(5)) + a7*(
    x1 - x(1)).*(x1 - x(2)).*(x1 - x(3)).*(x1 - x(4)).*(x1 -
    x(5)).*(x1 - x(6));
```

MATLAB cubic spline interpolation can also be employed as shown below and the resulting plot compared with the results of the Gregory-Newton method and with the given data points. This is done in Figure 5.14.

```
x2 = 0:1:12;
vs = spline(x,y,x2);

p = plot(x,y,'redo',x1,f,'blue',x2,vs,'green--*')
title('Interpolation - Speech Communication')
xlabel('x: Distance from speaker to listenter (ft)')
ylabel('y: Preferred speech interference level (dB)')
legend('Given data points','Gregory-Newton interpolation','
   Cubic spline interpolation')
p(1).LineWidth = 2;
p(2).LineWidth = 2;
```

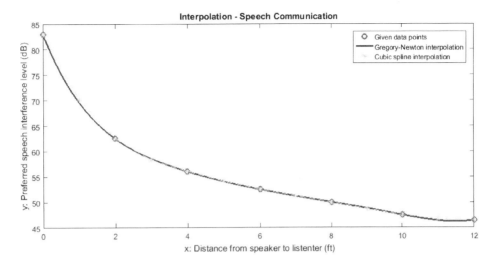

Fig. 5.14: Interpolation of speech communication data

5.9.4 Load-Deflection Data for Elastomeric Mounts

Elastomeric mounts are employed when small electrical and mechanical devices have to be isolated from high forcing frequencies [5, 6]. They are especially useful in the protection of delicate electronic instruments. Mount performance characteristics in the form of load versus static deflection data are provided by manufacturers of vibration control products to enable a designer to select an appropriate isolator for a given application.

The following data is available for an elastomeric mount.

Deflection (cm)	0	0.02	0.04	0.06	0.08	0.10
Load (N)	5	11	17.5	23.5	28	30.5

There are six data points prescribed. Thus, if a Lagrangian interpolating polynomial is to be generated, it will be of order 5, having the form

$$L(D) = \sum_{i=1}^{6} w_i(D) L_i$$

where

$$w_i(D) = \frac{\prod_{j=1}^{6} (D - D_j)}{\prod_{j=1}^{6} (D_i - D_j)}, \quad j \neq i.$$

The interpolating polynomial obtained by Lagrangian interpolation may now be obtained using:

```
D = [0  0.02 0.04 0.06 0.08 0.10];
L = [5 11 17.5 23.5 28 30.5];

D1 = 0.07;

w1 = ((D1 - D(2)).*(D1 - D(3)).*(D1 - D(4)).*(D1 - D(5)).*(
    D1 - D(6)))/((D(1) - D(2))*(D(1) - D(3))*(D(1) - D(4))*(D
    (1) - D(5))*(D(1) - D(6)));
w2 = ((D1 - D(1)).*(D1 - D(3)).*(D1 - D(4)).*(D1 - D(5)).*(
    D1 - D(6)))/((D(2) - D(1))*(D(2) - D(3))*(D(2) - D(4))*(D
    (2) - D(5))*(D(2) - D(6)));
w3 = ((D1 - D(1)).*(D1 - D(2)).*(D1 - D(4)).*(D1 - D(5)).*(
    D1 - D(6)))/((D(3) - D(1))*(D(3) - D(2))*(D(3) - D(4))*(D
    (3) - D(5))*(D(3) - D(6)));
w4 = ((D1 - D(1)).*(D1 - D(2)).*(D1 - D(3)).*(D1 - D(5)).*(
    D1 - D(6)))/((D(4) - D(1))*(D(4) - D(2))*(D(4) - D(3))*(D
    (4) - D(5))*(D(4) - D(6)));
w5 = ((D1 - D(1)).*(D1 - D(2)).*(D1 - D(3)).*(D1 - D(4)).*(
    D1 - D(6)))/((D(5) - D(1))*(D(5) - D(2))*(D(5) - D(3))*(D
    (5) - D(4))*(D(5) - D(6)));
w6 = ((D1 - D(1)).*(D1 - D(2)).*(D1 - D(3)).*(D1 - D(4)).*(
    D1 - D(5)))/((D(6) - D(1))*(D(6) - D(2))*(D(6) - D(3))*(D
    (6) - D(4))*(D(6) - D(5)));

L1 = L(1)*w1 + L(2)*w2 + L(3)*w3 + L(4)*w4 + L(5)*w5 + L(6)*
    w6

L1 =

 25.986328125000007
```

Thus, $L(0.07) = 25.9863$.

MATLAB cubic spline interpolation can also be employed as shown below and the resulting plot compared with the results of the Lagrangian interpolation and with the given data points. This is done in Figure 5.15.

```
D = [0  0.02 0.04 0.06 0.08 0.10];
L = [5 11 17.5 23.5 28 30.5];

D1 = 0:0.01:0.10;
```

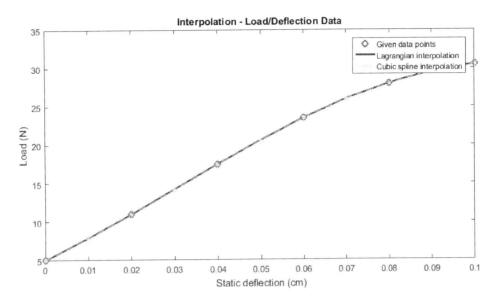

Fig. 5.15: Interpolation of load-deflection data for elastomeric mount

```
w1 = ((D1 - D(2)).*(D1 - D(3)).*(D1 - D(4)).*(D1 - D(5)).*(
    D1 - D(6)))/((D(1) - D(2))*(D(1) - D(3))*(D(1) - D(4))*(D
    (1) - D(5))*(D(1) - D(6)));
w2 = ((D1 - D(1)).*(D1 - D(3)).*(D1 - D(4)).*(D1 - D(5)).*(
    D1 - D(6)))/((D(2) - D(1))*(D(2) - D(3))*(D(2) - D(4))*(D
    (2) - D(5))*(D(2) - D(6)));
w3 = ((D1 - D(1)).*(D1 - D(2)).*(D1 - D(4)).*(D1 - D(5)).*(
    D1 - D(6)))/((D(3) - D(1))*(D(3) - D(2))*(D(3) - D(4))*(D
    (3) - D(5))*(D(3) - D(6)));
w4 = ((D1 - D(1)).*(D1 - D(2)).*(D1 - D(3)).*(D1 - D(5)).*(
    D1 - D(6)))/((D(4) - D(1))*(D(4) - D(2))*(D(4) - D(3))*(D
    (4) - D(5))*(D(4) - D(6)));
w5 = ((D1 - D(1)).*(D1 - D(2)).*(D1 - D(3)).*(D1 - D(4)).*(
    D1 - D(6)))/((D(5) - D(1))*(D(5) - D(2))*(D(5) - D(3))*(D
    (5) - D(4))*(D(5) - D(6)));
w6 = ((D1 - D(1)).*(D1 - D(2)).*(D1 - D(3)).*(D1 - D(4)).*(
    D1 - D(5)))/((D(6) - D(1))*(D(6) - D(2))*(D(6) - D(3))*(D
    (6) - D(4))*(D(6) - D(5)));

L1 = L(1)*w1 + L(2)*w2 + L(3)*w3 + L(4)*w4 + L(5)*w5 + L(6)*
    w6;

vs = spline(D,L,D1);
```

```
p = plot(D,L,'redo',D1,L1,'blue',D1,vs,'green--*')
title('Interpolation - Load/Deflection Data')
xlabel('Static deflection (cm)')
ylabel('Load (N)')
legend('Given data points','Lagrangian interpolation','Cubic
    spline interpolation')
p(1).LineWidth = 2;
p(2).LineWidth = 2;
```

Problems

5.1. Using the method of undetermined coefficients, derive an interpolating polynomial $f(x)$ of the form "$a + bx$", for the following data. Determine the interpolated value of $f(0.52)$.

x	0.45	0.55	0.65	0.75
y	0.075	0.136	0.227	0.372

5.2. For the same data as in Problem 5.1, use the method of undetermined coefficients to derive an interpolating polynomial $f(x)$ of form "$a + bx + cx^2$". Calculate $f(0.63)$. Check your results against functions obtained with MATLAB splines. Present these comparisons as MATLAB plots with proper labels and titles.

5.3. Using the method of undetermined coefficients, derive an interpolating polynomial $f(x)$ for the data given below.

x	0	20	40
y	892	853	725

Estimate $f(37)$.

5.4. The following table gives the values of $\cos(x)$ for selected angles x in degrees.

x	10	12	14	16
$f(x) = \cos(x)$	0.98481	0.97815	0.97030	0.96126

Using the method of undetermined coefficients, derive a cubic interpolating polynomial for the given interval . Estimate the value of $\cos(x)$ for $x = 12.75$ deg and $x = 13.5$ deg. Compare these results with the true values.

5.5. Given the following data set, derive an interpolating polynomial $f(x)$ using the Gregory-Newton method. Estimate $f(0.535)$ and $f(0.625)$. Compare the accuracy of the estimated values if the true values are 0.6022 and 0.6978, respectively.

x	0.50	0.55	0.60	0.65
y	0.5823	0.6124	0.6435	0.7869

5.6. The deflection, δ, of a structure under loading is measured at a point for four different values of the applied force, F. The measured data is given below. Using the Gregory-Newton method, compute the deflection for $F = 1.75$ kN.

F (kN)	0.5	1.5	2.0	2.5
δ (cm)	3.12	5.25	7.32	10.63

5.7. The amplitude of vibration of an automobile in the vertical direction after passing over a road bump is found to be as follows.

Time, t (seconds)	0	0.65	1.30	1.95
Amplitude, A (mm)	5.25	2.50	0.80	0.40

Using the Gregory-Newton method, compute the amplitude for $t = 1.80$ seconds.

5.8. The *Charpy* test [10] provides material toughness data under dynamic conditions. In this test, which is helpful in comparing several materials and in determining low-temperature brittleness and impact strength, the specimen is struck by a pendulum released from a fixed height and the energy absorbed by the specimen, termed the impact value, computed from the height of the swing after fracture. The following table gives the *impact value*, V, as a function of *temperature*, T, for a certain material. Using the Gregory-Newton method, derive an interpolating polynomial and estimate V for $T = -25$ deg F and -75 deg F.

T (deg F)	-200	-150	-100	-50	0
V (ft-lbs)	0	1.5	3	10	35

Check your results against functions obtained with MATLAB splines. Present these comparisons as MATLAB plots with proper labels and titles.

5.9. The data in the following table are the distances traveled by a motorcycle, which was stationary at time $t = 0$, for selected times.

Time, t (seconds)	0	2	4	6	8	10
Distance, D (ft)	0	10	50	150	330	610

Generate a finite-difference table and obtain an interpolating polynomial using Newton's method. Estimate the distance D traveled at $t = 7$ seconds.

5.10. For the given data, generate both a finite-difference table and an interpolating polynomial.

Angle, θ (degrees)	$\cos(\theta)$
0	1.00000
10	0.98481
20	0.93969
30	0.86603
40	0.76604
50	0.64279
60	0.50000

Evaluate the error of the estimated value of $\cos(25°)$. The true value is given to be 0.90631.

5.11. The following data gives the *notch sensitivity*, q, of a steel as a function of the *notch radius*, r [10]. Compute a finite-difference table and derive an interpolating polynomial by Newton's method. Estimate q for $r = 0.11$ inches.

q	0.45	0.65	0.75	0.78	0.785
r (in)	0.01	0.05	0.09	0.13	0.17

5.12. The *deflection*, δ, of a structure under loading is measured at a point for four different values of the *applied force*, F. The measured data is as follows.

F (kN)	0.5	1.5	2.0	2.5
δ (cm)	3.0	5.2	7.3	10.5

Using Lagrangian interpolation, compute the deflection, δ, for $F = 2.2$ kN. Check your results against functions obtained with MATLAB splines. Present these comparisons as MATLAB plots with proper labels and titles.

5.13. When a vibration problem is solved with nonlinearities included, the natural frequencies of vibration become dependent on the amplitudes of vibration [9, 16, 20, 21]. The following table relates the *nonlinear natural frequency/linear natural frequency ratio*, r, of a rotating blade vibrating in the plane of rotation to its *vibration amplitude*, A.

A (in)	10	8.5	5	0
r (%)	99.9325	99.9575	99.9921	100.0000

Derive a Lagrange interpolating polynomial and compute r for $A = 4.25$ in. Check your results against functions obtained with MATLAB splines. Present these comparisons as MATLAB plots with proper labels and titles.

5.14. The behavior of a mooring line employed to control the excursions of a floating ocean structure resembles that of a nonlinear spring with tension-displacement characteristics which depend upon its length, weight, elastic properties, anchor holding capacities and water depth [14]. In the table below, the *horizontal component of mooring line tension, H*, is given as a function of the *horizontal distance, X*, between the ends of the line.

X (ft)	440	470	485	492.5	495	498
H (Kips)	0	5	10	42	150	440

Using Lagrangian interpolation, generate an interpolating polynomial and compute H for $X = 487$ ft.

5.15. The following table gives the *pressure*, P, versus *temperature*, T, relationship in the liquid-vapor region for water [9].

T (Kelvin)	403.15	453.15	503.15	553.15	633.15
P (MPa)	0.2701	1.0021	2.795	6.412	18.651

Using Lagrangian interpolation, generate an interpolating polynomial and estimate P for $T = 525$ deg K.

5.16. While the value of the endurance limit, S_{end}, of a material is based on its tensile strength, S_{ult}, it is also dependent on the condition of its surface [11]. The following data relates to a machined, unnotched specimen subjected to reversed bending.

S_{ult} (kpsi)	60	80	100	140	180	220
S_{end} (kpsi)	22	30	38	50	60	64

Using Lagrangian interpolation, generate an interpolating polynomial and compute the values of S_{end} for $S_{ult} = 90$ kpsi and 160 kpsi.

Chapter 6
Curve Fitting

6.1 The Need to Fit a Function to Measured Data

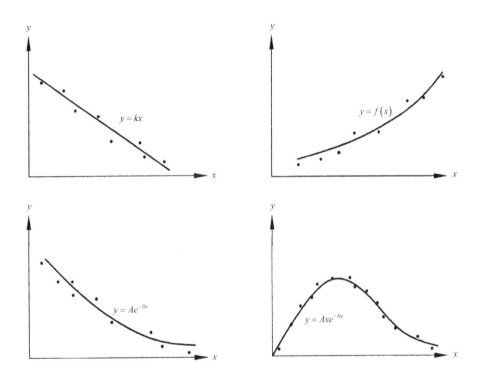

Fig. 6.1: Examples of functions employed in curve-fitting

Regression analysis plays an important role in analysis and interpretation of experimental as well as statistical data and in their correlation with mathematical models. It involves the determination of a function $f(x)$ that would "*best fit*" a bunch of experimentally measured values: (x_1, y_1), (x_2, y_2), ..., (x_n, y_n). This function can be a *linear function*, a *polynomial*, a *nonlinear function*, an *exponential function*, or a *linear combination of known functions*.

Some examples are shown in Figure 6.1. In curve-fitting a bunch of data points, typically the number of data points would be much larger than the number of undetermined coefficients in a given problem. Thus, there will be discrepancies between the function $f(x)$ determined and the data points given and it is very rare for a curve-fit to go through all the given data points exactly. However, these differences are minimized by an adaptation of the Method of Least Squares.

Handling of Weighted Data

When dealing with engineering, scientific and statistical data, situations may be encountered when certain data may be considered to be more accurate than other data and consequently must be assigned more weight in the process of generating a curve-fit. One way to include this weighting is to make multiple inclusions of the associated data point in the regression analysis. For example, if the following data is given and the point (2, 20) is to be assigned a *"weighting factor"* of 3, this data point must simply be considered thrice in coming up with a curve-fit as shown below.

Given data:

x	1	2	3	4
y	10	20	30	40

Information to be used for curve-fitting:

x	1	2	2	2	3	4
y	10	20	20	20	30	40

6.2 The Method of Least Squares

With a well-chosen approximating function, a *"least squares"* fit will yield a good representation of experimental data. Suppose you want to measure the distance between two points in a field, and let us say that you do this n times. You will come up with n measurements which are likely to be somewhat different from one another. Let these be $d_1, d_2, d_3, \ldots, d_n$. If the true distance is D, then the sum of the squares of the deviations from the true distance D is

$$S = (d_1 - D)^2 + (d_2 - D)^2 + \cdots + (d_n - D)^2. \tag{6.1}$$

This sum S will be a maximum or a minimum when $\frac{dS}{dD} = 0$, which yields

$$\sum_{i=1}^{n} d_i - nD = 0 \tag{6.2}$$

or

$$D = \frac{\sum_{i=1}^{n} d_i}{n}. \tag{6.3}$$

For S to be a minimum, $\frac{d^2S}{dD^2} > 0$, which it is since it comes out to be $2n$. Thus, S will be a minimum when

$$D = \frac{\sum_{i=1}^{n} d_i}{n},$$

that is, if n measurements are taken, the true distance will be the arithmetic mean of the n measurements if the sum of the squares of the deviations is to be a minimum.

6.3 Straight Line Regression

Let us assume that a plot of the given data suggests that we should fit it with a linear function. Let this function be

$$f(x) = C_1 + C_2 x \qquad (6.4)$$

where C_1 and C_2 are coefficients to be determined. If the given data is

$$(x_1, y_1), (x_2, y_2), \ldots, (x_n, y_n),$$

then the quantity S, which is the sum of the squares of the deviations of the measured values y from the function values $f(x)$ is

$$S = [y_1 - (C_1 + C_2 x_1)]^2 + [y_2 - (C_1 + C_2 x_2)]^2 + \cdots + [y_n - (C_1 + C_2 x_n)]^2. \qquad (6.5)$$

For S to be a minimum, the partial derivatives of S with respect to C_1 and C_2 must be zeros, which leads to

$$nC_1 + \sum_{i=1}^{n} x_i C_2 = \sum_{i=1}^{n} y_i,$$

$$\sum_{i=1}^{n} x_i C_1 + \sum_{i=1}^{n} x_i^2 C_2 = \sum_{i=1}^{n} x_i y_i. \qquad (6.6)$$

In matrix form, this is

$$\begin{pmatrix} n & \sum_{i=1}^{n} x_i \\ \sum_{i=1}^{n} x_i & \sum_{i=1}^{n} x_i^2 \end{pmatrix} \begin{pmatrix} C_1 \\ C_2 \end{pmatrix} = \begin{pmatrix} \sum_{i=1}^{n} y_i \\ \sum_{i=1}^{n} x_i y_i \end{pmatrix}. \qquad (6.7)$$

Using Cramer's rule or the inverse of the matrix on the right hand side of the above equation or the MATLAB "\" command, the undetermined coefficients C_1 and C_2 can now be found.

Example 6.1. Given the following data:

x_i	y_i
0.10	65.85
0.15	65.20
0.20	55.51
0.25	50.43
0.30	45.97
0.35	33.25
0.40	34.33
0.45	29.76
0.50	23.89
0.55	23.76
0.60	18.99

Fit a straight line $y = f(x) = C_1 + C_2 x$ to the above data.

In this case, C_1 and C_2 are determined using

$$\begin{pmatrix} n & \sum_{i=1}^{n} x_i \\ \sum_{i=1}^{n} x_i & \sum_{i=1}^{n} x_i^2 \end{pmatrix} \begin{pmatrix} C_1 \\ C_2 \end{pmatrix} = \begin{pmatrix} \sum_{i=1}^{n} y_i \\ \sum_{i=1}^{n} x_i y_i \end{pmatrix}.$$

```
x = 0.10:.05:0.60;
y = [65.85 65.20 55.51 50.43 45.97 33.25 34.33 29.76 23.89
   23.76 18.99];
n = size(x,2);

d = [n, sum(x); sum(x), sum(x.^2)]
m = [sum(y), sum(x); sum(x.*y), sum(x.^2)]
q = [n, sum(y); sum(x), sum(x.*y)]

C1 = det(m)/det(d)
C2 = det(q)/det(d)

f = C1 + C2*x;

p = plot(x,y,'redo',x,f,'blue')
title('Comparison: Fitted Function with Data')
xlabel('x')
ylabel('y')
legend('Given data','Fitted function')
p(1).LineWidth = 2;
p(2).LineWidth = 2;
```

```
d  =
    11.0000      3.8500
     3.8500      1.6225

m  =
   446.9400      3.8500
   129.0340      1.6225

q  =
    11.0000    446.9400
     3.8500    129.0340

C1  =
   75.4973

C2  =
  -99.6182
```

Thus, the fitted straight line function is then

$$f(x) = C_1 + C_2 x = 75.4973 - 99.6182x$$

which is compared with the given data in Figure 6.2. At $x = 0.20, 0.42$ and 0.52, the fitted function yields

$$f(0.20) = 55.574, \quad f(0.42) = 33.658, \quad f(0.52) = 23.696.$$

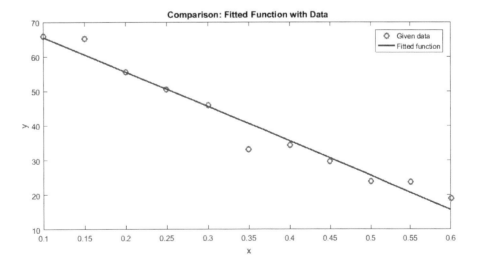

Fig. 6.2: Curve-fit with a linear function

6.4 Curve-Fitting with a Quadratic Function

For some types of data, it may be appropriate to resort to a quadratic function of the form:

$$f(x) = C_1 + C_2 x^2. \tag{6.8}$$

In this case S will be

$$S = [y_1 - (C_1 + C_2 x_1^2)]^2 + [y_2 - (C_1 + C_2 x_2^2)]^2 + \cdots + [y_n - (C_1 + C_2 x_n^2)]^2. \tag{6.9}$$

Taking the partial derivatives of S with respect to C_1 and C_2 yields

$$\begin{pmatrix} n & \sum_{i=1}^n x_i^2 \\ \sum_{i=1}^n x_i^2 & \sum_{i=1}^n x_i^4 \end{pmatrix} \begin{pmatrix} C_1 \\ C_2 \end{pmatrix} = \begin{pmatrix} \sum_{i=1}^n y_i \\ \sum_{i=1}^n x_i^2 y_i \end{pmatrix}, \tag{6.10}$$

which can be solved for the C_i's using algebraic or matrix methods or by accessing the MATLAB "\" command. The above can be expressed as

$$MC = A, \tag{6.11}$$

where

$$M = \begin{pmatrix} n & \sum_{i=1}^n x_i^2 \\ \sum_{i=1}^n x_i^2 & \sum_{i=1}^n x_i^4 \end{pmatrix}, \quad A = \begin{pmatrix} \sum_{i=1}^n y_i \\ \sum_{i=1}^n x_i^2 y_i \end{pmatrix}. \tag{6.12}$$

Example 6.2. A data set is given below:

x	y
0.5	0.51
1.0	2.35
1.5	7.54
2.0	13.23
2.5	17.65
3.0	24.21
3.5	28.94
4.0	37.63
4.5	58.32
5.0	63.21

Determine the quadratic function that will best fit the data given.

```
x = 0.5:0.5:5.0;
y = [0.51 2.35 7.54 13.23 17.65 24.21 28.94 37.63 58.32
   63.21];
```

```
n = size(x,2);

M = [n, sum(x.^2); sum(x.^2), sum(x.^4)]
A = [sum(y); sum(x.^2.*y)]

C = M\A

f = C(1) + C(2)*x.^2;

p = plot(x,y,'redo',x,f,'blue')
title('Comparison: Fitted Function with Data')
xlabel('x')
ylabel('y')
legend('Given data','Fitted function')
p(1).LineWidth = 2;
p(2).LineWidth = 2;

M =
   1.0e+03 *

     0.0100     0.0963
     0.0963     1.5833

A =
   1.0e+03 *

     0.2536
     4.1184

C =
     0.7790
     2.5538
```

The quadratic function fitted to the given data is $f(x)$,

$$f(x) = 0.7790 + 2.5538x^2$$

which is plotted and compared with the given data in Figure 6.3.

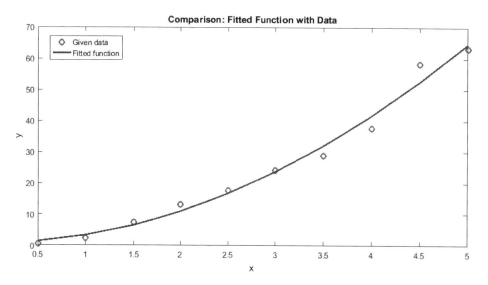

Fig. 6.3: Curve-fit with a quadratic function

6.5 Curve-Fitting with a Power Function

For some data types, it may be appropriate to do a curve-fit with a function of the form

$$f(x) = Ax^B, \tag{6.13}$$

where A and B are undetermined coefficients to be evaluated on a least squares basis.

Taking the logarithm of the above, we obtain

$$\ln(f(x)) = \ln(A) + B\ln(x) \tag{6.14}$$

or,

$$F = C + BX, \tag{6.15}$$

where

$$F = \ln(f(x)), \quad C = \ln(A), \quad X = \ln(x). \tag{6.16}$$

Thus, now the problem has been reduced to one of linear regression and can be handled as a linear fit.

Example 6.3. For the data set given below, find a power function that will serve as a least squares fit.

x	y	x	y
0.18	4.5921	3.12	7.9765
0.32	5.2345	3.61	8.4328
0.65	6.2321	3.92	9.6322
1.12	6.5467	4.51	8.8764
1.65	7.2976	4.72	9.0276
2.34	7.7654	5.25	9.2568
2.52	7.7237	6.75	8.6432
2.85	8.2543	7.85	10.2137

Using $f(x) = y(x) = Ax^B$, $F = Y = C + BX$, where $F = Y = \ln(y)$, $C = \ln(A)$ and $X = ln(x)$, we have the following matrix equation to solve for C and B

$$\begin{pmatrix} n & \sum_{i=1}^{n} X_i \\ \sum_{i=1}^{n} X_i & \sum_{i=1}^{n} X_i^2 \end{pmatrix} \begin{pmatrix} C \\ B \end{pmatrix} = \begin{pmatrix} \sum_{i=1}^{n} Y_i \\ \sum_{i=1}^{n} X_i Y_i \end{pmatrix}. \tag{6.17}$$

```
x = [0.18 0.32 0.65 1.12 1.65 2.34 2.52 2.85 3.12 3.61 3.92
   4.51 4.72 5.25 6.75 7.85];
y = [4.5921 5.2345 6.2321 6.5467 7.2976 7.7654 7.7237 8.2543
   7.9765 8.4328 9.6322 8.8764 9.0276 9.2568 8.6432
   10.2137];
n = size(x,2);

X = log(x);
Y = log(y);

D = [n, sum(X); sum(X), sum(X.^2)]
P = [sum(Y); sum(X.*Y)]
K = D\P

A = exp(K(1))
B = K(2)

f = A*x.^B;

p = plot(x,y,'redo',x,f,'blue')
title('Least Squares - Power Function Fit')
xlabel('x')
ylabel('y')
legend('Given data','Least squares/Power function fit')
p(1).LineWidth = 2;
p(2).LineWidth = 2;
```

```
D =
   16.0000    12.6248
   12.6248    27.4895

P =
   32.6438
   29.2567

K =
   1.8827
   0.1996

A =
   6.5714

B =
   0.1996
```

The function fitted to the given data is $f(x)$,

$$f(x) = 6.5714x^{0.1996}$$

which is plotted and compared with the given data in Figure 6.4.

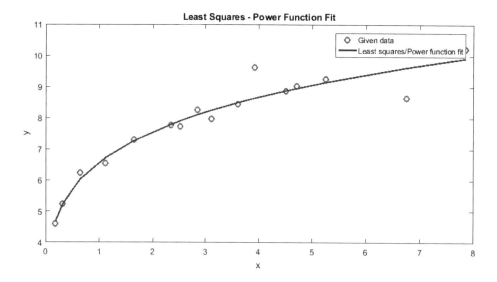

Fig. 6.4: Curve-fit with a power function

6.6 Curve-Fitting with an Exponential Function

Function Form of Ae^{Bx}

Exponential functions appear frequently in the analysis of business, science as well as engineering problems and are often employed to curve-fit experimental and statistical data. The function, in this case, has the form

$$f(x) = Ae^{Bx}, \tag{6.18}$$

where A and B are undetermined coefficients to be evaluated on a least squares basis. Taking the logarithm of the above gives

$$\ln(f(x)) = \ln(A) + Bx, \tag{6.19}$$

or

$$F = C + Bx, \tag{6.20}$$

where

$$F = \ln(f(x)) \text{ and } C = ln(A). \tag{6.21}$$

Thus, now the problem is again reduced to one of linear regression and can be handled as done earlier for a linear fit.

Example 6.4. For the data set given below, find an exponential function that will serve as a least squares fit.

x	y
0	16.45
1	4.47
2	1.06
3	0.45
4	0.15
5	0.03

Using $f(x) = y(x) = Ae^{Bx}$, $F = Y = C + Bx$, where $F = Y = \ln(y)$, and $C = \ln(A)$ we have the following matrix equation to solve for C and B

$$\begin{pmatrix} n & \sum_{i=1}^{n} x_i \\ \sum_{i=1}^{n} x_i & \sum_{i=1}^{n} x_i^2 \end{pmatrix} \begin{pmatrix} C \\ B \end{pmatrix} = \begin{pmatrix} \sum_{i=1}^{n} Y_i \\ \sum_{i=1}^{n} x_i Y_i \end{pmatrix} \tag{6.22}$$

which can be solved for C and B.

```
x = 0:1:5;
y = [16.45 4.47 1.06 0.45 0.15 0.03];
n = size(x,2);

Y = log(y);

D = [n, sum(x); sum(x), sum(x.^2)]
P = [sum(Y); sum(Y.*x)]
K = D\P

C = K(1)
B = K(2)
A = exp(C)

x1 = 0:0.01:5;
f = A*exp(B*x1);
logf = log(f);

subplot(1,2,1);
p1 = plot(x,y,'redo',x1,f,'blue')
axis([0 5 0 18])
title('Curve-Fit with an Exponential Function')
xlabel('x')
ylabel('y')
legend('Given data','Fitted function')
p1(1).LineWidth = 2;
p1(2).LineWidth = 2;

subplot(1,2,2);
p2 = plot(x,Y,'redo',x1,logf,'blue')
axis([0 5 -4 3])
title('Natural Log of Curve-Fit')
xlabel('x')
ylabel('y')
legend('Data','Fitted function')
p2(1).LineWidth = 2;
p2(2).LineWidth = 2;

D =
     6    15
    15    55
```

```
P  =
    -1.8462
   -25.9029

K  =
     2.7334
    -1.2164

C  =
     2.7334

B  =
    -1.2164

A  =
    15.3844
```

The unknown constants C and B can be computed using the "\" command and the coefficient A can then be calculated as shown. The curve-fit and its natural log are generated below and compared with the given data in Figures 6.5.

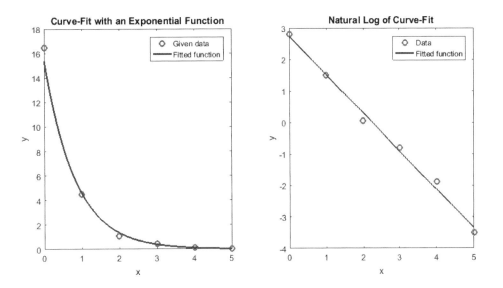

Fig. 6.5: Curve-fit with an exponential function of form Ae^{Bx} and the natural log of Curve-fit.

Function Form Axe^{Bx}

There are times when exponential functions of the following form appear in the analysis of practical problems

$$f(x) = y(x) = Axe^{Bx}, \tag{6.23}$$

where A and B are undetermined coefficients to be evaluated on a least squares basis.

Taking the logarithm of the above, we obtain

$$\ln(y) = \ln(f) = \ln(A) + \ln(x) + Bx,$$

or, $\ln(y/x) = \ln(A) + Bx$. That is,

$$Z = C + Bx, \tag{6.24}$$

where

$$Z = \ln\left(\frac{y}{x}\right) \text{ and } C = \ln(A). \tag{6.25}$$

Thus, now the problem is reduced again to one of linear regression and can be handled as a linear fit.

Example 6.5. For the stress versus strain data given below, find an exponential function of form $S = Ae\exp(Be)$ that will serve as a least squares fit.

Strain (e) (micro-in/in)	300	800	1300	1800	2300	2800
Stress (S) (psi)	1656	3521	4079	4354	4300	3675

Using $f(e) = y(e) = Ae\exp(Be)$, $Z = C + Be$, where $Z = \ln(S/e)$ and $C = \ln(A)$, we have the following matrix equation to solve for C and B.

$$\begin{pmatrix} n & \sum_{i=1}^{n} e_i \\ \sum_{i=1}^{n} e_i & \sum_{i=1}^{n} e_i^2 \end{pmatrix} \begin{pmatrix} C \\ B \end{pmatrix} = \begin{pmatrix} \sum_{i=1}^{n} Z_i \\ \sum_{i=1}^{n} e_i Z_i \end{pmatrix}. \tag{6.26}$$

Here, the x-coordinate is e and the y-coordinate is S.

```
e = 300:500:2800;
S = [1656 3521 4079 4354 4300 3675];
n = size(e,2);

Z = log(S./e);

D = [n, sum(e); sum(e), sum(e.^2)]
P = [sum(Z); sum(e.*Z)]

K = D\P

C = K(1)
B = K(2)
A = exp(C)
```

```
e1 = 300:1:2800;
f = A*e1.*exp(B*e1);

p = plot(e,S,'redo',e1,f,'blue')
title('Curve-Fit with an Exponential Function')
xlabel('Strain (e)')
ylabel('Stress (S)')
legend('Given data points','Exponential function fit')
p(1).LineWidth = 2;
p(2).LineWidth = 2;

D =

             6          9300
          9300      18790000

P =
    1.0e+03 *

      0.0061
      6.9751

K =
      1.9058
     -0.0006

C =
      1.9058

B =
    -5.7205e-04

A =
      6.7248
```

The function fitted to the given data is $f(e)$,

$$f(e) = 6.7248e * \exp(-0.00057205e)$$

which is plotted and compared with the given data in Figure 6.6.

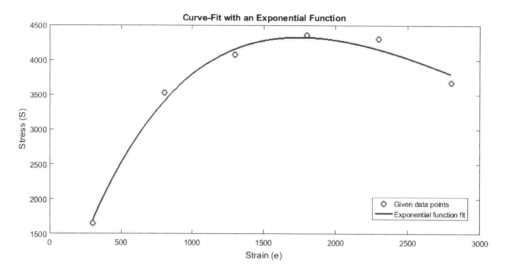

Fig. 6.6: Curve-fit with exponential function Axe^{Bx}

6.7 Curve-Fitting with a Linear Combination of Known Functions

In fitting a function to given data points, a linear combination of known functions may have to be used at times.

Given a set of data points: (x_1, y_1), (x_2, y_2), ..., (x_n, y_n), it is required to find a function:

$$f(x) = C_1 f_1(x) + C_2 f_2(x) + \cdots + C_m f_m(x), \qquad (6.27)$$

where the $f_i(x)$ are prescribed functions and the C_i's are undetermined coefficients to be evaluated. The total number of data points given is n while the total number of prescribed functions to be utilized is m.

In general, then, the function value at x_i will be

$$f(x_i) = \sum_{j=1}^{m} C_j f_j(x_i). \qquad (6.28)$$

In this case, the sum of the squares of the deviations from the true values y_i will be:

$$s = (y_1 - f(x_1))^2 + (y_2 - f(x_2))^2 + \cdots + (y_n - f(x_n))^2. \qquad (6.29)$$

For S to be a minimum, the partial derivatives of S with respect to C_1, C_2, ..., C_m must be zero and the second partials must be positive. These requirements lead to the following matrix equation in the unknowns, C_1, C_2, ..., C_m:

$$MC = L, \qquad (6.30)$$

where

$$C = \begin{pmatrix} C_1 \\ C_2 \\ \vdots \\ C_m \end{pmatrix}, \quad L = \begin{pmatrix} \sum_{i=1}^{n} f_1(x_i) y_i \\ \sum_{i=1}^{n} f_2(x_i) y_i \\ \vdots \\ \sum_{i=1}^{n} f_m(x_i) y_i \end{pmatrix}$$

and

$$M = \begin{pmatrix} \sum_{i=1}^{n} [f_1(x_i)]^2 & \sum_{i=1}^{n} f_1(x_i) f_2(x_i) & \cdots & \sum_{i=1}^{n} f_1(x_i) f_m(x_i) \\ \sum_{i=1}^{n} f_2(x_i) f_1(x_i) & \sum_{i=1}^{n} [f_2(x_i)]^2 & \cdots & \sum_{i=1}^{n} f_2(x_i) f_m(x_i) \\ \vdots & \vdots & \ddots & \vdots \\ \sum_{i=1}^{n} f_m(x_i) f_1(x_i) & \sum_{i=1}^{n} f_m(x_i) f_2(x_i) & \cdots & \sum_{i=1}^{n} [f_m(x_i)]^2 \end{pmatrix}.$$

The above equations can now be solved for the C_is.

Example 6.6. Fit the data points:

x	1.0	2.0	3.0	4.0	5.0
y	5.75	10.75	12.65	29.95	49.35

with a function of the form $y(x) = C_1 f_1(x) + C_2 f_2(x)$, where $f_1(x) = 1$ and $f_2(x) = x^3$.

In this case, $n = 5$ and $m = 2$. Equation (6.30) then gives the following matrix equation in C_1 and C_2:

$$\begin{pmatrix} \sum_{i=1}^{5} [f_1(x_i)]^2 & \sum_{i=1}^{5} f_1(x_i) f_2(x_i) \\ \sum_{i=1}^{5} f_2(x_i) f_1(x_i) & \sum_{i=1}^{5} [f_2(x_i)]^2 \end{pmatrix} \begin{pmatrix} C_1 \\ C_2 \end{pmatrix} = \begin{pmatrix} \sum_{i=1}^{5} f_1(x_i) y_i \\ \sum_{i=1}^{5} f_2(x_i) y_i \end{pmatrix}.$$

```
x = 1:1:5;
y = [5.75 10.75 12.65 29.95 49.35];
n = size(x,2);

f1 = ones(1,n);
f2 = x.^3;

M = [sum(f1.^2), sum(f1.*f2); sum(f2.*f1), sum(f2.^2)]
L = [sum(f1.*y); sum(f2.*y)]

C = M\L

C1 = C(1)
C2 = C(2)
```

```
x1 = 1:0.1:5;
f = C1 + C2*x1.^3;

p = plot(x,y,'redo',x1,f,'blue')
title('Analysis - Generated Fit/Given Data')
xlabel('x')
ylabel('y')
legend('Given data points','Results of analysis')
p(1).LineWidth = 2;
p(2).LineWidth = 2;

M =
              5           225
            225         20515

L =
    1.0e+03 *

      0.1084
      8.5189

C =
      5.9309
      0.3502

C1 =
      5.9309

C2 =
      0.3502
```

The fitted yield by this analysis is: $y = f(x) = 5.9309 + 0.3502x^3$, which is plotted in Figure 6.7 and compared with the given data.

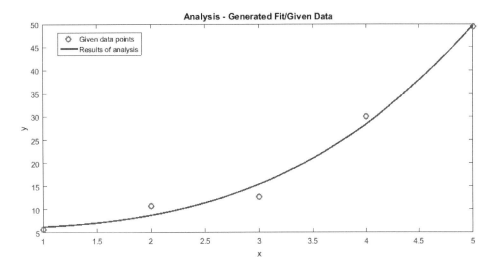

Fig. 6.7: Curve-fit with a linear combination of known functions

6.8 Curve-Fitting with Polynomials

If an mth order polynomial seems to be a good fit to the data points given, the procedure used in fitting a linear combination of known functions can still be resorted to. In this case,

$$f_1(x) = 1, \quad , f_2(x) = x, \quad f_3(x) = x^2, \quad f_4(x) = x^3, \ldots, f_{m+1}(x) = x^m \tag{6.31}$$

with

$$f(x) = C_1 f_1(x) + C_2 f_2(x) + \cdots + C_{m+1} f_{m+1}(x), \tag{6.32}$$

in which the C's must be solved by using

$$MC = L, \tag{6.33}$$

where

$$M = \begin{pmatrix} n & \sum_{i=1}^{n} x_i & \cdots & \sum_{i=1}^{n} x_i^m \\ \sum_{i=1}^{n} x_i & \sum_{i=1}^{n} x_i^2 & \cdots & \sum_{i=1}^{n} x_i^{m+1} \\ \sum_{i=i}^{n} x_i^2 & \cdots & \cdots & \sum_{i=1}^{n} x_i^{m+2} \\ \vdots & \vdots & \vdots & \vdots \\ \sum_{i=1}^{n} x_i^m & \cdots & \cdots & \sum_{i=1}^{n} x_i^{2m} \end{pmatrix}, \quad C = \begin{pmatrix} C_1 \\ C_2 \\ \vdots \\ C_{m+1} \end{pmatrix},$$

and

$$L = \begin{pmatrix} \sum_{i=1}^{n} y_i \\ \sum_{i=1}^{n} x_i y_i \\ \vdots \\ \sum_{i=1}^{n} x_i^m y_i \end{pmatrix},$$

where the (x_i, y_i) are the n given data points.

Example 6.7. Given the data points

x	0	1	2	3	4	5
y	0	8.47	17.48	19.57	14.69	11.23

obtain a curve-fit of the form $y(x) = f(x) = C_1 + C_2 x + C_3 x^2$.

Here, $n = 6$ and $m = 2$ and the matrix equation to be solved is

$$[M]\{C\} = \{L\},$$

where $[M]$ is a known 3×3 matrix and $\{L\}$ is a known column vector:

$$M = \begin{pmatrix} n & \sum_{i=1}^{n} x_i & \sum_{i=1}^{n} x_i^2 \\ \sum_{i=1}^{n} x_i & \sum_{i=1}^{n} x_i^2 & \sum_{i=1}^{n} x_i^3 \\ \sum_{i=1}^{n} x_i^2 & \sum_{i=1}^{n} x_i^3 & \sum_{i=1}^{n} x_i^4 \end{pmatrix}, \quad L = \begin{pmatrix} \sum_{i=1}^{n} y_i \\ \sum_{i=1}^{n} x_i y_i \\ \sum_{i=1}^{n} x_i^2 y_i \end{pmatrix}.$$

The column vector $\{C\}$, which involves the undetermined coefficients, is $\begin{pmatrix} C_1 \\ C_2 \\ C_3 \end{pmatrix}$.

```
x = 0:1:5;
y = [0 8.47 17.48 19.57 14.69 11.23];
n = size(x,2);

M = [n, sum(x), sum(x.^2); sum(x), sum(x.^2), sum(x.^3); sum
   (x.^2), sum(x.^3), sum(x.^4)]
L = [sum(y); sum(x.*y); sum(x.^2.*y)]

C = M\L

C1 = C(1)
C2 = C(2)
C3 = C(3)

x1 = 0:0.1:5;
f = C1 + C2*x1 + C3*x1.^2;

p = plot(x,y,'redo',x1,f,'blue')
title('Curve Fitted with a Second Order Polynomial')
xlabel('x')
ylabel('y')
legend('Given data points','Second order polynomial')
p(1).LineWidth = 2;
p(2).LineWidth = 2;
```

```
M  =
       6      15      55
      15      55     225
      55     225     979

L  =
    71.4400
   217.0500
   770.3100

C  =
   -0.4439
   12.4838
   -2.0573

C1  =
   -0.4439

C2  =
   12.4838

C3  =
   -2.0573
```

The polynomial fitting the given data is $f(x) = -0.4439 + 12.4838x - 2.0573x^2$. Figure 6.8 shows a comparison of the curve-fit generated with the given data points.

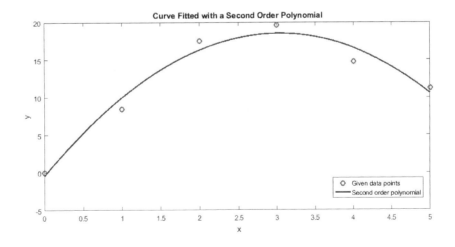

Fig. 6.8: Curve-fit with polynomial

6.9 Use of MATLAB's Regression Functions for Curve-Fitting

6.9.1 Linear Regression with MATLAB

In MATLAB, linear regression or least squares regression is done on data represented by vectors vx and vy by using the *polyfit* function. Taking $N = 1$, the function *polyfit(vx,vy,N)* returns a vector of values in the order $[C_1, C_2]$, representing the slope and intercept of the linear regression. Use of this function is demonstrated below.

Example 6.8. Determine a linear function that would fit the data of Example 6.1, using MATLAB's linear regression.

```
x = 0.10:0.05:0.60;
y = [65.85 65.20 55.51 50.43 45.97 33.25 34.33 29.76 23.89
   23.76 18.99];

C = polyfit(x,y,1)

m = C(1)
b = C(2)

yfit = 75.4973 -99.6182*x;
ylin = m*x + b;

p = plot(x,y,'redo',x,yfit,'blue',x,ylin,'green--')
title('Comparison: Fitted Functions with Data')
xlabel('x')
ylabel('y')
legend('Given data ','Curve fit from Example 6.1', 'MATLABs
   Linear Regression')
p(1).LineWidth = 2;
p(2).LineWidth = 2;
p(3).LineWidth = 2;

C =
  -99.6182    75.4973

m =
  -99.6182

b =
   75.4973
```

The straight line fit generated by MATLAB is $y(x) = -99.6182x + 75.4973$. Figure 6.9 shows a comparison of the data with the curve-fit generated in Example 6.1 and MATLAB's linear regression.

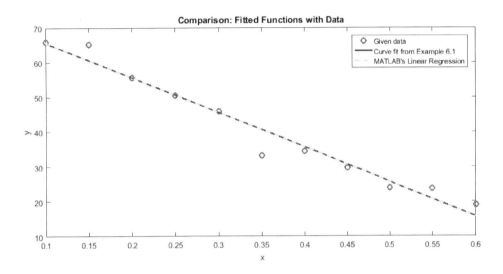

Fig. 6.9: Curve-fit with MATLAB's linear regression functions

6.9.2 Nonlinear Regression with MATLAB

In MATLAB, the function *polyfit* is used to fit a single polynomial of any desired order through all the given data points. In practice, however, there is no need to fit a polynomial of order higher than four ($N = 4$). This function will not work very well if your data does not fit into a single polynomial.

The format of this function is *polyfit(vx,vy,N)*, where *vx* and *vy* are vectors containing the given data points and N is the polynomial order required. The output will be a vector of the coefficients of the desired order N polynomial.

Example 6.9. Do a curve-fit on the data of Example 6.2, using MATLAB's nonlinear regression.

```
x = 0.5:0.5:5.0;
y = [0.51 2.35 7.54 13.23 17.65 24.21 28.94 37.63 58.32
   63.21];
```

```
C = polyfit(x,y,2)

yfit = 0.7790 + 2.5538*x.^2;
f = C(1)*x.^2 + C(2)*x + C(3);

p = plot(x,y,'redo',x,yfit,'blue',x,f,'green--')
title('Comparison: Fitted Functions with Data')
xlabel('x')
ylabel('y')
legend('Given data ','Curve fit from Example 6.2', 'MATLABs
   Linear Regression')
p(1).LineWidth = 2;
p(2).LineWidth = 2;
p(3).LineWidth = 2;

C =
    2.4930    0.3517    0.3963
```

The quadratic fit generated by MATLAB is $y(x) = 2.4930x^2 + 0.3517x + 0.3963$. Figure 6.10 shows a comparison of the data with the curve-fit generated in Example 6.2 and MATLAB's quadratic fit. Table 6.1 compares the data.

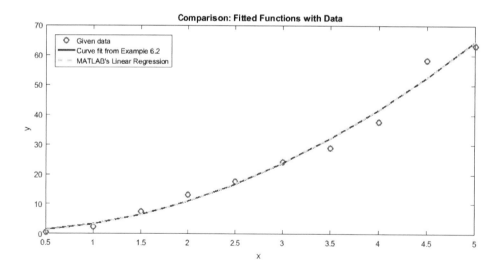

Fig. 6.10: Curve-fit with MATLAB's nonlinear regression function

	Given data	Quadratic Fit (Ex: 5.2)	MATLAB's Quadratic Fit
x_i	y_i	$yfit(x_i)$	$f(x_i)$
0.5	0.51	1.4175	1.1955
1.0	2.35	3.3328	3.2411
1.5	7.54	6.5250	6.5332
2.0	13.23	10.9942	11.0719
2.5	17.65	16.7403	16.8571
3.0	24.21	23.7632	23.8888
3.5	28.94	32.0631	32.1670
4.0	37.63	41.6398	41.6917
4.5	58.32	52.4935	52.4630
5.0	63.21	64.6240	64.4807

Table 6.1: Comparison of given data with generated curve-fits

6.9.3 Using MATLAB's lsqcurvefit Function

The MATLAB function *lsqcurvefit* evaluates the undetermined coefficients $C_1, C_2, \ldots$ in a regression function that is a linear combination of known functions $f_1(x), f_2(x), \ldots$. It has the form

$$C_1 f_1(x) + C_2 f_2(x) + \cdots.$$

The function *lsqcurvefit(F,x0,x,y)* returns a vector that contains the coefficients $C_1, C_2, \ldots$ in the linear combination of known functions that would best fit the given data based on the least squares principle. Here F is an anonymous function representing the function that is linearly combined to generate the best fit to the given data, vectors x and y. $x0$ is an initial point, specified as a vector of the same size as the number of coefficients for which you are solving. One should pick a value near the data set being entered. Often an initial guess of zero (as a vector) is sufficient.

Example 6.10. Apply the MATLAB function *lsqcurvefit* to the data and solution found in Example 6.6.

```
x = 1:1:5;
y = [5.75 10.75 12.65 29.95 49.35];
n = size(x,2);

%From Example 6.6
f1 = ones(1,n);
f2 = x.^3;

M = [sum(f1.^2), sum(f1.*f2); sum(f2.*f1), sum(f2.^2)];
L = [sum(f1.*y); sum(f2.*y)];
```

```
C = M\L;

C1 = C(1)
C2 = C(2)

x1 = 1:0.1:5;
f = C1 + C2*x1.^3;

%Using MATLAB's Nonlinear Regression
F = @(c,x)  c(1)+c(2)*x.^3;
x0 = [0, 0];
c = lsqcurvefit(F,x0,x,y);
f1 = F(c,x1);

p = plot(x,y,'redo',x1,f,'blue',x1,f1,'green^')
title('Comparison of Results')
xlabel('x')
ylabel('y')
legend('Given data points ','Curve fit from Example 6.6', '
   MATLABs Linear Regression')
p(1).LineWidth = 2;
p(2).LineWidth = 2;
p(3).LineWidth = 2;

c =
    5.9309    0.3502
```

The linear combination of functions generated by MATLAB then is $f(x) = 5.9309 + 0.3502x^3$. Figure 6.11 shows a comparison of the data with the curve fit in Example 6.6 and MATLAB's nonlinear regression fit.

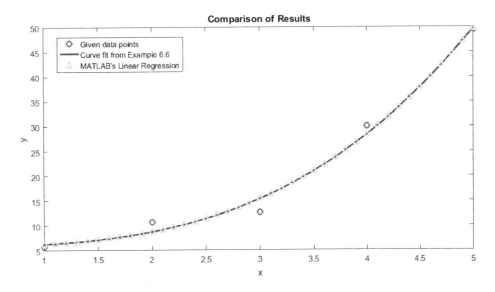

Fig. 6.11: Comparison of *lsqcurve fit* results with given data

Example 6.11. Given the following data,

x	0.3	0.4	1	1.4	2	4
y	9.4	11.2	5	3	6	0

fit the data with a function of the form $e^{u_1 + u_2 x + u_3 x^2}$.

```
x = [0.3 0.4 1 1.4 2 4];
y = [9.4 11.2 5 3 6 0];

F = @(u,x) exp(u(1) + u(2)*x + u(3)*x.^2);
x0 = [0,0,0];

u = lsqcurvefit(F,x0,x,y)

x1 = 0.3:0.1:4;
f = F(u,x1);

p = plot(x,y,'redo',x1,f,'blue')
title('Comparison of Curve-Fit with Given Data')
xlabel('x')
ylabel('y')
legend('Given data points ','MATLABs Nonlinear Regression')
p(1).LineWidth = 2;
p(2).LineWidth = 2;
```

```
u =
    2.5654    -0.7882     0.0364
```

The function generated by MATLAB then is $f(x) = e^{2.5654-0.7882x+0.0364x^2}$. Figure 6.12 shows a comparison of the data with this function.

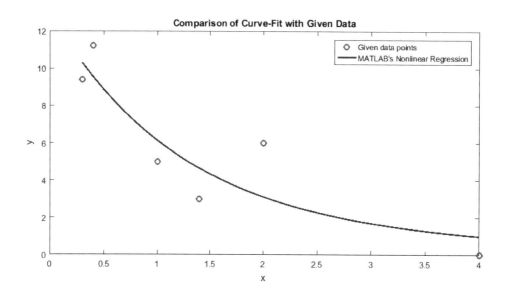

Fig. 6.12: Curve-fit with *lsqcurvefit*

Example 6.12. Given the following data,

x	0	1	2	3	4	5
y	4	5	5.5	5.8	6.2	6.5

fit the data with a function of the form $a\ln(x+b)+c$. Use initial guess $[2,1,5]$.

```
x = 0:1:5;
y = [4 5 5.5 5.8 6.2 6.5];

F = @(c,x) c(1)*log(x + c(2)) + c(3)
x0 = [2, 1, 5];

c = lsqcurvefit(F,x0,x,y)

x1 = 0:.1:5;
f = F(c,x1);
```

```
p = plot(x,y,'redo',x1,f,'blue')
title('Comparison of Curve-Fit with Given Data')
xlabel('x')
ylabel('y')
legend('Given data points ','MATLABs Nonlinear Regression')
p(1).LineWidth = 2;
p(2).LineWidth = 2;


c =
    1.3879    1.0435    3.9538
```

The function generated by MATLAB then is $f(x) = 1.3879 \ln(x + 1.0435) + 3.9538$. Figure 6.13 shows a a comparison of the data with this function.

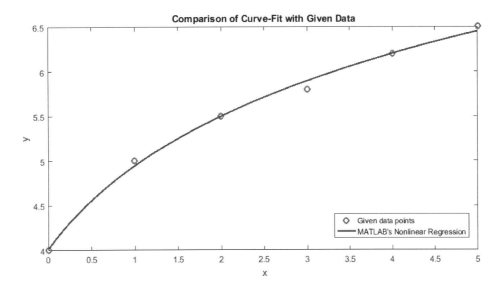

Fig. 6.13: Curve-fit with *lsqcurvefit*

Example 6.13. Given the following data,

x	1	2	3	4	5	6
y	5	6.5	7.25	7.80	8.25	8.63

fit the data with a function of the form $a \ln(x) + b$.

```
x = 1:1:6;
y = [5 6.5 7.25 7.80 8.25 8.63];
```

```
F = @(c,x) c(1)*log(x) + c(2);
x0 = [0, 0];

c = lsqcurvefit(F,x0,x,y)

x1 = 1:.1:6;
f = F(c,x1);

p = plot(x,y,'redo',x1,f,'blue')
title('Comparison of Curve-Fit with Given Data')
xlabel('x')
ylabel('y')
legend('Given data points ','MATLABs Nonlinear Regression')
p(1).LineWidth = 2;
p(2).LineWidth = 2;

c =
    2.0048    5.0400
```

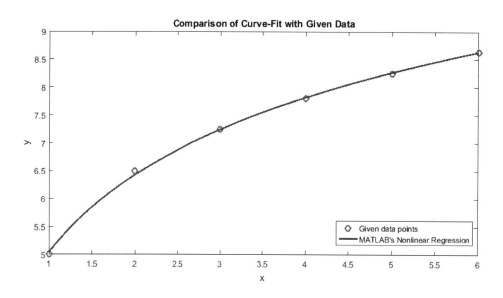

Fig. 6.14: Curve-fit with *lsqcurvefit*

The function generated by MATLAB then is $f(x) = 2.0048\ln(x) + 5.0400$. Figure 6.14 shows comparison of the data with this function.

Example 6.14. Given the following data,

x	0	1	2	3	4	5	6	7
y	5	9	50	192	517	1123	2121	3635

fit the data with a function of the form $ax^b + c$. Use initial guess $[3, 4, 10]$.

```
x = 0:1:7;
y = [5 9 50 192 517 1123 2121 3635];


F = @(c,x) c(1)*x.^(c(2)) + c(3);
x0 = [3, 4, 10];


c = lsqcurvefit(F,x0,x,y)


x1 = 0:.1:7;
f = F(c,x1);


plot(x,y,'redo',x1,f,'blue')
title('Comparison of Curve-Fit with Given Data')
xlabel('x')
ylabel('y')
legend('Given data points ','MATLABs Nonlinear Regression')
p(1).LineWidth = 2;
p(2).LineWidth = 2;


c =
    3.9977    3.5003    4.9612
```

The function generated by MATLAB then is $f(x) = 3.9977x^{3.5003} + 4.9612$. Figure 6.15 shows a a comparison of the data with this function.

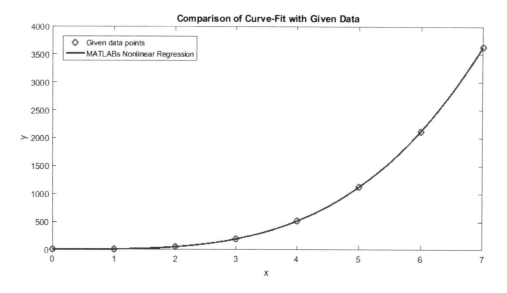

Fig. 6.15: Curve-fit with *lsqcurvefit*

Example 6.15. Given the following data,

x	0	1	2	3	4	5	6	7	8
y	21	24.892	31.31	41.89	59.334	88.095	135.513	213.693	342.5889

fit the data with a function of the form $ae^{bx} + c$. Use initial guess $[3, 2, 10]$.

```
x = 0:1:8;
y = [21 24.892 31.31 41.89 59.334 88.095 135.513 213.693
   342.589];

F = @(c,x) c(1)*exp(c(2)*x) + c(3);
x0 = [3, 2, 10];

c = lsqcurvefit(F,x0,x,y)

x1 = 0:.1:8;
f = F(c,x1);

p = plot(x,y,'redo',x1,f,'blue')
title('Comparison of Curve-Fit with Given Data')
xlabel('x')
ylabel('y')
legend('Given data points ','MATLABs Nonlinear Regression')
p(1).LineWidth = 2;
```

```
p(2).LineWidth = 2;

c =
    6.0000    0.5000    14.9999
```

The function generated by MATLAB then is $f(x) = 6.0000e^{0.5000x} + 14.9999$. Figure 6.16 shows a comparison of the data with this function.

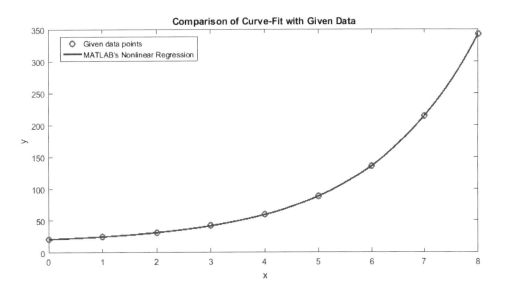

Fig. 6.16: Curve-fit with *lsqcurvefit*

6.9.4 More Examples with MATLAB

Example 6.16. Using MATLAB's linear regression, generate a curve-fit in the form of the exponential function Ae^{Bx} for the data of Example 6.4. Compare this with the given data and with the analytical results of Example 6.4.

```
x = 0:1:5;
y = [16.45 4.47 1.06 0.45 0.15 0.03];
n = size(x,2);

Y = log(y);

%From Example 6.4
D = [n, sum(x); sum(x), sum(x.^2)];
```

```
P = [sum(Y); sum(Y.*x)];
K = D\P;


C = K(1);
B = K(2);
A = exp(C);


x1 = 0:0.01:5;
f = A*exp(B*x1);

%Use of MATLAB's Linear Regression
C1 = polyfit(x,Y,1)


m1 = C1(1)
b1 = C1(2)
A1 = exp(b1)


x2 = 0:.1:5;
f1 = A1*exp(m1*x2);


p = plot(x,y,'redo',x1,f,'blue',x2,f1,'green^')
title('Curve-Fitting with an Exponential Function')
xlabel('x')
ylabel('y')
legend('Given data points','Curve fit from Example 6.4','
   MATLABs Linear Regression')
p(1).LineWidth = 2;
p(2).LineWidth = 2;
p(3).LineWidth = 2;

C1 =
   -1.2164     2.7334

m1 =
   -1.2164

b1 =
    2.7334

A1 =
   15.3844
```

The function generated by MATLAB then is $f(x) = 15.3844e^{-1.2164x}$. Figure 6.17 shows a a comparison of the data and the results from Example 6.4 with this function.

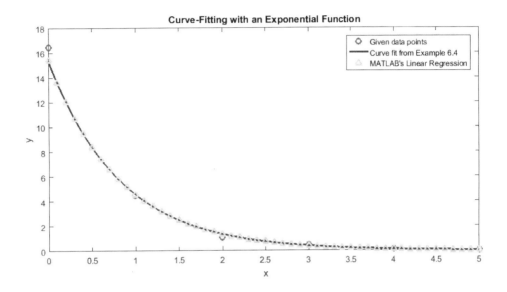

Fig. 6.17: Curve-fit with an exponential function Ae^{Bx} using MATLAB's linear regression

Example 6.17. Using MATLAB's linear regression, generate a fit in the form of the exponential function Axe^{Bx} for the problem of Example 6.5. Compare this with the results of Example 6.5 and with the given data.

```
e = 300:500:2800;
S = [1656 3521 4079 4354 4300 3675];
n = size(e,2);

Z = log(S./e);

%From Example 6.5
D = [n, sum(e); sum(e), sum(e.^2)];
P = [sum(Z); sum(e.*Z)];

K = D\P;

C = K(1);
B = K(2);
A = exp(C);

e1 = 300:1:2800;
```

```
f = A*e1.*exp(B*e1);

%Use of MATLAB's Linear Regression
C1 = polyfit(e,Z,1)

m1 = C1(1)
b1 = C1(2)
A1 = exp(b1)

e2 = 300:100:2800;
f1 = A1*e2.*exp(m1*e2);

p = plot(e,S,'redo',e1,f,'blue',e2,f1,'green^')
title('Comparion of Curve-Fit')
xlabel('Strain values (e)')
ylabel('Stress values (S)')
legend('Given data points','Curve fit from Example 6.5','
   MATLABs Linear Regression')
p(1).LineWidth = 2;
p(2).LineWidth = 2;
p(3).LineWidth = 2;

C1 =
   -0.0006    1.9058

m1 =
  -5.7205e-04

b1 =
    1.9058

A1 =
    6.7248
```

The function generated by MATLAB then is $f(x) = 6.7248e\exp^{-0.00057205e}$. Figure 6.18 shows a comparison of the data and the results from Example 6.5 with this function.

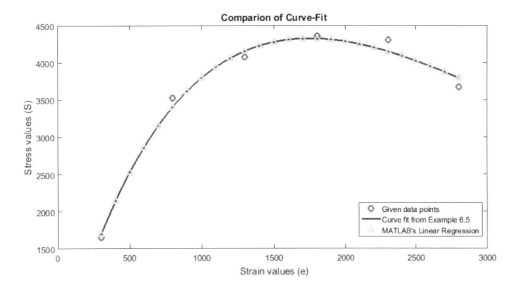

Fig. 6.18: Curve-fit with an exponential function Axe^{Bx} using MATLAB's linear regression

Example 6.18. Using MATLAB, generate a nonlinear fit for the data of Example 6.7. Compare these results with the fit of form $y = f(x) = C_1 + C_2 x + C_3 x^2$ generated in Example 6.7 and with the given data.

```
x = 0:1:5;
y = [0 8.47 17.48 19.57 14.69 11.23];
n = size(x,2);

%From Example 6.7
M = [n, sum(x), sum(x.^2); sum(x), sum(x.^2), sum(x.^3); sum
   (x.^2), sum(x.^3), sum(x.^4)];
L = [sum(y); sum(x.*y); sum(x.^2.*y)];

C = M\L;

C1 = C(1);
C2 = C(2);
C3 = C(3);

x1 = 0:0.1:5;
f = C1 + C2*x1 + C3*x1.^2;

%Use of MATLAB's Nonlinear Regression
F = @(c,x) c(1) + c(2)*x + c(3)*x.^2;
```

```
x0 = [0,0,0];

c = lsqcurvefit(F,x0,x,y)
f1 = F(c,x1);

p = plot(x,y,'redo',x1,f,'blue',x1,f1,'green^')
title('Comparison - Polynomial Method/MATLAB')
xlabel('x')
ylabel('y')
legend('Given data points','Curve fit from Example 6.7','
  MATLABs Nonlinear Regression')
p(1).LineWidth = 2;
p(2).LineWidth = 2;
p(3).LineWidth = 2;

c =
   -0.4439    12.4838    -2.0573
```

The function generated by MATLAB then is $f(x) = -0.4439 + 12.4838x - 2.0573x^2$. Figure 6.19 shows a comparison of the data and the results from Example 6.7 with this function.

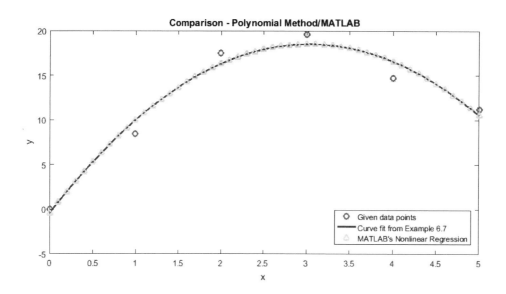

Fig. 6.19: Comparison of MATLAB's fit with the polynomial method

Example 6.19. Fit the data points:

x	0.1	0.2	0.3	0.4	0.5	0.6	0.7	0.8
y	0.59	0.83	0.90	0.95	1.02	1.43	1.75	3.15

with a function of the form $y = C_1 f_1(x) + C_2 f_2(x) + C_3 f_3(x) + C_4 f_4(x)$, where $f_1(x) = 1$, $f_2(x) = x^2$, $f_3(x) = \sin(2x)$, and $f_4(x) = e^{0.95x}$.

In this case, we have the following matrix equation

$$[M]\{C\} = \{L\},$$

where $\{C\}$ is the column vector of unknown coefficients C_1, C_2, C_3, and C_4, and $[M]$ and $\{L\}$ are known matrices, as generated below.

```
x = 0.1:0.1:0.8;
y = [0.59 0.83 0.90 0.95 1.02 1.43 1.75 3.15];
n = size(x,2);

f1 = ones(1,n);
f2 = x.^2;
f3 = sin(2*x);
f4 = exp(0.95*x);

M = [sum(f1.^2), sum(f1.*f2), sum(f1.*f3), sum(f1.*f4);
     sum(f2.*f1), sum(f2.^2), sum(f2.*f3), sum(f2.*f4);
     sum(f3.*f1), sum(f3.*f2), sum(f3.^2), sum(f3.*f4);
     sum(f4.*f1), sum(f4.*f2), sum(f4.*f3), sum(f4.^2)];

L = [sum(f1.*y); sum(f2.*y); sum(f3.*y); sum(f4.*y)];

C = M\L;

C1 = C(1)
C2 = C(2)
C3 = C(3)
C4 = C(4)

x1 = 0.1:0.01:0.8;
f = C1 + C2*x1.^2 + C3*sin(2*x1) + C4*exp(0.95*x1);

C1 =
  -45.6119

C2 =
  -49.7351

C3 =
```

```
    -16.6999

C4 =
    45.4596
```

The fit yielded by the analysis is then $f(x) = -45.6119 - 49.7351x^2 - 16.6999\sin(2x) + 45.4596e^{0.95x}$.

The use of *lsqcurvefit*, as applied to this problem, is illustrated as follows:

```
F =@(c,x) c(1) + c(2)*x.^2 + c(3)*sin(2*x) + c(4)*exp(0.95*x
    );
x0 = [0, 0, 0, 0];
c = lsqcurvefit(F,x0,x,y)
F1 = F(c,x1);

p = plot(x,y,'redo',x1,f,'blue',x1,F1,'green^')
title('Comparison of Results')
xlabel('x')
ylabel('y')
legend('Given data points','Analysis results','MATLABs
    Nonlinear Regression')
p(1).LineWidth = 2;
p(2).LineWidth = 2;
p(3).LineWidth = 2;

c =
    -45.6119   -49.7351   -16.6999    45.4596
```

The function generated by MATLAB then is $f(x) = -45.6119 - 49.7351x^2 - 16.6999\sin(2x) + 45.4596e^{0.95x}$. The MATLAB results and the linear combination results are both presented in Figure 6.20 and compared with the given data points.

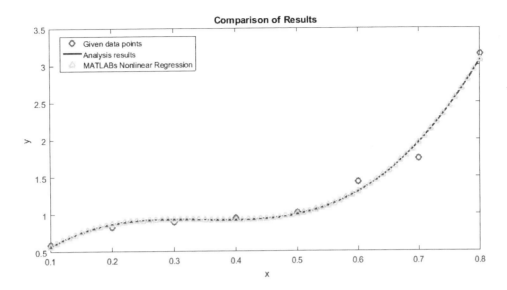

Fig. 6.20: Curve-fit with a linear combination of functions

Example 6.20. Given the following data:

x	0	1	2	3	4	5	6	7
y	3	6.2	9.75	20.13	24.25	33.21	37.54	41.95

Using MATLAB's *lsqcurvefit*, fit the data with a function of the form $f(x) = u_1 \sin(2x) + u_2 \sin(4x) + u_3 x$, where the u's are constants to be determined using the least squares principle. Use initial guess $[1, 2, 3]$.

```
x = 0:1:7;
y = [3 6.2 9.75 20.13 24.25 33.21 37.54 41.95];

F = @(u,x) u(1)*sin(2*x) + u(2)*cos(4*x) + u(3)*x;
u0 = [1, 2, 3];

u = lsqcurvefit(F,u0,x,y)

x1 = 0:0.1:7;
f = F(u,x1);

p = plot(x,y,'redo',x1,f,'blue')
title('Curve-fitting with MATLABs lsqcurvefit')
xlabel('x')
ylabel('y')
legend('Given data points','MATLABs Nonlinear Regression')
```

```
p(1).LineWidth = 2;
p(2).LineWidth = 2;

u =
    1.9347    3.1747    6.2514
```

The function generated by MATLAB then is $f(x) = 1.9347\sin(2x) + 3.1747\cos(4x) + 6.2514x$. Figure 6.21 shows a comparison of the data with this function.

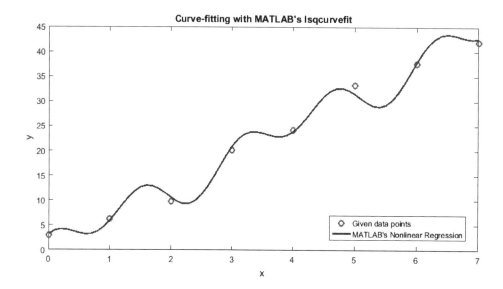

Fig. 6.21: Curve-fit with a linear combination of functions

6.10 Using MATLAB's *Basic Fitting* Toolbox

MATLAB has a *Basic Fitting UI* that allows you to interactively model different curve-fits. You can also extrapolate the model for interpolation outside of the data. To use this toolbox, you first must plot your data, then from the menu bar select *Tools>Basic Fitting*. This will produce a window with different curve-fit options. The use of this *Basic Fitting* toolbox is illustrated as follows, applied to the data from Example 6.6.

Example 6.21. First, plot the data from Example 6.6.

```
x = 1:1:5;
y = [5.75 10.75 12.65 29.95 49.35];
plot(x,y,'*')
```

From the menu bar select *Tools>Basic Fitting*. A window will pop up as illustrated in Figure 6.22.

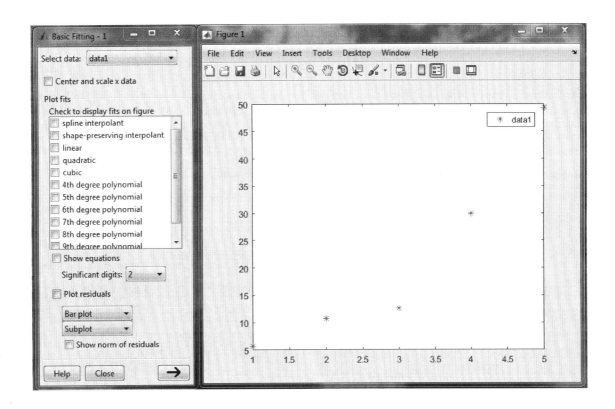

Fig. 6.22: Use of MATLAB's Basic Fitting toolbox

Click through the different fit options, one at a time, clicking each one off before trying the next. Note that the spline, the shape-preserving interpolant, and the 4th degree polynomial produce very nice curves.

To see the equation of a curve, click on the arrow button in the lower left corner of the *Basic Fitting* toolbox. The window will expand and you can see the polynomial that is being plotted, in addition to some other information. You can also have the equation of the polynomial display on the plot by clicking the "Show equations" option (see Figure 6.23).

To evaluate the curve-fit at a data point (given or additional), click on the next right-pointing arrow button in the lower left corner of the *Basic Fitting* toolbox. The window will expand once again and you can enter a value or values and click "Evaluate". MATLAB will then produce a table of the function values at the entered points (see Figure 6.24).

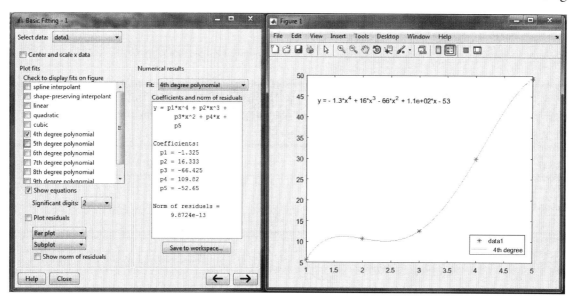

Fig. 6.23: Use of MATLAB's Basic Fitting toolbox

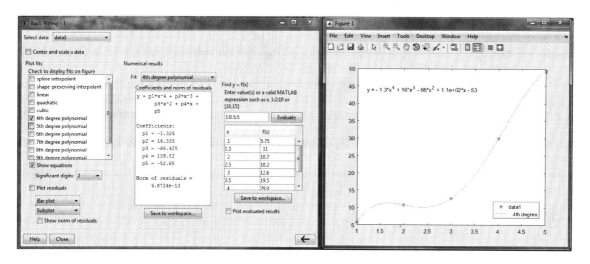

Fig. 6.24: Use of MATLAB's Basic Fitting toolbox

6.11 Applications in Curve-Fitting

In the world of engineering, science, and business, it is very common to see a function in the form of data prescribed at many points, and in addition, there may also be considerable scatter in the available data. The methods discussed in the earlier sections of this chapter will now be used to generate appropriate curve-fits to actual data from several practical applications.

6.11.1 Fatigue Failure Curve for Loading in the Finite Life Range

The fatigue failure curve of a material provides useful information pertinent to the design of machinery for finite life [2]. It is essentially a relationship between the completely reversed applied stress, S, and fatigue life, L, which is measured in terms of the number of stress reversals to failure.

The following data pertains to a steel with an endurance limit of 40 kpsi and an ultimate strength of 90 kpsi. It is required to curve-fit the data with a suitable function.

L (million cycles)	Stress (kpsi)
0.02	80
0.03	70
0.04	65
0.05	61
0.075	57
0.1	55
0.2	50
0.4	45
0.6	42
0.8	40.5
1.0	40.1
1.1	40
1.2	39.9
1.3	39.85

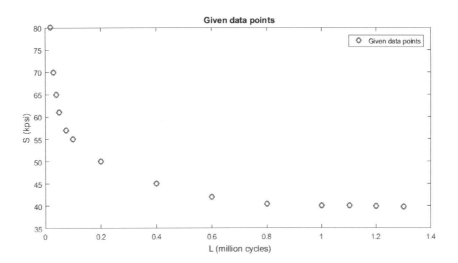

Fig. 6.25: Fatigue life data

From the plot of the given data shown in Figure 6.25, it appears that a power function would furnish a reasonable curve-fit. This has the form

$$S(L) = AL^B,$$

where A and B are undetermined coefficients to be evaluated on a least squares basis.

Using $S(L) = AL^B$, $S^* = C + BL^*$, where $L^* = \ln(L)$, $C = \ln(A)$ and $S^* = \ln(S)$, the matrix equation $[D]\{X\} = \{P\}$ is obtained, where $\{X\}$ is the column vector containing the unknowns C and B.

$$D = \begin{pmatrix} n & \sum_{i=1}^{n} L_i^* \\ \sum_{i=1}^{n} L_i^* & \sum_{i=1}^{n} (L_i^*)^2 \end{pmatrix}, \quad P = \begin{pmatrix} \sum_{i=1}^{n} S_i^* \\ \sum_{i=1}^{n} S_i^* L_i^* \end{pmatrix}$$

```
L = [0.02 0.03 0.04 0.05 0.075 0.1 0.2 0.4 0.6 0.8 1.0 1.1
   1.2 1.3];
S = [80 70 65 61 57 55 50 45 42 40.5 40.1 40 39.9 39.85];
n = size(L,2);

Last = log(L);
Sast = log(S);

D = [n, sum(Last); sum(Last), sum(Last.^2)];
P = [sum(Sast); sum(Sast.*Last)];

X = D\P;

C = X(1);
A = exp(C)
B = X(2)

L1 = 0.02:0.01:1.3;
S1 = A*L1.^B;

A =
   39.8083

B =
   -0.1553
```

The curve-fit generated by the linear regression analysis is $S(L) = 39.8083L^{-0.1553}$. MATLAB's linear regression can also be performed on this problem and the curve-fit is obtained as follows:

```
X1 = polyfit(Last,Sast,1);

C1 = X1(2)
A1 = exp(C1)
B1 = X1(1)

S2 = A1*L1.^B1;

p = plot(L,S,'redo',L1,S1,'blue',L1,S2,'green^')
title('Curve-Fitting with a Power Function')
xlabel('L (million cycles)')
ylabel('S (kpsi)')
legend('Given data points','Analysis generated fit','MATLABs
    Linear Regression')
p(1).LineWidth = 2;
p(2).LineWidth = 2;
p(3).LineWidth = 2;

C1 =
    3.6841

A1 =
    39.8083

B1 =
    -0.1553
```

The function generated by MATLAB then is $S(L) = 39.8083L^{-0.1553}$. Figure 6.26 shows a comparison of curve-fits generated with the given data points.

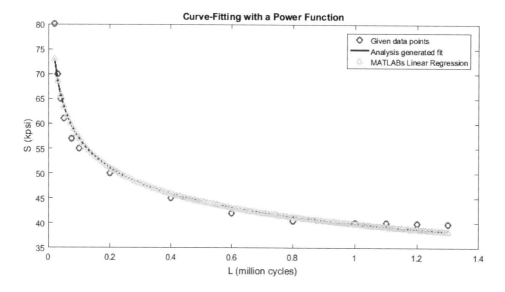

Fig. 6.26: Fatigue failure curve for loading in the finite life range

6.11.2 *Temperature Response of an Object Placed in a Hot Stream of Air*

The following data pertains to the temperatures of a solid steel sphere suspended in a hot stream of air measured at several instances of time [9]. It is required to curve-fit the data with a suitable function.

t = time (secs)	T = temp (deg C)
0	14
100	28
200	37.5
300	44
400	48
500	51
600	54
700	55
800	57.8
900	59.1

The given data is put in as follows and plotted in Figure 6.27.

```
t = 0:100:900;
T = [14 28 37.5 44 48 51 54 55 57.8 59.1];

p = plot(t,T,'redo')
xlabel('t (sec)')
ylabel('T (deg C')
legend('Given data points')
p(1).LineWidth = 2;
```

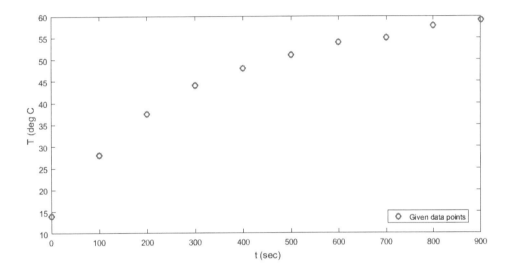

Fig. 6.27: Given temperature versus time data

A glance at the plot of Figure 6.27 suggests that a function of the following form would provide a reasonable fit to the given data

$$f(t) = A + Be^{-t/\tau},$$

where $f(t)$ is a linear combination of functions in which A and B are constants to be determined on a least squares basis. From the data plot, it appears that the temperature profile attains steady state in approximately 1200 seconds, which, when equated to four time constants, will yield a time constant, τ, of 300 seconds. Thus, the coefficient of t in the exponential term can be selected as $-1/300$.

In this case, the matrix equation to be solved is

$$[M]\{C\} = \{A\},$$

in which $[M]$ and $\{A\}$ contain the function $f_1(t) = 1$ and $f_2(t) = e^{-1/300t}$ as shown,

$$M = \begin{pmatrix} \sum_{i=1}^{n} [f_1(t_i)]^2 & \sum_{i=1}^{n} [f_1(t_i)f_2(t_i)] \\ \sum_{i=1}^{n} [f_1(t_i)f_2(t_i)] & \sum_{i=1}^{n} [f_2(t_i)]^2 \end{pmatrix},$$

$$C = \begin{pmatrix} C_1 \\ C_2 \end{pmatrix}, \quad A = \begin{pmatrix} \sum_{i=1}^{n} [f_1(t_i)T_i] \\ \sum_{i=1}^{n} [f_2(t_i)T_i] \end{pmatrix}.$$

In the above, note that $n = 10$ and $m = 2$, and the unknown constants are C_1 and C_2 which are determined below.

```
t = 0:100:900;
T = [14 28 37.5 44 48 51 54 55 57.8 59.1];
n = size(t,2);

f1 = ones(1,n);
f2 = exp(-1/300*t);

M = [sum(f1.^2), sum(f1.*f2); sum(f1.*f2), sum(f2.^2)];
A = [sum(f1.*T); sum(f2.*T)];

C = M\A;

A = C(1)
B = C(2)

t1 = 0:1:900;
f = A + B*exp(-1/300*t1);

A =
    60.4774

B =
   -45.9669
```

The function fitting the given data, then, is $f(t) = 60.4774 - 45.9669e^{-1/300t}$. Mathcad's function *lsqcurvefit* can also be used to evaluate the undetermined coefficients A and B in the regression function employed which is a linear combination of the functions selected for the curve-fit. This can be done as shown in the following steps.

```
F = @(c,t) c(1) + c(2)*exp(-1/300*t);
t0 = [0;0];

c = lsqcurvefit(F,t0,t,T)
```

```
t2 = 0:25:900;
F1 = F(c,t2);

p = plot(t,T,'redo',t1,f,'blue',t2,F1,'green^')
title('Comparison of Curve-Fits with Data')
xlabel('t (sec)')
ylabel('T (deg C)')
legend('Given data points','Analysis  fit','MATLABs Linear
    Regression')
p(1).LineWidth = 2;
p(2).LineWidth = 2;
p(3).LineWidth = 2;
```

The *lsqcurvefit* results and those of the linear combination analysis are presented in Figure 6.28 and compared with the given data.

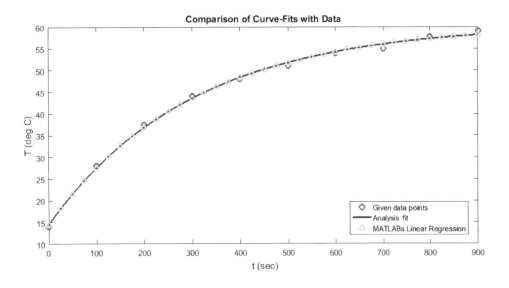

Fig. 6.28: Temperature response of an object placed in a hot stream of air

6.11.3 The Effect of Operating Temperature on the Strength of a Mechanical Element

When a mechanical element is subjected to reversed stresses at temperatures below room temperature, there is a strong possibility of the occurrence of brittle fracture. On the other hand, when the operating temperatures are higher than room temperature, the yield strength of the material drops off very rapidly with increase in temperature, and yielding can take place. The temperature-corrected value of tensile strength to be used in design calculations is obtained by multiplying the tensile strength at room temperature by a factor K_d which is a function of the temperature of the operating environment.

The following data was collected from tests done on carbon and alloy steels and shows the effect of operating temperature on tensile strength [10]. An appropriate curve-fit to the given data is sought.

Temperature (deg F)	K_d
0	0.975
100	1.008
200	1.020
300	1.024
400	1.018
500	0.995
600	0.963
700	0.927
800	0.872
900	0.797
1000	0.698
1100	0.567

The given data points, which are plotted in Figure 6.29 below, are put in as follows.

```
T = 0:100:1100;
K = [0.975 1.008 1.020 1.024 1.018 0.995 0.963 0.927 0.872
   0.797 0.698 0.567];

p = plot(T,K,'redo')
xlabel('Temperature (deg F)')
ylabel('Factor K_d')
legend('Given data points')
p(1).LineWidth = 2;
```

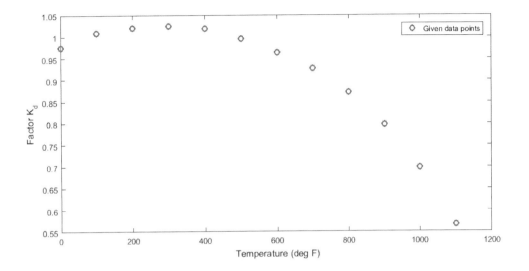

Fig. 6.29: Given K_d versus temperature data

We will fit the given data with a second-order polynomial of the following form.

$$K_d(T) = f(T) = C_1 + C_2 T + C_3 T^2.$$

Here, $n = 12$ and $m = 2$ and the matrix equation to be solved is:

$$MC = A,$$

where M is a known 3×3 matrix and A is a known column vector as shown

$$C = \begin{pmatrix} C_1 \\ C_2 \\ C_3 \end{pmatrix}$$

The M and A matrices are

$$M = \begin{pmatrix} n & \sum_{i=1}^{n} T_i & \sum_{i=1}^{n} T_i^2 \\ \sum_{i=1}^{n} T_i & \sum_{i=1}^{n} T_i^2 & \sum_{i=1}^{n} T_i^3 \\ \sum_{i=1}^{n} T_i^2 & \sum_{i=1}^{n} T_i^3 & \sum_{i=1}^{n} T_i^4 \end{pmatrix} \text{ and } A = \begin{pmatrix} \sum_{i=1}^{n} K_{di} \\ \sum_{i=1}^{n} T_i K_{di} \\ \sum_{i=1}^{n} T_i^2 K_{di} \end{pmatrix}.$$

```
T = 0:100:1100;
K = [0.975 1.008 1.020 1.024 1.018 0.995 0.963 0.927 0.872
    0.797 0.698 0.567];
n = size(T,2);

M = [n, sum(T), sum(T.^2); sum(T), sum(T.^2), sum(T.^3); sum
    (T.^2), sum(T.^3), sum(T.^4)];
```

```
A = [sum(K); sum(T.*K); sum(T.^2.*K)];

C = M\A;

C1 = C(1)
C2 = C(2)
C3 = C(3)

T1 = 0:1:1100;
f = C1 + C2*T1 + C3*T1.^2;

C1 =
    0.9681

C2 =
   4.1992e-04

C3 =
  -6.9655e-07
```

Using MATLAB, we obtain

$$f(T) = 0.9681 + 0.00041992T - 0.000000669655T^2.$$

The *polyfit* function in MATLAB can also be employed as shown below to generate curve-fits to the given data.

```
c = polyfit(T,K,2);
c1 = c(1)
c2 = c(2)
c3 = c(3)

f = c1*T1.^2 + c2*T1 + c3;

c1 =
  -6.9655e-07

c2 =
   4.1992e-04

c3 =
    0.9681
```

```
p = plot(T,K,'redo',T1,f,'blue',T,f1,'green^')
title('Curve-Fits Generated')
xlabel('Temperature (deg F)')
ylabel('Multiplying Factor K_d')
legend('Given data points','Analysis  fit','MATLABs Linear
    Regression')
p(1).LineWidth = 2;
p(2).LineWidth = 2;
p(3).LineWidth = 2;
```

Figure 6.30 shows a comparison of the various curve-fits generated with the given data points.

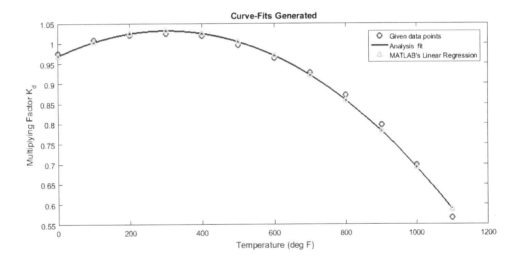

Fig. 6.30: Effect of operating temperature on the strength of a mechanical element

6.11.4 Drop-Testing of Packaged Articles

An interesting parameter that often warrants investigation is the height from which a package can be dropped before it suffers any accountable damage, which can be assessed from the maximum acceleration imparted to the package at the end of the drop [12]. This is a question that arises when packages must be properly cushioned before shipment to another location. The maximum acceleration to gravity ratio, a, has been found to be a function of the ratio, h, of twice the distance dropped to the static deflection of the package.

The following a versus h data is provided, for which a reasonable curve-fit is to be generated.

h	1	2	3	4	5	6	7	8
a	1.4	1.8	2	2.25	2.65	2.8	2.9	3.01
h	9	10	11	12	13	14	15	16
a	3.25	3.3	3.55	3.65	3.75	3.85	4.2	4.3

These data points are plotted in Figure 6.31.

```
h = 1:1:16;
a = [1.4 1.8 2 2.25 2.65 2.8 2.9 3.01 3.25 3.3 3.55 3.65
    3.75 3.85 4.2 4.3];

p = plot(h,a,'redo')
xlabel('2h/Static Deflection Ratio')
ylabel('Max Acceleration/Gravity Ratio')
legend('Given data points')
p(1).LineWidth = 2;
```

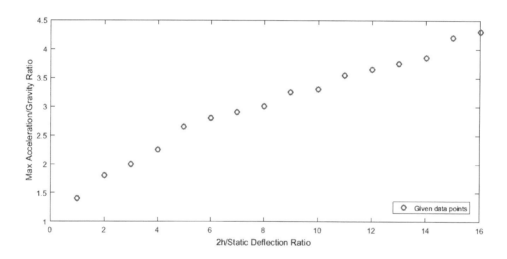

Fig. 6.31: Given acceleration ratio versus height ratio data

We will generate a curve-fit of the form:

$$a = f(h) = C_1 + C_2 h + C_3 h^2 + C_4 h^3.$$

Here, $n = 16$ and $m = 3$ and the matrix equation to be solved is:

$$MC = A,$$

where M is a known 4×4 matrix and A is a known column vector as shown below. The column vector C, which involves the undetermined coefficients, is

$$C = \begin{pmatrix} C_1 \\ C_2 \\ C_3 \\ C_4 \end{pmatrix},$$

$$M = \begin{pmatrix} n & \sum_{i=1}^{n} h_i & \sum_{i=1}^{n} h_i^2 & \sum_{i=1}^{n} h_i^3 \\ \sum_{i=1}^{n} h_i & \sum_{i=1}^{n} h_i^2 & \sum_{i=1}^{n} h_i^3 & \sum_{i=1}^{n} h_i^4 \\ \sum_{i=1}^{n} h_i^2 & \sum_{i=1}^{n} h_i^3 & \sum_{i=1}^{n} h_i^4 & \sum_{i=1}^{n} h_i^5 \\ \sum_{i=1}^{n} h_i^3 & \sum_{i=1}^{n} h_i^4 & \sum_{i=1}^{n} h_i^5 & \sum_{i=1}^{n} h_i^6 \end{pmatrix}, \text{ and } A = \begin{pmatrix} \sum_{i=1}^{n} a_i \\ \sum_{i=1}^{n} h_i a_i \\ \sum_{i=1}^{n} h_i^2 a_i \\ \sum_{i=1}^{n} h_i^3 a_i \end{pmatrix}.$$

```
h = 1:1:16;
a = [1.4 1.8 2 2.25 2.65 2.8 2.9 3.01 3.25 3.3 3.55 3.65
    3.75 3.85 4.2 4.3];
n = size(h,2);


M = [n, sum(h), sum(h.^2), sum(h.^3); sum(h), sum(h.^2), sum
    (h.^3), sum(h.^4); sum(h.^2), sum(h.^3), sum(h.^4), sum(h
    .^5); sum(h.^3), sum(h.^4), sum(h.^5), sum(h.^6)];
A = [sum(a); sum(h.*a); sum(h.^2.*a); sum(h.^3.*a)];


C = M\A;
C1 = C(1)
C2 = C(2)
C3 = C(3)
C4 = C(4)


C1 =
    0.9972


C2 =
    0.4333


C3 =
   -0.0292


C4 =
    9.4725e-04


h1 = 1:0.1:16;
a1 = C1 + C2*h1 + C3*h1.^2 + C4*h1.^3;
```

Using MATLAB, we obtain $f(T) = 0.9972 + 0.4333h - 0.0292h^2 + 0.00094725h^3$. The *polyfit* function in MATLAB also can be utilized as shown below to generate curve-fits to the given data.

```
c = polyfit(h,a,3);
c1 = c(1)
c2 = c(2)
c3 = c(3)
c4 = c(4)

h2 = 1:0.5:16;
a2 = c1*h2.^3 + c2*h2.^2 + c3*h2 + c4;

c1 =
   9.4725e-04

c2 =
   -0.0292

c3 =
    0.4333

c4 =
    0.9972

p = plot(h,a,'redo',h1,a1,'blue',h2,a2,'green--')
title('Curve-Fits Generated')
xlabel('2h/Static Deflection Ratio')
ylabel('Max Acceleration/Gravity Ratio')
legend('Given data points','Analysis  fit','MATLAB Nonlinear
    Regression')
p(1).LineWidth = 2;
p(2).LineWidth = 2;
p(3).LineWidth = 2;
```

Figure 6.32 shows a comparison of the various curve-fits obtained with the given data points.

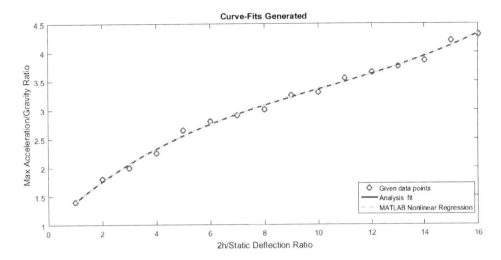

Fig. 6.32: Acceleration ratio versus height ratio curve-fits

Problems

6.1. Given the following data

x	1.3	3.2	4.6	6.1
y	52	46	38	26

fit a straight line $y = f(x) = C_1 + C_2 x$ to the above data. Determine $y(5.1)$. Verify your result with MATLAB's *polyfit*.

6.2. Given

x	0	1	2	3	4
y	11.25	12.34	18.56	28.69	44.73

generate a MATLAB script to determine a least squares quadratic fit. Determine $y(3.75)$. Verify with MATLAB's *polyfit*. Draw plots and compare results.

6.3. Generate a least squares fit of the form $f(x) = Ax^B$ to the following data

x	1	2	4	5
y	2	10	60	110

Apply a weighting factor of 3 to the last data point and determine $f(3.5)$.

6.4. The thermal conductivity, K, of a material varies with temperature, T, as follows:

T (Kelvin)	200	600	1000	1400
K (W/(cm-Kelvin))	1.0	0.40	0.30	0.25

Generate a MATLAB script to determine a least squares fit of the form $K = AT^B$. Determine K for $T = 1200$ Kelvin. Obtain an answer that is good to two decimal places. Verify with MATLAB's *polyfit*. Draw plots and compare results.

6.5. For the data set given below, determine a power function that will serve as a least squares fit.

x	1	2	3	4	5	6	7	8
y	0.43	0.71	0.94	1.07	1.19	1.27	1.32	1.47

Compute $y(4.5)$.

6.6. For the data set given below, find an exponential function of form: $y = f(x) = Ae^{Bx}$ that will serve as a least squares fit.

x	0	1	2	2.75	3.5
y	2.5	6.75	15.42	28.86	52.03

Determine $y(3.0)$.

6.7. For the data set given below, find an exponential function of form: $y = f(x) = Ae^{Bx}$ that will serve as a least squares fit.

x	0	1	2	3	4
y	2.01	1.37	0.83	0.55	0.33

Determine $y(1.5)$.

6.8. For the experimental data given below

Strain, x (μ-in/in)	40	50	70	90
Displacement, y (inches)	0.015	0.028	0.045	0.072

Determine a least squares fit of the form $f(x) = Axe^{Bx}$. Determine $f(45)$ and $f(60)$.

6.9. For the strain (e) and displacement (d) data shown below:

e (micro-in/in)	43	57	68	84	99	115
d (inches)	0.009	0.017	0.029	0.043	0.067	0.097

determine a least squares fit using an approximation of the form $d = Ae\exp(Be)$. Determine $d(72)$.

6.10. The temperature of a a hot surface varies sinusoidally with time. The data which is in terms of temperatures, T (deg C), measured at several time intervals , τ, where τ is the number of hours from midnight, is given below.

τ (hours)	2	4	8
T (deg C)	80	120	105

Obtain a curve fit to the given data of the form $T = A\sin(\pi\tau/12) + B\cos(\pi\tau/12)$. Determine $T(6)$.

6.11. Fit the data points given below with a function of the form $y(x) = C_1 f_1(x) + C_2 f_2(x)$ where $f_1(x) = x$ and $f_2(x) = x^3$. Compute $y(3.75)$.

x	2.25	3.30	4.40
y	9.75	15.60	28.27

6.12. The following data pertains to the temperatures of an object suspended in a hot stream of air measured at several instances of time.

t, Time (seconds)	0.0	400	1200
T, Temperature (deg C)	20	50	61.5

Generate a MATLAB script to curve-fit the data with a function of the form $f(t) = A + Be^{-0.0033t}$ and estimate the temperature attained by the object at time $t = 600$ seconds. Verify your results with MATLAB's *lsqcurvefit*. Draw plots and compare results.

6.13. Fit a linear combination of known functions

$$f(x) = A + Bx + C\sin(\pi x) + D\sin(3\pi x)$$

to

x	0.1	0.2	0.3	0.4	0.5
y	0.5541	2.1456	2.8021	2.5645	3.2458
x	0.6	0.7	0.8	0.9	1.0
y	2.9765	2.8521	2.4379	1.7872	0.1315

Determine $y(0.85)$. Verify your results with MATLAB's *lsqcurvefit*. Draw plots and compare results.

6.14. Given the four data points

x	0	2.5	4.75	6.26
y	0	12.45	22.67	36.89

generate a MATLAB script to obtain a curve-fit of the form: $y = f(x) = C_1 + C_2 x + C_3 x^2 + C_4 x^3$. Apply a weighting factor of 2 to the last two data points. Determine $y(3.5)$. Verify with MATLAB's *polyfit*. Draw plots and compare results.

6.15. Data defining the stress (S) versus strain (e) curve for an aluminum alloy is given below.

Strain, e (%)	Stress, S (Kpsi)
10	63
20	63.6
40	62
60	60
80	58
100	56
120	52
140	48
150	47

Using an approximating polynomial of the form

$$S = C_1 + C_2 e + C_3 e^2$$

obtain a least squares fit to the given data. Determine $S(105\%)$.

6.16. The following data relating the distance traveled by an object to time was obtained from a test in an experimental test track. The distance traveled, S, is in meters and the time, t, is in seconds.

Time, t (secs)	0.1	0.5	1.5	3.0
Distance, S (m)	0.26	1.56	7.41	30.90

Generate a curve-fit of the form $S(t) = A + Bt + Ct^2$. Compute S for $t = 2$ seconds.

6.17. The pressure drag, D_P, on an object can be reduced in comparison with the total drag, D_T, by streamlining it, that is, making its length, L, in the direction of flow larger with respect to its maximum thickness or diameter, D [9]. The following data is provided to demonstrate the effect of streamlining on the pressure drag of a body of symmetrical airfoil cross section.

$\frac{L}{D}$	1	2	3	4	5	6	7	8	9	10	11
$\frac{D_P}{D_T}$	1.25	0.65	0.42	0.25	0.20	0.10	0.08	0.06	0.04	0.02	0.01

Curve-fit the given data with a power function and determine D_P/D_T for $L/D = 5.5$.

6.18. The following data, in which the time, t, is given in seconds provides the response $c(t)$ of a control system to a step input.

t (sec)	0.0	0.75	1.5	2.0	3.0	4.0	5.0	6.0
$c(t)$	0.0	1.30	1.40	1.10	0.85	1.02	1.01	1.009

Generate a MATLAB script to obtain a least-squares fit of the form

$$c(t) = A + Be^{-t}\sin(2.828t) + Ce^{-t}\cos(2.828t)$$

and determine c at $t = 3.5$ seconds. Verify with MATLAB's *lsqcurvefit*. Draw plots and compare results.

6.19. The Brinell hardness number, Bhn, for steel [10] is given as a function of the tempering temperature, T, in the following table.

T (deg F)	400	600	800	1000	1200
Bhn	540	500	445	375	310

Curve-fit the given data with a second-order polynomial and determine the Brinell hardness number for $T = 850$ deg F.

6.20. The average strain rate used in obtaining stress/strain data for a material specimen is about 0.001 in/(in-sec). However, when the strain rate, SR, is increased, as it happens, under conditions of impact loading, the strength of the material also increases [10]. The following data shows the influence of the increase in strain rate on the yield strength, $SYLD$, of a steel specimen.

SR in/(in-sec)	10^{-6}	10^{-5}	10^{-4}	10^{-2}	1	10^2	10^3
$SYLD$ kpsi	30	28	30	37	45	65	78

Curve-fit the given data with a function of the form

$$f(SR) = D \cdot SR^2 + E \cdot SR^{0.049},$$

where $f(SR)$ is a linear combination of functions and D and E are constants to be determined. Determine $SYLD$ corresponding to an SR of 50. Verify your results with MATLAB's *lsqcurvefit*. Draw plots and compare results.

6.21. The endurance limit of a steel specimen is typically a function of the condition of its surface [11]. For an unnotched ground specimen in reversed bending, the endurance limit, S_{end}, is related to its tensile strength, S_{ult}, as given in the following table of data.

S_{ult} kpsi	60	80	100	120	140	160	180	200	220
S_{end} kpsi	25	35	45	55	65	72	80	85	90

Curve-fit the given data with a second-order polynomial. Determine S_{end} corresponding to $S_{ult} = 135$ kpsi.

6.22. Expected voice levels required for speech communication with various background noise levels and separations between the speaker and the listener [6] are given in the following table of data.

	Background Noise Levels (dBA)				
Speaker/ Listener Distance (m)	Normal Voice	Raised Voice	Very Loud Voice	Loud Shouting	Peak Shouting
0.25	90		95	100	118
0.5	80		88	92	112
1.0	72		78	84	103
2.0	63		72	77	96
3.0	57	62	68	74	92.5
4.0	54.5	60	66	72	90
5.0	52	57	64	68	88
6.0	50	56.5	62.5	67.5	86.5
7.0	49.5	55	61.5	66	86
8.0	49	54	60	65	85
9.0	48	53.5	58	64.5	84.5
9.5	47.5	52.5	57.5	64	84

Generate a MATLAB script to obtain curve-fits to the given data in the form of separate curves for (a) Peak shouting (b) Shouting (c) Very loud voice (d) Raised voice and (e) Normal voice. Use second-order polynomial forms.

Determine the voice levels required in the following situations:

(1) Speaker listener distance = 2.5 m, background noise level = 68 dBA
(2) Speaker listener distance = 4.5 m, background noise level = 86 dBA
(3) Speaker listener distance = 8.5 m, background noise level = 45 dBA
(4) Speaker listener distance = 6.5 m, background noise level = 65 dBA

6.23. Given the following data

x	0	1	2	3	4	5	6	7	8	9	10
y	0	0.47	0.395	0.011	-0.182	-0.079	-0.064	0.02	0.038	0.004	-0.003

use MATLAB's *lsqcurvefit* to fit the data with a function of the form

$$f(x) = e^{-u_0 x} \sin(u_1 x)$$

where u_0 and u_1 are constants to be determined. Show a comparison of your results with the given data by means of a plot.

6.24. Given the following data

x	-1	-0.6	-0.2	0.2	0.6	1.0
y	-3	-2.17	-0.73	0.07	0.23	1

use MATLAB's *lsqcurvefit* to fit the data with a function of the form

$$f(x) = ax + b + e^{cx^2}$$

where a, b and c are constants to be determined. Show a comparison of your results with the given data by means of a plot.

Chapter 7
Numerical Differentiation

7.1 Introduction to Numerical Differentiation and the Use of the MATLAB *diff* Command

In the process of generating a solution to a science or an engineering problem, the need to come up with a numerical estimate of a derivative is often encountered. We will discuss two methods of computing derivatives as follows:

1. Method of finite differences
2. Interpolating polynomial method

These methods will be discussed in detail in the paragraphs following.

To compute the derivative of a function using the MATLAB *diff* command, first define the variables of the function to be differentiated symbolically using *syms*. Then apply the *diff* command to either a predefined function or a function input, as follows.

```
syms x
f(x) = sin(x^2);
diff(f,x)

ans(x) =
2*x*cos(x^2)

diff(exp(-x^2),x)

ans =
-2*x*exp(-x^2)
```

The *diff* command can be used to find derivatives of multivariate expressions, as well as higher-order derivatives, as follows.

```
syms x t
diff(cos(x*t^2),t)

ans =
-2*t*x*sin(t^2*x)

diff(cos(x*t^2),x)

ans =
-t^2*sin(t^2*x)

diff(cos(x*t^2),x,2)

s =
-t^4*cos(t^2*x)

diff(cos(x*t^2),x,12)

ans =
t^24*cos(t^2*x)
```

7.2 Method of Finite Differences

In traditional calculus, a derivative of a function $f(x)$ is defined as

$$\frac{d}{dx}f(x) = \lim_{\Delta x \to 0} \frac{f(x+\Delta x)-f(x)}{\Delta x}. \tag{7.1}$$

In numerical methods, taking the above limit as Δx goes to zero is not possible, and, although Δx can be very small, it certainly cannot be zero. The process by which this increment Δx is made small and utilized in calculations paves the way for the method of finite differences.

If the dependent variable x is incremented by Δx, as shown in Figure 7.1, the difference between the function value at $x + \Delta x$ and that at x is called a forward difference. In this case, the derivative of the function $f(x)$ at x is

$$\frac{d}{dx}f(x) = \frac{f(x+\Delta x)-f(x)}{\Delta x}. \tag{7.2}$$

However, if the dependent variable is incremented by $-\Delta x$, the difference between the function values is a backward difference, and the derivative in this case is

$$\frac{d}{dx}f(x) = \frac{f(x)-f(x-\Delta x)}{\Delta x}. \tag{7.3}$$

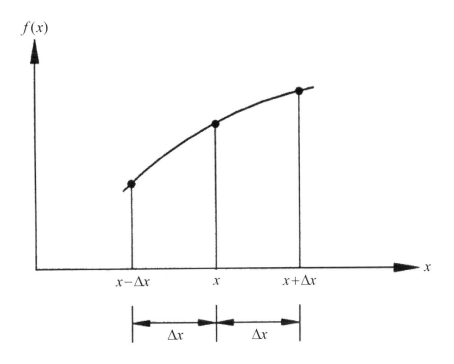

Fig. 7.1: Finite differences

If a *two-step difference* is employed, the method of computing derivatives is called the *two-step method*. An estimate of the derivative, in this case, is

$$\frac{d}{dx}f(x) = \frac{f(x+\Delta x) - f(x-\Delta x)}{2\Delta x}. \tag{7.4}$$

For obtaining an estimate of the second derivative of $f(x)$, we will consider the following Taylor series expansions.

$$f(x+\Delta x) = f(x) + \Delta x \frac{d}{dx}f(x) + \frac{\Delta x^2}{2!}\frac{d^2}{dx^2}f(x) + \cdots \tag{7.5}$$

and

$$f(x-\Delta x) = f(x) - \Delta x \frac{d}{dx}f(x) + \frac{\Delta x^2}{2!}\frac{d^2}{dx^2}f(x) - \cdots \tag{7.6}$$

Adding equations (7.5) and (7.6) with terms beyond the second derivative terms ignored will give an estimate of the second derivative as

$$\frac{d^2}{dx^2}f(x) = \frac{1}{\Delta x^2}(f(x+\Delta x) - 2f(x) + f(x-\Delta x)). \tag{7.7}$$

By following a similar procedure, the third and fourth derivatives can also be estimated as

$$\frac{d^3}{dx^3}f(x) = \frac{1}{\Delta x^3}(f(x+2\Delta x) - 2f(x+\Delta x) + 2f(x-\Delta x) - f(x-2\Delta x)) \tag{7.8}$$

and

$$\frac{d^4}{dx^4} f(x) = \frac{1}{\Delta x^4} (f(x+2\Delta x) - 4f(x+\Delta x) + 6f(x) - 4f(x-\Delta x) + f(x-2\Delta x)). \quad (7.9)$$

Example 7.1. Using the data given, compute the first derivative at $x = 4$ using the forward, backward as well as the two-step finite difference approximations. Also compute the second derivative at $x = 4$.

x	2	3	4	5	6
$f(x)$	0.703	1.212	1.456	1.723	1.853

The first derivative at $x = 4$ using equation (7.2), which is the forward difference approximation is

$$f'(4) \approx \frac{1.723 - 1.456}{5 - 4} = 0.267.$$

The first derivative at $x = 4$ using equation (7.3), which is the backward difference approximation is

$$f'(4) \approx \frac{1.456 - 1.212}{4 - 3} = 0.244.$$

The first derivative at $x = 4$ using equation (7.4), which is the two-step difference approximation is

$$f'(4) \approx \frac{1.723 - 1.212}{5 - 3} = 0.2555.$$

The second, third and fourth derivatives at $x = 4$ are given by equations (7.7), (7.8) and (7.9), and these are

$$f''(4) \approx \frac{1}{1^2} (1.723 - 2(1.456) + 1.212) = 0.023,$$

$$f'''(4) \approx \frac{1}{1^3} (1.853 - 2(1.723) + 2(1.212) - 0.703) = 0.128,$$

and

$$f^{(4)}(4) \approx \frac{1}{1^4} (1.853 - 4(1.723) + 6(1.456) - 4(1.212) - 0.703) = -0.448.$$

7.3 Interpolating Polynomial Method

In the interpolating polynomial method, an interpolating polynomial passing through given data points is determined by any of the methods discussed in Chapter 5. Then, the polynomial generated can be differentiated as is done in traditional calculus. If the polynomial derived, for instance, is

$$f(x) = a_0 + a_1 x + a_2 x^2 + a_3 x^3 + \cdots + a_n x^n, \quad (7.10)$$

then, its derivative can be obtained as

$$\frac{d}{dx}f(x) = a_1 + 2a_2 x + 3a_3 x^2 + \cdots + na_n x^{n-1}. \tag{7.11}$$

Example 7.2. Given the following data:

x	2	3	4	5	6
y	0.80354	1.23591	1.62312	1.89765	1.96789

Use the Method of Undetermined Coefficients to fit an interpolating polynomial to the given data and estimate: $y'(4.5)$, $y'(2.7)$, $y''(4.5)$ and $y''(2.7)$.

Since five data points are given, we can generate a 4th order polynomial.

Let $y(x) = f(x) = a + bx + cx^2 + dx^3 + ex^4$.

Substituting the given values of (x, y) in the assumed polynomial above yields the following matrix equation:

$$MA = V,$$

where

$$M = \begin{pmatrix} 1 & 2 & 2^2 & 2^3 & 2^4 \\ 1 & 3 & 3^2 & 3^3 & 3^4 \\ 1 & 4 & 4^2 & 4^3 & 4^4 \\ 1 & 5 & 5^2 & 5^3 & 5^4 \\ 1 & 6 & 6^2 & 6^3 & 6^4 \end{pmatrix}, \quad V = \begin{pmatrix} 0.80354 \\ 1.23591 \\ 1.62312 \\ 1.89765 \\ 1.96789 \end{pmatrix}.$$

Using the MATLAB "\" command, the unknown coefficients in the column vector A can be found.

```
M = [1 2 2^2 2^3 2^4; 1 3 3^2 3^3 3^4; 1 4 4^2 4^3 4^4; 1 5
    5^2 5^3 5^4; 1 6 6^2 6^3 6^4];
V = [0.80354; 1.23591; 1.62312; 1.89765; 1.96789];
A = M\V

A =
   -0.0471
    0.4073
    0.0074
    0.0028
   -0.0010
```

The coefficients a, b, c, d and e of the assumed polynomial are the elements of A. The polynomial derived is, then,

$$y(x) = -0.0471 + 0.4073x + 0.0074x^2 + 0.0028x^3 - 0.0010x^4,$$

with first and second derivatives as follows.

First derivative:

$$y'(x) = 0.4073 + 2(0.0074)x + 3(0.0028)x^2 - 4(0.0010)x^3,$$

$$y'(4.5) = 0.27835, \quad y'(2.7) = 0.42959.$$

Second derivative:

$$y''(x) = 2(0.0074) + 6(0.0028)x - 12(0.0010)x^2,$$

$$y''(4.5) = -0.15347, \quad y''(2.7) = -0.02759.$$

Use of the MATLAB *diff* operator yields:

```
syms x
y(x) = A(1) + A(2)*x + A(3)*x^2 + A(4)*x^3 + A(5)*x^4;
yprime(x) = diff(y);
ydblprime(x) = diff(y,2);
double(yprime(4.5))

ans =
    0.2783

double(ydblprime(4.5))

ans =
   -0.1535

double(yprime(2.7))

ans =
    0.4296

double(ydblprime(2.7))

ans =
   -0.0276
```

Notice that the MATLAB *diff* function yields the same results as those obtained through the manual process of differentiation. These are presented in Figures 7.2 and 7.3.

```
x = 2:0.5:6;
Y = A(1) + A(2)*x + A(3)*x.^2 + A(4)*x.^3 + A(5)*x.^4;
YPrime = A(2) + 2*A(3)*x + 3*A(4)*x.^2 + 4*A(5)*x.^3;
YDblPrime =2*A(3) + 6*A(4)*x + 12*A(5)*x.^2;
```

```
p = plot(x,YPrime,'blueo-')
hold on
p1 = fplot(yprime,[2 6])
title('A Comparison of the First Derivative Results')
xlabel('x')
ylabel('y')
legend('Interpolated polynomial','MATLAB diff results')
p(1).LineWidth = 2;
p1(1).LineWidth = 2;
p1(1).Color = 'red';
```

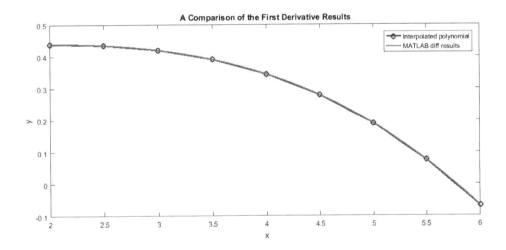

Fig. 7.2: Graph of the first derivative

```
p = plot(x,YDblPrime,'blueo-')
hold on
p1 = fplot(ydblprime,[2 6])
title('A Comparison of the Second Derivative Results')
xlabel('x')
ylabel('y')
legend('Interpolated polynomial','MATLAB diff results')
p(1).LineWidth = 2;
p1(1).LineWidth = 2;
p1(1).Color = 'red';
```

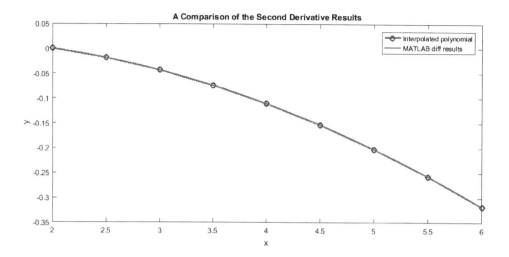

Fig. 7.3: Graph of the second derivative

7.4 Applications in Numerical Differentiation

The following examples illustrate situations where numerical differentiation can be applied and used to our advantage in generating realistic solutions to practical problems.

7.4.1 Determination of Velocities and Accelerations from Given Displacement Data

The following position versus time data for a train has been experimentally obtained.

Time t (secs)	0	10	20	30	35	40
Position s (m)	0	75	175	360	480	600

Determine the velocity and acceleration of the train as functions of time. Estimate the velocity and acceleration of the train at $t = 32$ seconds.

We first use the method of undetermined coefficients to fit an interpolating polynomial to the given data. Since six data points are given, a fifth order polynomial of the following form will be generated,

$$s(t) = f(t) = a + bt + ct^2 + dt^3 + et^4 + ft^5.$$

Substituting the given values of (t, s) in the assumed polynomial above yields the following matrix equation:

$$MA = V,$$

where

$$M = \begin{pmatrix} 1 & 0 & 0^2 & 0^3 & 0^4 & 0^5 \\ 1 & 10 & 10^2 & 10^3 & 10^4 & 10^5 \\ 1 & 20 & 20^2 & 20^3 & 20^4 & 20^5 \\ 1 & 30 & 30^2 & 30^3 & 30^4 & 30^5 \\ 1 & 35 & 35^2 & 35^3 & 35^4 & 35^4 \\ 1 & 40 & 40^2 & 40^3 & 40^4 & 40^5 \end{pmatrix}, \quad V = \begin{pmatrix} 0 \\ 75 \\ 175 \\ 360 \\ 480 \\ 600 \end{pmatrix}.$$

Using the MATLAB "\" command, the unknown coefficients in the column vector A can be found.

```
format long
M = ones(6,6);
T = [0 10 20 30 35 40];
for i = 1:6
    for j = 2:6
        M(i,j) = T(i)^(j-1);
    end
end

V   = [0; 75; 175; 360; 480; 600];

A = M\V

A =
                     0
   9.414285714285715
  -0.361309523809524
   0.016666666666667
   0.000077380952381
  -0.000004523809524
```

The coefficients a, b, c, d, e and f of the assumed polynomial are the elements of A. The polynomial derived is, then,

$$s(t) = 9.414286t - 0.361310t^2 + 0.016667t^3 + 0.000077t^4 - 0.000005t^5,$$

with first and second derivatives as follows.

First derivative:

$$s'(t) = 9.4143 - 2(0.3613)t + 3(0.0167)t^2 + 4(0.00008)t^3 - 5(0.000005)t^4,$$

Velocity: $s'(32) = 23.91516 \text{m/sec}$

Second derivative:

$$s''(t) = -2(0.3613) + 6(0.0167)t + 12(0.00008)t^2 - 20(0.000005)t^3,$$

$$\text{Acceleration: } s''(32) = 0.46351\,\text{m/sec}^2$$

Use of the MATLAB *diff* function yields:

```
syms x
s(x) =  A(1) + A(2)*x + A(3)*x^2 + A(4)*x^3 + A(5)*x^4 + A
    (6)*x^5;
sprime(x) = diff(s);
sdblprime(x) = diff(s,2);
double(sprime(32))
double(sdblprime(32))

ans =

  23.915161904761906
ans =
   0.463514285714286
```

As is expected, the results of the MATLAB *diff* function are the same as those obtained through the process of manual differentiation of the interpolating polynomial. They are presented in Figure 7.4.

```
x = 0:1:40;
S = A(1) + A(2)*x + A(3)*x.^2 + A(4)*x.^3 + A(5)*x.^4 + A(5)
    *x.^5;
SPrime = A(2) + 2*A(3)*x + 3*A(4)*x.^2 + 4*A(5)*x.^3 + 5*A
    (6)*x.^4;
SDblPrime =2*A(3) + 6*A(4)*x + 12*A(5)*x.^2 + 20*A(6)*x.^3;

subplot(3,1,1);
p = plot(x,S,'blueo-')
title('Position vs. Time')
xlabel('Time (secs)')
ylabel('Position (m)')
legend('s(t)')
p(1).LineWidth = 2;

subplot(3,1,2);
p = plot(x,SPrime,'blueo-')
hold on
p1 = fplot(sprime,[0 40])
title('Velocity vs. Time')
```

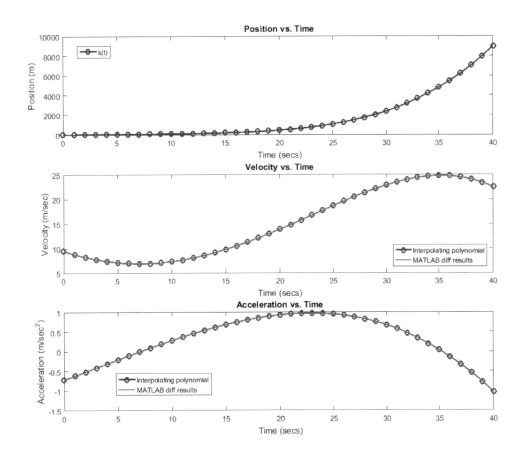

Fig. 7.4: Position, velocity and acceleration versus time

```
xlabel('Time (secs)')
ylabel('Velocity (m/sec)')
legend('Interpolating polynomial','MATLAB diff results')
p(1).LineWidth = 2;
p1(1).LineWidth = 2;
p1(1).Color = 'red';
hold off

subplot(3,1,3);
p = plot(x,SDblPrime,'blueo-')
hold on
p1 = fplot(sdblprime,[0 40])
title('Acceleration vs. Time')
xlabel('Time (secs)')
ylabel('Acceleration (m/sec^2)')
```

```
legend('Interpolating polynomial','MATLAB diff results')
p(1).LineWidth = 2;
p1(1).LineWidth = 2;
p1(1).Color = 'red';
hold off
```

7.4.2 Determination of Shock Absorber Parameters, and Damper and Spring Restoring Forces from Given Vehicle Displacement Data

The following displacement x versus time t data is provided for a 200 kg motorcycle with a shock absorber.

t (secs)	0	0.5	1.0	1.5	2.0	2.5
x (mm)	0	0.23	0	-0.075	0.025	0

Generate an interpolating polynomial for the displacement data given and obtain velocity and acceleration profiles using MATLAB. Determine

(a) the stiffness and the damping constant of the shock absorber; and
(b) the damper and spring restoring forces of the shock absorber as functions of time.

The given data is plotted in Figure 7.5 below.

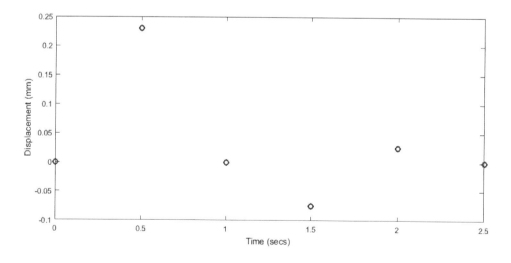

Fig. 7.5: Given data

As done in the preceding problem, we first use the method of undetermined coefficients to fit an interpolating polynomial to the given data. Since six data points are prescribed, a fifth order polynomial of the following form can be generated,

$$x(t) = f(t) = a + bt + ct^2 = dt^3 + et^4 + ft^5.$$

Substituting the given values of (t, x) in the assumed polynomial above yields the following matrix equation:

$$MA = V,$$

where

$$M = \begin{pmatrix} 1 & 0 & 0^2 & 0^3 & 0^4 & 0^5 \\ 1 & 0.5 & 0.5^2 & 0.5^3 & 0.5^4 & 0.5^5 \\ 1 & 1.0 & 1.0^2 & 1.0^3 & 1.0^4 & 1.0^5 \\ 1 & 1.5 & 1.5^2 & 1.5^3 & 1.5^4 & 1.5^5 \\ 1 & 2.0 & 2.0^2 & 2.0^3 & 2.0^4 & 2.0^5 \\ 1 & 2.5 & 2.5^2 & 2.5^3 & 2.5^4 & 2.5^5 \end{pmatrix}, \quad \begin{pmatrix} 0 \\ 0.23 \\ 0 \\ -0.075 \\ 0.025 \\ 0 \end{pmatrix}$$

Using the MATLAB "\" command, the unknown coefficients in the column vector A can be found.

```
M = ones(6,6);
T = 0:0.5:2.5;
for i = 1:6
    for j = 2:6
        M(i,j) = T(i)^(j-1);
    end
end

V  = [0; 0.23; 0; -0.075; 0.025; 0];

A = M\V

A =
                 0
    1.737499999999997
   -3.699166666666650
    2.651666666666647
   -0.763333333333325
    0.073333333333332
```

The coefficients a, b, c, d, e and f of the assumed polynomial are the elements of A. The interpolated polynomial which is

$$x(t) = 1.7374t - 3.6992t^2 + 2.6517t^3 - 0.7633t^4 + 0.0733t^5$$

is plotted in Figure 7.6. As follows, MATLAB's *spline* function can also be used to generate a cubic spline interpolation which is compared with the undetermined coefficients method and with the given data.

```
t = 0:0.1:2.5;
X = A(1) + A(2)*t + A(3)*t.^2 + A(4)*t.^3 + A(5)*t.^4 + A(6)
   *t.^5;

y = spline(T,V,t);

p = plot(T,V,'blueo',t,X,'red',t,y,'green--')
title('Motorcycle Displacement Profile')
xlabel('Time (secs)')
ylabel('Displacement (mm)')
legend('Given data','Interpolating polynomial','MATLAB
   spline')
p(1).LineWidth = 2;
p(2).LineWidth = 2;
p(3).LineWidth = 2;
```

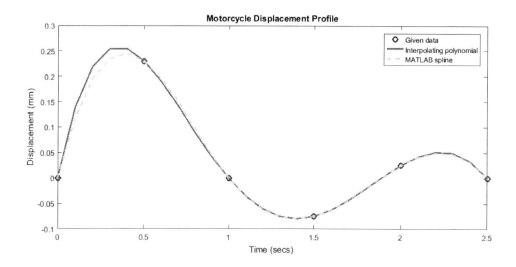

Fig. 7.6: Polynomials generated

Using MATLAB's *diff* function, the velocity and the acceleration of the vehicle are also plotted as functions of time in Figure 7.7.

```
syms t
x(t) = A(1) + A(2)*t + A(3)*t^2 + A(4)*t^3 + A(5)*t^4 + A(6)
   *t^5;
xprime(t) = diff(x);
xdblprime(t) = diff(x,2);
```

```
p = fplot(x,[0 2.5],'blue')
hold on
p1 = fplot(xprime,[0 2.5],'red--')
hold on
p2 = fplot(xdblprime,[0 2.5],'green-.')
title('Displacement, Velocity and Acceleration Profiles')
xlabel('Time (secs)')
legend('Displacement (mm)','Velocity (mm/sec)','Acceleration
    (mm/sec^2')
p(1).LineWidth = 2;
p1(1).LineWidth = 2;
p2(1).LineWidth = 2;
```

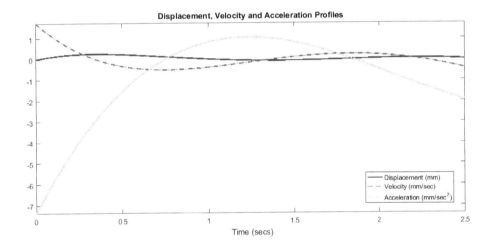

Fig. 7.7: Displacement, velocity and acceleration profiles

The system settling time is the time taken for the free vibration of the motorcycle to completely die down. This, in this case, is 2.5 seconds. Since the settling time is approximately equal to four time constants for a 2% error, the system time constant τ can be computed:

$$\tau = \frac{2.5}{4} = 0.625 \text{ seconds.}$$

The displacement profile also indicates a natural period, τ_d, of one oscillation to be approximately two seconds, yielding the natural frequency of the system as

$$\omega_d = 2\frac{\pi}{\tau_d} = 3.142 \text{ rad/sec.}$$

As shown below, the damping c and stiffness k furnished by the shock absorber can be computed using the pertinent formulas available in textbooks in *Vibrations and Con-*

trols [3, 5, 7, 8, 12, 13].

Damping factor × *undamped natural frequency* = 1/(*system time constant*):

$$\zeta \omega_n = \frac{1}{\tau} = 1.6.$$

Since $\zeta \omega_n$ and ω_d are known, the damping factor ζ can be calculated. Then,

$$\omega_d = \omega_n \sqrt{1 - \zeta^2},$$

but

$$\omega_d = 2\frac{\pi}{\tau_d} = 3.142 \text{ rad/sec.}$$

Thus,

$$\zeta = \sqrt{\frac{(\zeta \omega_n)^2}{\omega_d^2 + (\zeta \omega_n)^2}} = 0.454.$$

The undamped natural frequency of the system along with the stiffness and damping coefficients of the shock absorber can now be computed using

$$\omega_n = \frac{\zeta \omega_n}{\zeta} = 3.526 \text{ rad/sec.}$$

The stiffness and damping coefficients of the shock absorber can now be determined, as follows.

$$m = 200 \text{ kg}, \quad k = m\omega_n^2 = 2.486 \times 10^3 \text{ N/m},$$

$$c = 2m\omega_n\zeta = 640 \text{ N-sec/m.}$$

The shock absorber spring and damper restoring forces which can now be calculated as functions of time using

$$F_{spring}(t) = k\frac{x(t)}{1000} \quad \text{and} \quad F_{damper}(t) = c\frac{d}{dt}\frac{x(t)}{1000}$$

are plotted in Figure 7.8.

```
tau = 2.5/4;
taud = 2;
omegad = 2*pi/taud;
zetaomegan = 1/tau;
zeta = sqrt(zetaomegan^2/(omegad^2 + zetaomegan^2));
omegan = zetaomegan/zeta;
m = 200;
k = m*omegan^2;
c = 2*m*omegan*zeta;
```

```
Fspring(t)  = k*x(t)/1000;
Fdamper(t)  = c/1000*xprime(t);


p = fplot(Fspring,[0 2.5],'blue--')
hold on
p1 = fplot(Fdamper,[0 2.5],'red--')
title('Shock Absorber Spring/Damper Restoring Forces')
xlabel('Time (secs)')
ylabel('Force (N)')
legend('F_{spring}(t)','F_{damper}(t)')
p(1).LineWidth = 2;
p1(1).LineWidth = 2;
```

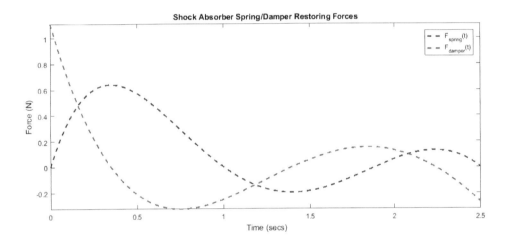

Fig. 7.8: Shock absorber spring and damper restoring forces

Problems

7.1. Given the following function

θ	4	5	6	7	8
$\cos(\theta)$	0.99756	0.99619	0.99452	0.99252	0.99027

determine the first derivative of $\cos(\theta)$ at $\theta = 7$ degrees, using forward, backward and two-step finite difference approximations. Compare the results with the true value. Generate a MATLAB script to fit an interpolating polynomial to the given data using the Method of Undetermined Coefficients and obtain the derivative with MATLAB's *diff* function. Graph the interpolating polynomial and its derivative in the given range with proper labels and titles.

7.2. Given the following:

x	1.0	1.2	1.4	1.6	1.8	2.0
$f(x)$	1.1	0.9283	0.8972	0.9015	0.9422	1.1

compute first and second derivatives at $x = 1.4$, using finite differences.

7.3. Given $f(x)$ versus x as follows:

x	1	2	3	4	5
$f(x)$	5.25	155.2	458.1	1682	6489

generate a MATLAB script to fit an interpolating polynomial to the given data using the Method of Undetermined Coefficients and obtain the first derivative at $x = 3.5$ and $x = 4.5$ with MATLAB's *diff* function. Graph the interpolating polynomial and its derivative in the given range with proper labels and titles.

7.4. Generate a MATLAB script to fit an interpolating polynomial to the data of Problem 7.2 using the Method of Undetermined Coefficients and obtain the first and second derivatives at $x = 1.4$ with MATLAB's *diff* function. Graph the interpolating polynomial and its derivatives in the given range with proper labels and titles.

7.5. The horizontal and vertical positions of a weather balloon with respect to a station are furnished below at various instants of time.

t (secs)	Horizontal Distance x (ft)	Vertical Distance y (ft)
0	0	0
1	8	6.4
2	16	25.6
3	24	57.6
4	32	102.4
5	40	160
6	48	230.4
7	54	291.6

Write a MATLAB script to fit interpolating polynomials to the given data using the Method of Undetermined Coefficients and generate x versus time and y versus time curves. Estimate horizontal and vertical velocities and horizontal and vertical accelerations using MATLAB's *diff* function. Show a comparison of all results generated with the help of appropriate plots.

7.6. The deflection curve of a cantilevered beam is given by the following data, in which x is the distance in feet from the fixed end and y is the deflection in feet at x.

x	0	1	2	3	4	5	6	7	8
y	0	0.015	0.05	0.1	0.2	0.3	0.4	0.5	0.6

Write a MATLAB script to fit an interpolating polynomial to the given data using the Method of Undetermined Coefficients. Using MATLAB's *diff* function, estimate the beam slopes at $x = 5.5$ ft and $x = 6.5$ ft. Also plot the deflection versus x and slope versus x curves.

7.7. In a slider-crank mechanism, the crank angle θ and the position x of the slider are prescribed below at various instants of time. The position x is in feet while the angle θ is in radians.

θ	0	0.393	0.785	1.178	1.571	1.963	2.356	2.749	3.142
x	0.667	0.65	0.604	0.539	0.471	0.412	0.368	0.342	0.333

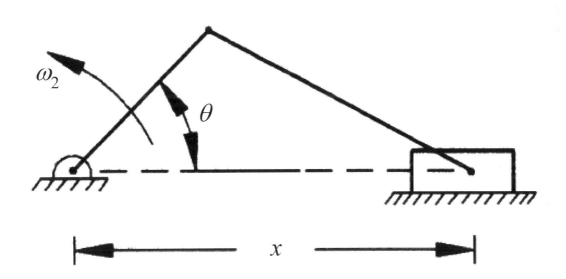

Write a MATLAB script to fit an interpolating polynomial to the given data using the Method of Undetermined Coefficients. If the rotational speed of the crank is $\omega_2 = 1000$ RPM, counterclockwise, and it is maintained constant, estimate the velocity and acceleration of the slider at $\theta = \pi/2$ and $3\pi/4$ radians using MATLAB's *diff* function. Plot the position x, velocity dx/dt and acceleration d^2x/dt^2 as functions of the crank angle θ.

7.8. The data in the following table are the distances D traveled by a motorcycle for selected times t.

t (secs)	0	2	4	6	8	10
D (ft)	0	10	50	150	330	610

(a) Determine the velocity and acceleration of the motorcycle at $t = 4$, 6, and 8 seconds, using finite differences.

(b) Using only three relevant data points, determine the velocity and acceleration at $t = 6$ seconds by the Interpolating Polynomial method. Compare these results with those of part (a).

7.9. The deflection curve of a cantilevered beam is given by the following data, in which x is the distance in feet from the fixed end and y is the deflection at x.

x	1	4	8
y	0.015	0.20	0.60

Using the Interpolating Polynomial method, compute the first and second derivatives of $y(x)$ at $x = 3$ ft and $x = 6$ ft.

7.10. The displacements of an instrument subjected to a random vibration test are given below.

Time t (secs)	0.05	0.10	0.15	0.20	0.25	0.30
Displacement y (in)	0.144	0.172	0.213	0.296	0.070	0.085

Using finite differences, determine the velocity and acceleration of the instrument at $t = 0.15$, 0.20 and 0.25 seconds.

Chapter 8
Numerical Integration

8.1 Introduction to Numerical Integration and the Use of the MATLAB Integral Operator

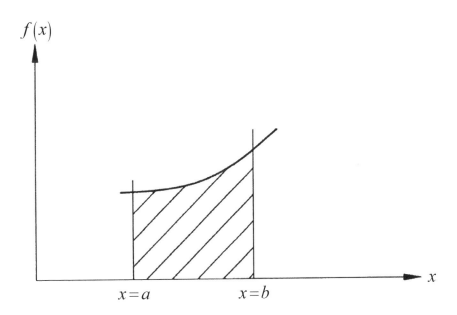

$f(x)$

$x = a$ $x = b$

x

Fig. 8.1: Integral of a function

In traditional calculus, an integral of a function $f(x)$ between limits a and b is the shaded area shown in Figure 8.1 and is defined as

$$I = \int_a^b f(x)\,dx. \tag{8.1}$$

This analytical solution is possible only when $f(x)$ is explicitly known. When the evaluation of this integral becomes either impossible or extremely difficult, it is advantageous to resort to numerical techniques.

In many science and engineering problems, data is often presented as a given bunch of numbers for given values of the independent variable. In this case, the evaluation of the integral is also done by a numerical process.

There are several methods available for evaluating an integral numerically. However, only the following will be discussed here:

1. The interpolating polynomial method
2. Trapezoidal rule
3. Simpson's rules
4. Romberg integration

To compute the definite integral of a function using the MATLAB *int* command, first define the variables of the function symbolically using *syms*. Then apply the *int* command to either a predefined function or a function input, as follows.

```
syms x
f(x) = x^5;
int(f,x)

ans(x) =
x^6/6

int(sin(x),x)

ans =
-cos(x)
```

The *int* command can be used to find the values of definite integrals, as well as find integrals of multivariate functions, as follows.

```
syms x t
int(exp(x)*log(x),x,0,10)

ans =
eulergamma - ei(10) + exp(10)*log(10)

double(ans)

ans =
   4.8226e+04
```

```
int(x/(1 + t^2),x)

ans =
x^2/(2*(t^2 + 1))

int(x/(1 + t^2),t)

ans =
x*atan(t)

int(x/(1 + t^2),t,0, pi)

ans =
x*atan(pi)
```

8.2 The Interpolating Polynomial Method

In this method, an interpolating polynomial passing through the given data points is generated as was done in the chapter on numerical differentiation and then the polynomial is integrated analytically over the prescribed limits of integration. If the polynomial generated is of the form

$$y(x) = a + bx + cx^2 + dx^3 + \cdots, \tag{8.2}$$

its integral is

$$I = ax + b\frac{x^2}{2} + c\frac{x^3}{3} + d\frac{x^4}{4} + \cdots, \tag{8.3}$$

which can be evaluated analytically over any prescribed integration limits.

Example 8.1. Given the data of Example 7.2 of Chapter 7, which is

x	2	3	4	5	6
y	0.80354	1.23591	1.62312	1.89765	1.96789

estimate the integral of $y(x)$ over the range from $x = 2$ to $x = 6$.

The interpolating polynomial generated in Example 7.2 for the data given was

$$y(x) = -0.0471 + 0.4073x + 0.0074x^2 + 0.0028x^3 - 0.0010x^4.$$

```
M = [1 2 2^2 2^3 2^4; 1 3 3^2 3^3 3^4; 1 4 4^2 4^3 4^4; 1 5
    5^2 5^3 5^4; 1 6 6^2 6^3 6^4];
```

```
V = [0.80354; 1.23591; 1.62312; 1.89765; 1.96789];
A = M\V;

syms z
y(z) = A(1) + A(2)*z + A(3)*z^2 + A(4)*z^3 + A(5)*z^4;

inty(z) = int(y,z,2,6);

double(inty(z))

ans =
    6.1845
```

Thus, the required integral is

$$\int_2^6 y(x)\,dx = 6.1845.$$

8.3 Trapezoidal Rule

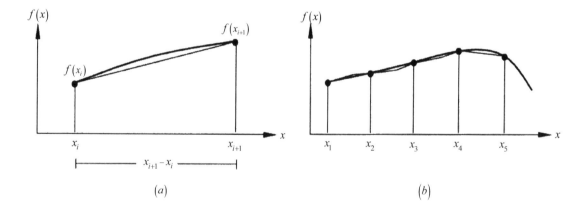

Fig. 8.2: The trapezoidal rule

The trapezoidal rule estimates the integral of a function on the basis of linear interpolation between the given data points. If the integral of a given function $f(x)$ is to be evaluated between limits a and b, the interval from a to b is divided into n equal subintervals each of width H, where

$$H = \frac{b-a}{n}. \tag{8.4}$$

The desired integral which is, in fact, the sum of the areas in the subintervals under the curve $f(x)$ is then (See Figure 8.2)

$$I = \frac{1}{2}H \sum_{i=1}^{n} (f(x_{i+1}) + f(x_i)), \tag{8.5}$$

where the (x_i, y_i) are the x- and y- coordinates of the given data points at the beginning and end of each subinterval. An alternative form of the above integral is

$$I = \frac{1}{2}h \sum_{i=1}^{m-1} (f(x_{i+1}) + f(x_i)), \tag{8.6}$$

where m is the number of data points given on the curve and h is, accordingly,

$$h = \frac{b-a}{m-1}. \tag{8.7}$$

For example, if five data points are prescribed as shown in Figure 8.3, there will be four segments and the trapezoidal rule will estimate the integral of the function from the first to the last data point as

$$I = \frac{1}{2}h(y_1 + 2y_2 + 2y_3 + 2y_4 + y_5). \tag{8.8}$$

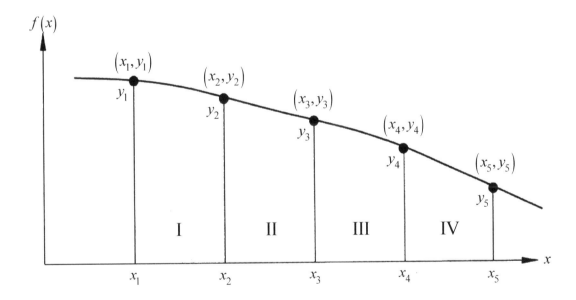

Fig. 8.3: Trapezoidal rule with five data points

If the intervals are not of equal width, the following equation should be used in place of Equation (8.6).

$$I = \frac{1}{2} \sum_{i=1}^{m-1} [(x_{i+1} - x_i)(f(x_{i+1}) + f(x_i))]. \tag{8.9}$$

Example 8.2. Given:

θ (deg)	0	15	30	45	60	75	90
$\sin(2\theta)$	0	0.5	0.86603	1	0.86603	0.5	0

use the trapezoidal rule to determine the area under the curve from $\theta = 0$ to 90 degrees. Compare the result with the true value of the integral.

The subinterval width, in this case, is

$$h = 15\frac{\pi}{180} = 0.2618.$$

The value of the desired integral can be estimated by the trapezoidal rule as

$$I = 0.5h(y_1 + 2y_2 + 2y_3 + 2y_4 + 2y_5 + 2y_6 + y_7) = 0.97705.$$

The true value and the error between the true and estimated values of the integral are

$$\text{True Value } = 1.0 \quad \Rightarrow \quad \%\text{ Error } = \frac{1.0 - 097705}{1.0} \times 100 = 2.2949\%.$$

Using MATLAB, the following estimate of the integral is obtained:

```
syms x
int(sin(2*x),x,0,pi/2)

ans =
1
```

8.4 Simpson's Rules

Simpson's rules are two in number. They are the Simpson's one-third rule and the Simpson's three-eighth rule. The first is based on the area under a parabola passing through three equally spaced points, while the second is based on the area under a third-order interpolating polynomial passing through four points.

8.4.1 Simpson's One-Third Rule

It can be easily shown that the area under a parabola passing through the equally spaced points (x_1, y_1), (x_2, y_2) and (x_3, y_3), shown in Figure 8.4, is

$$A = \frac{h}{3}(y_1 + 4y_2 + y_3). \tag{8.10}$$

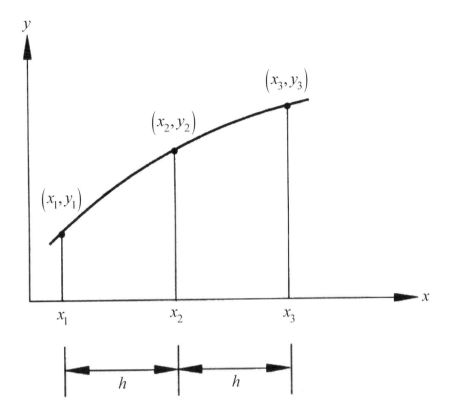

Fig. 8.4: Basis of Simpson's one-third rule

In general, if the area under a curve is divided into n segments, there are $n+1$ points on the curve

$$(x_1, y_1), (x_2, y_2), \ldots, (x_{n+1}, y_{n+1}).$$

If each segment is of width h and there are n segments, n being an even number, the area under the parabola passing through the first three points will be

$$A_1 = \frac{h}{3}(y_1 + 4y_2 + y_3). \tag{8.11}$$

Similarly, the areas under the parabolas passing through the third, fourth and fifth points, and through the last three points on the curve will be

$$A_2 = \frac{h}{3}(y_3 + 4y_4 + y_5), \ldots, A_{\text{last}} = \frac{h}{3}(y_{n-1} + 4y_n + y_{n+1}). \tag{8.12}$$

The integral according to Simpson's one-third rule is the sum of the above areas and can be written as

$$I = \frac{h}{3}\left(y_1 + 4 \sum_{i \text{ even}} y_i + 2 \sum_{i \text{ odd except last}} y_i + y_{n+1} \right). \tag{8.13}$$

For example, if there are seven data points, this integral can be estimated as

$$I = \frac{h}{3}(y_1 + 4y_2 + 2y_3 + 4y_4 + 2y_5 + 4y_6 + y_7).$$ (8.14)

Figure 8.5 shows a comparison between the function approximations obtained with the trapezoidal rule and Simpson's one-third rule, and the consequent integrals which are the respective areas under these functions.

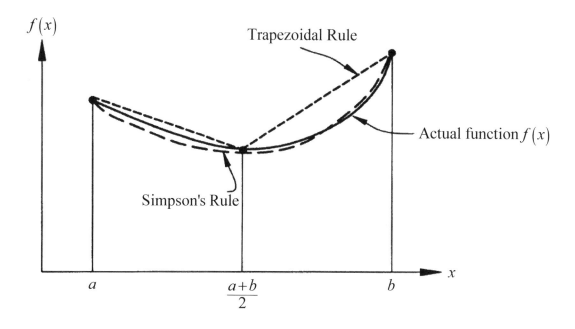

Fig. 8.5: Comparison between the trapezoidal and Simpson's one-third rules

Example 8.3. For the data of Example 8.2, compute the area under the curve by Simpson's three-eighth rule and compare the estimated value with the true value.

An estimate of the desired integral by Simpson's one-third rule is then

$$I_1 = h\frac{y_1 + 4y_2 + 2y_3 + 4y_4 + 2y_5 + 4y_6 + y_7}{3} = 1.0004.$$

The true value of the integral is

$$\int_0^{\pi/2} \sin(2\theta)\, d\theta = 1.0.$$

The percentage error between the true and estimated values is

$$\% \text{ Error } = \frac{1.0 - 1.0004}{1.0} \times 100 = -0.0433\%.$$

8.4.2 Simpson's Three-Eighth Rule

Simpson's 3/8th rule is based on the area under a third order interpolating polynomial passing through four points. If these points are

$$(x_1, y_1), \ (x_2, y_2), \ (x_3, y_3), \ \text{and} \ (x_4, y_4)$$

as shown in Figure 8.6, then this area can be shown to be

$$A = \frac{3}{8} h(y_1 + 3y_3 + 3y_3 + y_4). \tag{8.15}$$

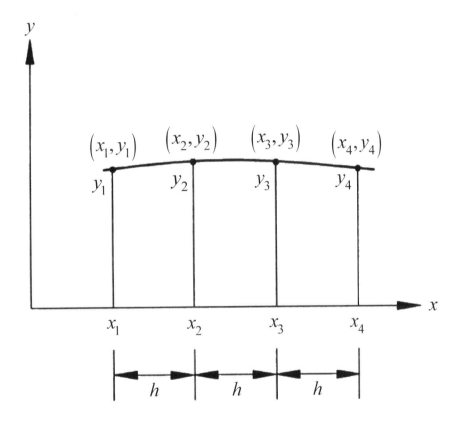

Fig. 8.6: Basis of Simpson's three-eighth rule

If the area under a curve is divided into n segments of equal width h giving $n + 1$ points on the curve, equation (8.15) will give the area under the third-order interpolating polynomial passing through the first four points. Similarly, the area under the polynomial passing through the fourth, fifth, sixth and seventh points will be

$$A_2 = \frac{3}{8} h(y_4 + 3y_5 + 3y_6 + y_7) \tag{8.16}$$

and that under the polynomial passing through the last four points will be

$$A_{\text{last}} = \frac{3}{8}h(y_{n-2} + 3y_{n-1} + 3y_n + y_{n+1}). \tag{8.17}$$

The integral according to Simpson's 3/8th rule is then the sum of the above areas and can be written as

$$I = \frac{3}{8}h(y_1 + 3y_2 + 3y_3 + 2y_4 + 3y_5 + 3y_6 + 2y_7 + 3y_8 + 3y_9 + 2y_{10} + \cdots + y_{n+1}). \tag{8.18}$$

8.4.3 Limitations of Simpson's Rules

While the one-third rule requires the number of segments under the curve to be even, the minimum number being two, the three-eighth rule requires the number of segments to be a number divisible by three, the minimum number being three. That is, for computation by the one-third rule, the number of segments can be 2, 4, 6, and so on while the number of segments required by the 3/8th rule is 3, 6, 9, 12, etc.

Example 8.4. For the data of Example 8.3, compute the area under the curve by Simpson's three-eighth rule and compare the estimated value with the true value.

The integral, according to Simpson's three-eighth rule, can be estimated as

$$I_2 = \frac{3}{8}h(y_1 + 3y_2 + 3y_3 + 2y_4 + 3y_5 + 3y_6 + y_7) = 1.001.$$

The true value, as computed in Example 9.3, is 1.0 and the percentage error is

$$\% \text{ Error } = \frac{1.0 - 1.001}{1.0} \times 100 = -0.1008\%.$$

8.5 Romberg Integration

Romberg integration is a very powerful and efficient method of computing an integral. It uses a combination of the trapezoidal rule with an extrapolation technique known as Richardson extrapolation, and provides much better accuracy than the trapezoidal rule. The procedure for computing the integral of $f(x)$ over a prescribed range of $x = a$ to $x = b$ by the Romberg method is as follows.

1. For a range of integration from $x = a$ to $x = b$, as shown in Figure 8.7(a), obtain the first trapezoidal estimate $I_{0,1}$ of the integral of the given function $f(x)$ by the trapezoidal rule as

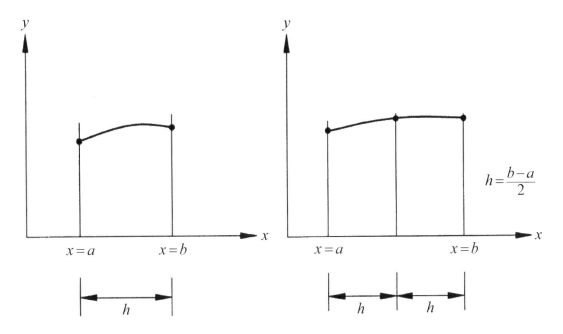

Fig. 8.7: Basis of Romberg integration

$$I_{0,1} = \frac{h}{2}(f(a)+f(b)), \qquad (8.19)$$

where

$$h = b-a. \qquad (8.20)$$

2. Divide the given range into two segments as shown in Figure 8.7(b) and obtain the second trapezoidal estimate $I_{1,1}$ as

$$I_{1,1} = \frac{h}{2}(y_1 + 2y_2 + y_3) \qquad (8.21)$$

where

$$h = \frac{b-a}{2},$$

$$y_1 = f(a) \leftarrow \text{Value of function at the beg. of the range of int.,}$$

$$y_2 = f(a+h) \leftarrow \text{Value at the middle of the range of integration,}$$

$$y_3 = f(a+2h) \leftarrow \text{Value at the end of the range of integration.} \qquad (8.22)$$

3. Now divide the given range further into four segments and obtain the third trapezoidal estimate $I_{2,1}$ with $h =$ one-half of the previous h, that is, $h = (b-a)/4$.
4. Obtain a fourth trapezoidal estimate $I_{3,1}$ with eight segments and $h = (b-a)/8$.
5. Obtain a fifth trapezoidal estimate $I_{4,1}$ with sixteen segments and $h = (b-a)/16$.

$$R = \begin{pmatrix} I_{0,1} \cdots \\ I_{1,1} \; I_{1,2} \cdots \\ I_{2,1} \; I_{2,2} \; I_{2,3} \cdots \\ I_{3,1} \; I_{3,2} \; I_{3,3} \; I_{3,4} \cdots \\ I_{4,1} \; I_{4,2} \; I_{4,3} \; I_{4,4} \; I_{4,5} \cdots \\ I_{5,1} \; I_{5,2} \; I_{5,3} \; I_{5,4} \; I_{5,5} \; I_{5,6} \cdots \\ \vdots \qquad\qquad\qquad\qquad \ddots \end{pmatrix}$$

Fig. 8.8: The Romberg table

6. Using the *Richardson extrapolation formula* which is

$$I_{i,j} = I_{i,j-1} + \frac{1}{4^{j-1} - 1}(I_{i,j-1} - I_{i-1,j-1}), \qquad (8.23)$$

compute the other unknown components of the matrix I, namely,

$$I_{1,2}, I_{2,2}, I_{2,3}, I_{3,2}, I_{3,3}, I_{3,4}, I_{4,2}, I_{4,3}, I_{4,4}, I_{4,5}, \ldots$$

and fill in the Romberg table which is shown in Figure 8.8. Keep filling in the table until the integral values converge, *i.e.*,

$$I_{3,3} = I_{3,2} \text{ or } I_{4,3} = I_{4,2} \text{ or } I_{4,4} = I_{4,3},$$

whichever occurs earlier.

The procedure of this method should be clear from the examples that follow.

Example 8.5. Use Romberg integration to find the integral of e^{-x^3} between the limits of $a = 0.1$ and $b = 1.75$ Use an h equal to $b - a$ to begin.

Computation of the first trapezoidal estimate:

$$h = b - a = 1.65, \quad f(a) = 0.999, \quad f(b) = 4.70382 \times 10^{-3},$$

$$I_{0,1} = 0.5h(f(a) + f(b)) = 0.82806 \quad \leftarrow \text{ First trapezoidal estimate}$$

Computation of the second trapezoidal estimate: In this case, the interval size must be halved, giving y_1, y_2 and y_3 as the function values at the beginning, middle and end of the integration range.

$$h = \frac{b - a}{2} = 0.825, \quad y_1 = f(a) = 0.999,$$

$$y_2 = f(a + h) = 0.45319, y_3 = f(a + 2h) = 4.70385 \times 10^{-3},$$

$$I_{1,1} = 0.5h(y_1 + 2y_2 + y_3) = 0.78791 \quad \leftarrow \text{Second trapezoidal estimate}$$

Computation of the third trapezoidal estimate: The h must be halved again giving $h = (b - a)/4$:

$$h = \frac{h}{2} = 0.4125.$$

In this case, the computation of the number of subintervals to be used in the integration process, n, the coordinates of the resulting data points and the third trapezoidal estimate is done as shown below.

$$n = \frac{b-a}{h} = 4, \quad i = 1, \ldots, n+1, \quad x_i = a + (i-1)h, \quad y_i = f(x_i),$$

x_i	y_i
0.1	0.999
0.5125	0.87406
0.925	0.45319
1.3375	0.09139
1.75	4.70385×10^{-3}

$$I_{2,1} = 0.5h\left(y_1 + 2\sum_{j=2}^{4} y_j + y_5\right) = 0.7922 \quad \leftarrow \text{Third trapezoidal estimate}$$

Computation of the fourth and fifth trapezoidal estimates: These are very similar to that of the third estimate and are presented below.

Fourth estimate:

$$h = \frac{h}{2} = 0.20625, \quad n = \frac{b-a}{h} = 8,$$

x_i	y_i
0.1	0.999
0.30625	0.97169
0.5125	0.87406
0.71875	0.68983
0.925	0.45319
1.13125	0.23511
1.3375	0.09139
1.54375	0.02525
1.75	4.70385×10^{-3}

$$I_{3,1} = 0.5h\left(y_1 + 2\sum_{j=2}^{8} y_j + y_9\right) = 0.79249 \quad \leftarrow \text{Fourth trapezoidal estimate}$$

Fifth estimate:

$$h = \frac{h}{2} = 0.10313, \quad n = \frac{b-a}{h} = 16,$$

x_i	y_i
0.1	0.999
0.20313	0.99165
0.30625	0.97169
0.40937	0.93369
0.5125	0.87406
0.61563	0.7919
0.71875	0.68983
0.82188	0.57398
0.925	0.45319
1.02812	0.3373
1.13125	0.23511
1.23438	0.15274
1.3375	0.09139
1.44063	0.05029
1.54375	0.02525
1.64688	0.01149
1.75	4.70385×10^{-3}

$$I_{4,1} = 0.5h\left(y_1 + 2\sum_{j=2}^{16} y_j + y_{17}\right) = 0.79253 \quad \leftarrow \text{ Fifth trapezoidal estimate}$$

Using the Richardson extrapolation formula for improved estimates, which is

$$I_{i,j} = I_{i,j-1} + \frac{1}{4^{j-1} - 1}(I_{i,j-1} - I_{i-1,j-1})$$

or

$$I_{i,j} = \frac{4^{j-1}I_{i,j-1} - I_{i-1,j-1}}{4^{j-1} - 1},$$

improved estimates of the integral can be computed as shown below.

$I_{2,2}$	0.79363
$I_{2,3}$	0.7949
$I_{3,2}$	0.79258
$I_{3,3}$	0.79251
$I_{3,4}$	0.79247
$I_{4,2}$	0.79254
$I_{4,3}$	0.79254
$I_{4,4}$	0.79254

However, the Romberg procedure requires the following quantities to be zeros.

$$I_{1,3} = 0, \quad I_{1,4} = 0, \quad I_{2,4} = 0$$

The Romberg Table for the integration of e^{-x^3} is shown below.

$$I = \begin{pmatrix} 0.82806 & 0 & 0 & 0 \\ 0.78791 & 0.77452 & 0 & 0 \\ 0.7922 & 0.79363 & 0.7949 & 0 \\ 0.79249 & 0.79258 & 0.79251 & 0.79247 \\ 0.79253 & 0.79254 & 0.79254 & 0.79254 \end{pmatrix}$$

Notice that convergence has taken place at an integral value of 0.79254 as shown in the tabular presentation.

Use of the MATLAB integral operator yields the same result.

```
syms x
int(exp(-x^3),x,.1,1.75)

ans =
igamma(1/3, 1/1000)/3 - igamma(1/3, 343/64)/3

double(ans)

ans =
   0.792542496047428
```

Example 8.6. Use Romberg integration to find the integral of $\ln(1+x^3)$ between the limits of $a = 1.0$ and $b = 4.5$. Use an h value equal to $(b-a)/2$ to begin.

Computation of the first trapezoidal estimate:

$$h = \frac{b-a}{2} = 1.75, \quad y_1 = f(a) = 0.69315,$$

$$y_2 = f(a+h) = 3.08177, \quad y_3 = f(a+2h) = 4.52315,$$

$$I_{1,1} = 0.5h(y_1 + 2y_2 + y_3) = 9.95735 \quad \leftarrow \text{First trapezoidal estimate}$$

Computation of the second trapezoidal estimate:

$$h = \frac{h}{2} = 0.875, \quad n = \frac{b-a}{h} = 4,$$

x_i	y_i
1	0.69315
1.875	2.02707
2.725	3.08177
3.625	3.88434
4.5	4.52315

$$I_{2,1} = 0.5h \left(y_1 + 2 \sum_{j=2}^{4} y_j + y_5 \right) = 10.15116 \quad \leftarrow \text{Second trapezoidal estimate}$$

Computation of the third trapezoidal estimate:

$$h = \frac{h}{2} = 0.4375, \quad n = \frac{b-a}{h} = 8,$$

x_i	y_i
1	0.69315
1.4375	1.37888
1.875	2.02707
2.3125	2.59275
2.725	3.08177
3.1875	3.50812
3.625	3.88434
4.0625	4.2202
4.5	4.52315

$$I_{3,1} = 0.5h \left(y_1 + 2 \sum_{j=2}^{8} y_j + y_9 \right) = 10.19431 \quad \leftarrow \text{Third trapezoidal estimate}$$

Computation of the fourth trapezoidal estimate:

$$h = \frac{h}{2} = 0.21875, \quad n = \frac{b-a}{h} = 16,$$

x_i	y_i
1	0.69315
1.21875	1.03328
1.4375	1.37888
1.65625	1.7126
1.875	2.02707
2.09375	2.32028
2.3125	2.59275
2.53125	2.84597
2.725	3.08177
2.96875	3.30193
3.1875	3.50812
3.40625	3.70182
3.625	3.88434
3.84375	4.0568
4.0625	4.2202
4.28125	4.3754
4.5	4.52315

$$I_{4,1} = 0.5h\left(y_1 + 2\sum_{j=2}^{16} y_j + y_{17}\right) = 10.20455 \quad \leftarrow \text{Fourth trapezoidal estimate}$$

Use of the Richardson extrapolation formula for improved estimates:

$$I_{i,j} = \frac{4^{j-1}I_{i,j-1} - I_{i-1,j-1}}{4^{j-1} - 1}$$

$I_{2,2}$	10.215576
$I_{3,2}$	10.20869
$I_{3,3}$	10.20822
$I_{4,2}$	10.20796
$I_{4,3}$	10.20791
$I_{4,4}$	10.20791

The Romberg procedure requires the following quantities to be zeros.

$$I_{0,1} = I_{1,2} = I_{1,3} = I_{1,4} = I_{2,3} = I_{2,4} = I_{3,4} = 0$$

Thus, the estimates computed can be assembled in the tabular form (Romberg Table) shown below.

$$I = \begin{pmatrix} 9.957348 & 0 & 0 & 0 \\ 10.151155 & 10.215758 & 0 & 0 \\ 10.194307 & 10.20869 & 10.208219 & 0 \\ 10.204548 & 10.207962 & 10.207914 & 10.207909 \end{pmatrix}$$

The tabular presentation of integral values shows that convergence has taken place at an integral value of 10.2079.

Use of the MATLAB integral operator yields the same result.

```
syms x
int(log(1 + x^3),x,1,4.5)

ans =
log((48438181913*2^(1/2)*67^(1/2)*737^(1/2))/65536) + (pi
    *3^(1/2))/3 - 3^(1/2)*atan(3^(1/2)/8) - 21/2

double(ans)

ans =
   10.207912447530623
```

Example 8.7. Use Romberg integration to find the integral of the given function $f(x)$ between the limits of $a = 0$ and $b = 8$. Begin with $h = b - a$ to compute the first trapezoidal estimate $I_{0,1}$. Compute four trapezoidal estimates, then complete the Romberg table.

x	$f(x)$
0.0	3.2
0.50	2.6
1.0	1.7
1.50	1.0
2.0	0.62
2.5	0.45
3.0	0.40
3.5	0.27
4.0	0.20

Computation of the first trapezoidal estimate:

$$h = b - a = 4, \quad y_1 = f(a) = 3.2, \quad y_2 = f(b) = 0.20,$$

$$I_{0,1} = 0.5h(f(a) + f(b)) = 6.8 \quad \leftarrow \text{First trapezoidal estimate}$$

Computation of the second trapezoidal estimate:

$$h = \frac{h}{2} = 2, \quad n = \frac{b - a}{h} =,$$

x_i	y_i
0	3.2
2	0.62
4	0.20

$$I_{1,1} = 0.5h(y_1 + 2y_2 + y_3) = 4.64 \quad \leftarrow \text{Second trapezoidal estimate}$$

Computation of the third trapezoidal estimate:

$$h = \frac{h}{2} = 1, \quad n = \frac{b - a}{h} = 4,$$

x_i	y_i
0	3.2
1	1.7
2	0.62
3	0.40
4	0.20

$$I_{2,1} = 0.5h\left(y_1 + 2\sum_{j=2}^{4} y_j + y_5\right) = 4.42 \quad \leftarrow \text{ Third trapezoidal estimate}$$

Computation of the fourth trapezoidal estimate:

$$h = \frac{h}{2} = 0.5, \quad n = \frac{b-a}{h} = 8,$$

x_i	y_i
0	3.2
0.5	2.6
1	1.7
1.5	1.0
2	0.62
2.5	0.45
3	0.40
3.5	0.27
4	0.20

$$I_{2,1} = 0.5h\left(y_1 + 2\sum_{j=2}^{8} y_j + y_9\right) = 4.37 \quad \leftarrow \text{ Fourth trapezoidal estimate}$$

Use of the Richardson extrapolation formula for improved estimates:

$$I_{i,j} = \frac{4^{j-1} I_{i,j-1} - I_{i-1,j-1}}{4^{j-1} - 1}$$

$I_{1,2}$	3.92
$I_{2,2}$	4.34667
$I_{2,3}$	4.37511
$I_{3,1}$	4.37
$I_{3,2}$	4.35333
$I_{3,3}$	4.35378
$I_{3,4}$	4.35344

The Romberg procedure requires the following quantities to be zeros.

$$I_{1,3} = I_{1,4} = I_{2,4} = I_{0,2} = I_{0,3} = I_{0,4} = I_{4,1} = I_{4,2} = I_{4,3} = I_{4,4} = 0$$

Thus, the estimates computed can be assembled in the tabular form (Romberg Table) shown below.

$$I = \begin{pmatrix} 6.8 & 0 & 0 & 0 \\ 4.64 & 3.92 & 0 & 0 \\ 4.42 & 4.34667 & 4.37511 & 0 \\ 4.37 & 4.35333 & 4.35378 & 4.35344 \end{pmatrix}$$

The tabular presentation of integral values shows that convergence has taken place at an integral value of 4.353.

8.6 Applications in Numerical Integration

Applications of numerical integration can be encountered in situations dealing with location of centroids, determination of moments of inertia of cross sectional shapes and computation of periods of oscillations in nonlinear vibration problems. Some examples are dealt with below.

8.6.1 Centroid of a Rod Bent into the Shape of a Parabola

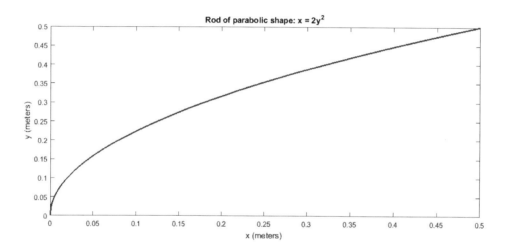

Fig. 8.9: Rod bent into a parabolic shape

The length of an element dL of a rod bent into the shape of the parabola shown in Figure 8.9 can be expressed in terms of the differentials dx and dy as [4]

$$dL = \sqrt{dx^2 + dy^2} \text{ or } dL = \sqrt{1 + \left(\frac{dx}{dy}\right)^2}\, dy. \qquad (8.24)$$

Since $x = 2y^2$

$$\frac{dx}{dy} = 4y \text{ and } dL = \sqrt{1 + 16y^2}\, dy.$$

The length of the rod can then be written as

$$L = \int 1\, dL \text{ or } L = \int_0^{0.5} \sqrt{1 + 16y^2}\, dy = 0.739 \text{ meters.}$$

The location of the centroid (x_{CG}, y_{CG}) can then be calculated using

$$x_{CG} = \frac{\int x\, dL}{L} \text{ and } y_{CG} = \frac{\int y\, dL}{L}$$

giving

$$x_{CG} = \frac{1}{L} \int_0^{0.5} 2y^2 \sqrt{1 + 16y^2}\, dy = 0.205 \text{ meters,}$$

and

$$y_{CG} = \frac{1}{L} \int_0^{0.5} y\sqrt{1 + 16y^2}\, dy = 0.287 \text{ meters.}$$

```
syms y
intL(y) = int(sqrt(1+16*y^2),y,0,0.5);
L = double(intL(y))

intxcg(y) = 1/L*int(2*y^2*sqrt(1+16*y^2),y,0,0.5);
double(intxcg(y))

intycg(y) = 1/L*int(y*sqrt(1+16*y^2),y,0,0.5);
double(intycg(y))

L =
    0.7395

ans =
    0.2050

ans =
    0.2868
```

8.6.2 Moment of Inertia of a Beam of Semi-Elliptic Cross Section

For the semi-elliptic beam cross section shown in Figure 8.10, its moments of inertia about the x and y axes can be calculated using [4]

$$I_{xx} = \int y^2\, dA \text{ and } I_{yy} = \int x^2\, dA, \tag{8.25}$$

where

$$dA = 2x\, dy \text{ with } x(y) = \sqrt{1 - \frac{y^2}{b^2}}\, a \text{ and } a = 4 \text{ in}, b = 2 \text{ in}$$

$$dA = y\, dx \text{ with } y(x) = \sqrt{1 - \frac{x^2}{a^2}}\, b \text{ and } a = 4 \text{ in}, b = 2 \text{ in.}$$

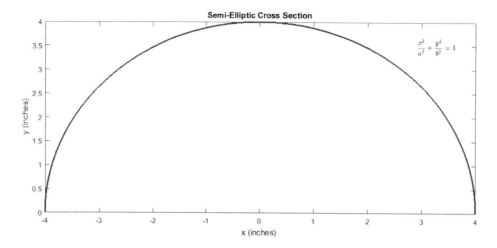

Fig. 8.10: Beam cross section

The moments of inertia, I_{xx} and I_{yy}, can now be computed as follows, using (8.25), yielding

$$I_{xx} = 2\frac{a}{b} \int_0^b y^2 \sqrt{b^2 - y^2}\, dy = 12.566 \text{ in}^4$$

and

$$I_{yy} = \frac{b}{a} \int_{-a}^{a} x^2 \sqrt{a^2 - x^2}\, dx = 50.266 \text{ in}^4.$$

```
syms x y
a = 4; b = 2;

intIxx(y) = 2*a/b*int(y^2*sqrt(b^2-y^2),y,0,b);
double(intIxx(y))

intIyy(x) = b/a*int(x^2*sqrt(a^2-x^2),x,-a,a);
double(intIyy(x))

ans =
   12.5664

ans =
   50.2655
```

8.6.3 Launch of a Projectile

A projectile is launched with an initial vertical velocity vy_{init} from a height y_0 above the ground. Neglecting air resistance, the relationship between its vertical velocity v_y at any time t and the height y above the ground that it attains on the way up is given by [4]

$$v_y = \sqrt{vy_{init}^2 + 2G(y_0 - y)}, \tag{8.26}$$

where G is the acceleration due to gravity (32.2 ft/sec^2 or 9.81 m/sec^2). Equating the above quantity to dy/dt, and then integrating with respect to time from 0 to t seconds, the following expression can be derived for the time t taken by the projectile to attain the height y above the ground

$$t = \int_{y_0}^{y} \frac{1}{\sqrt{vy_{init}^2 + 2G(y_0 - y)}}\, dy. \tag{8.27}$$

The time taken to reach the maximum height, y_{max}, is then the above integral with y_{max} as the upper limit of integration, where

$$y_{max} = \frac{vy_{init}^2}{2G} + y_0. \tag{8.28}$$

For an initial velocity of 55 ft/sec at an angle of 65 degrees from a height of 3.5 ft above ground, the time taken to attain the maximum height is calculated below using (8.27) and (8.28).

$$v_{init} = 55 \text{ ft/sec}, \quad \theta = 65 \text{ deg}, \quad \sin(\theta) = 0.906, \quad G = 32.2 \text{ ft/sec}^2,$$

$$vy_{init} = v_{init}\sin(\theta) = 49.847 \text{ ft/sec}, \quad y_0 = 3.5 \text{ ft},$$

$$\Rightarrow \quad y_{max} = \frac{vy_{init}^2}{2G} + y_0 = 42.083 \text{ ft}$$

$$\Rightarrow \quad t_{max\,height} = \int_{y_0}^{y_{max}} \frac{1}{\sqrt{vy_{init}^2 + 2G(y_0 - y)}}\, dy = 1.548 \text{ sec}$$

```
syms y
vinit = 55;
theta = 65*pi/180;

vyint = vinit*sin(theta);
G = 32.2;
y0= 3.5;
ymax = vyint^2/(2*G) + y0;

inttmax(y) = int(1/(sqrt(vyint^2 + 2*G*(y0-y))),y,y0,ymax);
double(inttmax(y))
```

```
ans =
    1.5480
```

8.6.4 Large Oscillations of a Simple Pendulum

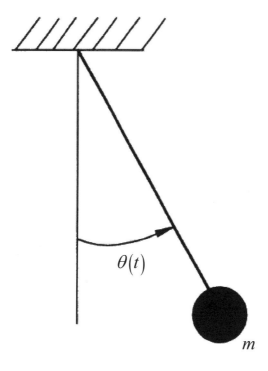

Fig. 8.11: Vibration of a simple pendulum

A simple pendulum, which is a mass attached to one end of a light rigid rod, is shown in Figure 8.11.

The large-amplitude motion of this pendulum is governed by the following nonlinear differential equation [3, 5, 8, 12]

$$\frac{d^2\theta}{dt^2} + \frac{G}{L}\sin(\theta(t)) = 0, \tag{8.29}$$

where L is the length of the rod and G is the acceleration due to gravity.
However, if the amplitudes of vibration are considered small, the above differential equation assumes its linear form

$$\frac{d^2\theta}{dt^2} + \frac{G}{L}\theta(t) = 0 \tag{8.30}$$

and the motion, then, has a natural period

$$\tau_{linear} = 2\pi\sqrt{\frac{L}{G}} \text{ seconds.} \tag{8.31}$$

For the nonlinear problem, it can be shown that the period of one oscillation, which is now a function of the amplitude of vibration, is given by the integral

$$\tau_{nonlinear}(A) = 2\sqrt{\frac{L}{G}} \int_0^{A\frac{\pi}{180}} \frac{1}{\sqrt{\sin\left(A\frac{\pi}{360}\right)^2 - \sin\left(\frac{\theta}{2}\right)^2}} \, d\theta \text{ seconds,} \tag{8.32}$$

where A is the maximum vibration amplitude in degrees that the pendulum attains. The corresponding linear and nonlinear natural frequencies in Hertz can be computed using

$$f_{linear} = \frac{1}{\tau_{linear}} \text{ and } f_{nonlinear}(A) = \frac{1}{\tau_{nonlinear}(A)}. \tag{8.33}$$

In a nonlinear problem, the percentage variation between the linear and nonlinear natural frequencies is typically expressed in the following form

$$\text{Percent Difference}(A) = \left|\frac{f_{nonlinear}(A) - f_{linear}}{f_{linear}}\right| \times 100\%. \tag{8.34}$$

This variation, which is plotted in Figure 8.12 below as a function of the maximum amplitude of vibration of the pendulum, confirms that there is a sharp increase in the variation from the linear natural frequency with increase in the amplitude of vibration.

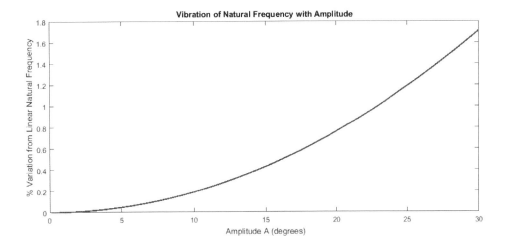

Fig. 8.12: Variation of nonlinear natural frequency with amplitude

```
G = 32.2;
L = 1;
tlin = 2*pi*sqrt(L/G);

f = @(theta,A) 1./sqrt((sin(A*pi/360)).^2 - (sin(theta/2))
   .^2);

A = 0.1:0.1:30;
n = size(A,2);
tnonlin = zeros(n,1);

for i = 1:n
tnonlin(i) = 2*sqrt(L/G)*integral(@(theta)f(theta,A(i)),0,A(
   i)*pi/180);
end

flin = 1/tlin*ones(n,1);
fnonlin = 1./tnonlin;

pda = abs((fnonlin - flin)./flin)*100;

plot(A,pda)
```

Problems

8.1. Use the trapezoidal rule to estimate the integral of $x^{2/3}$ over the range $a = 0$ to $b = 4$ for interval widths of $h = 1.0, 0.5$ and 0.25. Also obtain an answer using the MATLAB integral operator.

8.2. Using Simpson's rules, with $h = 0.25$, 0.5 and 1.5, obtain estimates of the following integral:

$$I = \int_0^3 x^{4/3}\, dx.$$

Also obtain an answer using the MATLAB integral operator.

8.3. Using Simpson's rules, with $n = 4, 8$ and 10 subdivisions of the given range of x, obtain estimates of the following integral:

$$I = \int_1^4 \frac{1}{6 + 5e^{2x}}\, dx.$$

Also obtain an answer using the MATLAB integral operator.

8.4. Use Romberg integration to find the integral of $x^3 e^{2x}$ between the limits of $a = 0$ and $b = 2.0$. Use an h equal to $b - a$ to begin when computing the first trapezoidal estimate. Also obtain an answer using the MATLAB integral operator.

8.5. Use Romberg integration to find the integral of $1/x$ between the limits of $a = 1.0$ and $b = 2.0$. Use an h equal to $b - a$ to begin. The completion of three rows of the Romberg table should be sufficient.

8.6. Use Romberg integration to find the integral of $\ln(x)$ between the limits of $a = 1.0$ and $b = 2.0$. Use an h equal to $b - a$ to begin. Compute 3 trapezoidal estimates before completing the Romberg table.

8.7. Use Romberg integration to find the integral of

$$\frac{3}{1 + x^2}$$

between the limits of $a = 0$ and $b = 4.0$. Use an h equal to $b - a$ to begin. Compute 3 trapezoidal estimates before completing the Romberg table.

8.8. Use Romberg integration to find the integral of $x e^{2x}$ between the limits of $a = 0$ and $b = 0.5$. Use an h equal to $b - a$ to begin. Compute 3 trapezoidal estimates before completing the Romberg table.

8.9. Use Romberg integration to find the integral of $x \sin(x)$ between the limits of $a = 1.0$ and $b = 2.0$. Use an h equal to $b - a$ to begin. Compute an answer that is good to at least 3 decimal places.

8.10. Use Romberg integration to find the integral of the following function $f(x)$ between the limits of $a = 1.8$ and $b = 3.4$. Begin with $h = (b - a)/2 = 0.8$, that is, use the values marked by asterisks to compute the first trapezoidal estimate $I_{1,1}$. Also obtain an answer by writing a MATLAB script to generate an interpolating polynomial using the Method of Undetermined Coefficients and then additionally using MATLAB's integral operator.

x	$f(x)$
1.6	4.751
1.8	6.152*
2.0	7.412
2.2	9.038
2.4	11.151
2.6	13.475*
2.8	16.521
3.0	20.08
3.2	24.7
3.4	30.114*
3.6	36.617
3.8	44.701

8.11. Use Romberg integration to find the integral of the following function $f(x)$ between the limits of $a = 0.3$ and $b = 1.1$. Begin with $h = b - a$ to compute the first trapezoidal estimate $I_{0,1}$. Compute four trapezoidal estimates, then complete the Romberg table.

x	$f(x)$
0.3	55
0.4	42
0.5	37
0.6	35
0.7	39
0.8	48
0.9	53
1.0	51
1.1	39

8.12. Use Romberg integration to find the integral of the function $f(x)$ given in the following table between the limits of $a = 0$ and $b = 4$. Begin with $h = b - a$ to compute the first trapezoidal estimate $I_{0,1}$. Compute four trapezoidal estimates, then complete the Romberg table. Obtain an answer that is good to at least two decimal places. Also obtain an answer by writing a MATLAB script to generate an interpolating polynomial using the Method of Undetermined Coefficients and then additionally using MATLAB's integral operator.

x	$f(x)$
0	3
0.5	2.4
1.0	1.5
1.5	0.92
2.0	0.60
2.5	0.41
3.0	0.30
3.5	0.23
4.0	0.18

8.13. Use Romberg integration to find the integral of the following function $f(x)$ between the limits of $a = 0$ and $b = 0.80$. Begin with $h = b - a$ to compute the first trapezoidal estimate $I_{0,1}$. Compute four trapezoidal estimates, then complete the Romberg table.

x	$f(x)$
0	0
0.1	0.12
0.2	0.30
0.3	0.55
0.4	0.89
0.5	1.36
0.6	1.99
0.7	2.84
0.8	3.96

8.14. Use Romberg integration to determine the integral of the following function $f(x)$ between the limits of $a = 1.0$ and $b = 2.0$. Use an h equal to $b - a$ to begin. Compute three trapezoidal estimates and then complete the Romberg table. Obtain an answer that is good to at least three decimal places.

x	$f(x)$
1	0
1.25	0.2231
1.50	0.4055
1.75	0.5596
2.00	0.6931

8.15. The time T required to raise or lower the water surface in a tank with inflow as well as outflow through an orifice at the bottom is given by the following integral

$$T = \int_{H_1}^{H_2} \frac{A}{Q - kh^{0.5}} \, dh$$

where H_1 and H_2 are the initial and final heights of the water surface above the base of the tank, A is the cross sectional area of the tank, Q is the inflow rate, and k is a constant that depends on the coefficient of discharge and the area of the orifice. Determine how long it will take for the water level to fall 10 ft in a tank 50 ft long by 30 ft wide with vertical sides, when water enters the tank at the rate of 6 cu. ft/sec and the initial level of the water surface in the tank is 16 ft above the bottom. Take k to be 3. Obtain an estimate of the integral using Romberg integration.

8.16. The motion of bodies moving with moderate speed in fluids such as water or air is resisted by a damping force that is proportional to the square of the speed. In order to estimate the resonant amplitude of the motion, the equivalent linear viscous damping, C_{eq}, is needed which is found by equating the energy dissipated by the viscous damping in one cycle to that of the nonviscous damping [12]. The equivalent viscous damping, in this case, can be shown to be

$$C_{eq} = \frac{2a\omega\chi}{\pi} \int_0^\pi \sin^3(\theta) \, d\theta$$

where a is a proportionality constant that depends on the body geometry and the properties of the fluid medium, ω is the frequency of excitation and χ is the amplitude of the resulting vibration. If $a = 0.85$ N-sec^2/m, $\omega = 550$ rads/sec and $\chi = 16$ mm, use the Trapezoidal rule with (a) 3 segments, (b) 6 segments, and (c) 12 segments to estimate C_{eq}.

8.17. The moment of inertia of a sphere of radius R about a diametral axis is given by the integral [4]

$$I_{dia} = \frac{1}{2}\rho\pi \int_{-R}^{R} (R^2 - x^2)^2 \, dx$$

where ρ is the mass density of the material of the sphere. Using Simpson's 1/3, as well as 3/8 rules with (a) two segments, (b) 6 segments and (c) 12 segments, estimate I_{dia} for a 1 m diameter sphere made of steel with $\rho = 7.8$ Mg/m^3.

8.18. The shear stress distribution in a beam cross section subjected to a shear force V is given by [10]

$$\tau = \frac{VQ}{Ib}$$

where V is the shear force acting on the cross section, I is the moment of inertia of the entire cross section about the neutral axis, b is the cross sectional width at the level of interest in the cross section, and Q is the first moment of the part of the area of the cross section above the level of interest about the neutral axis. For a circular cross section of radius R, the shear stress at a height y_1 above the neutral axis is given by the integral

$$\tau = \frac{V}{I2\sqrt{R^2 - y_1^2}} 2 \int_{y_1}^{R_1} y\sqrt{R^2 - y^2} \, dy.$$

Using the MATLAB integral operator, determine the shear stress distribution in the case of a beam with a circular cross section of radius 1 inch and subjected to a shear force of magnitude 500 lbs.

8.19. The time taken by an object to slide down under the action of gravity from a point $O(0,0)$ on a curved ramp described by the function $y = y(x)$ to a point B is given by the integral

$$T = \int_0^{x_B} \sqrt{\frac{1 + \left(\frac{dy}{dx}\right)^2}{2Gy(x)}} \, dx,$$

where G is the acceleration due to gravity (32.2 ft/sec^2). Using the Trapezoidal Rule with (a) 25, (b) 50, (c) 100, (d) 200, (e) 1000, (f) 2000, (g) 10000, (h) 20000, (i) 30000, and (j) 40000 subintervals, estimate the time required for a sack to slide from the top $O(0,0)$ of a ramp described by

$$y(x) = Ax^2 + Bx,$$

with $A = 0.02551$ and $B = 0.01$, to its bottom at $x = 28$ ft. Obtain answers by generating a MATLAB script.

Chapter 9
Numerical Solution of Ordinary Differential Equations

9.1 Introduction

A differential equation is an equation that expresses a relationship between a dependent variable y, an independent variable x and derivatives of y. The order of the differential equation is the order of the highest derivative in the equation. The following equation has only the first derivative of y in it and is, therefore, a first order differential equation.

$$\frac{dy}{dx} = f(x, y), \tag{9.1}$$

while one that has both first and second derivatives or just the second derivative is a second order differential equation. Its general form is given below.

$$\frac{d^2y}{dx^2} = f(x, y, \frac{dy}{dx}) \tag{9.2}$$

Applications of differential equations can be seen in heat transfer, electrical circuit analysis, vibration analysis, control systems analysis and a host of other areas in science as well as engineering.

The two broad classes of problems involving differential equations are

1. initial value problems and
2. boundary value problems.

In an initial value problem, conditions are specified at only one value of the independent variable. An example of an initial value problem is given below.

$$m\frac{d^2y}{dt^2} + c\frac{dy}{dt} + ky = f(t), \quad y(0) = disp_{init}, \quad y'(0) = vel_{init} \tag{9.3}$$

Although the independent variable in the above equation represents time, it can just as well represent a spatial coordinate such as x. In a boundary value problem, conditions are prescribed at two values of the independent variable, as in the following.

$$A\frac{d^2y}{dx^2} + B\frac{dy}{dx} + Cy = g(x), \quad y(0) = y_0, \quad y(L) = y_L \tag{9.4}$$

There are many methods of solving differential equations numerically. However, our discussion is going to be limited to the Taylor series method, the Euler and Modified Euler methods, and the Runge-Kutta methods.

9.2 Taylor Series Method

Given $y = y(x)$ and the value of the independent variable at $x = x_0$ as $y(x_0)$, a Taylor series will give the value of y at any value of the dependent variable x as

$$y(x) = y(x_0) + (x - x_0)\frac{dy(x_0)}{dx} + \frac{(x - x_0)^2}{2!}\frac{d^2y(x_0)}{dx^2} + \cdots . \tag{9.5}$$

If the problem to be solved is a first-order differential equation of the form

$$\frac{dy}{dx} = f(x), \tag{9.6}$$

with initial condition

$$y = y_0 \text{ at } x = x_0, \tag{9.7}$$

the Taylor series expansion of (9.5) can, clearly, be made use of in generating a solution to the given differential equation. The following example should clarify this issue.

Example 9.1. Given the differential equation

$$\frac{dy}{dx} = 7x^4 - 3x^2 + 9$$

with initial condition

$$y = 4 \text{ at } x = 1,$$

estimate values of the function using a Taylor series expansion for $x = 1$ to $x = 1.3$. Take Δx to be 0.05. Compare the accuracy of the solution by comparing the computed values with the true values computed from the true solution, which is:

$$y = \frac{7}{5}x^5 - x^3 + 9x - \frac{27}{5}.$$

The initial condition prescribed is

$$x_0 = 1 \text{ and } y_0 = 4.$$

The first, second, third, fourth and fifth derivatives of $f(x)$ are

$$y'(x) = 7x^4 - 3x^2 + 9 \quad \leftarrow \text{ First derivative (given)} \tag{9.8}$$

$$y''(x) = 28x^3 - 6x \quad \leftarrow \text{ Second derivative}$$

$$y'''(x) = 84x^2 - 6 \quad \leftarrow \text{ Third derivative}$$

$$y^{(4)}(x) = 168x \quad \leftarrow \text{ Fourth derivative}$$

$$y^{(5)}(x) = 168 \quad \leftarrow \text{ Fifth derivative}$$

$$y^{(6)}(x) = 0 \quad \leftarrow \text{ Sixth derivative}$$

The Taylor series of (9.5) expanded to seven terms up to the sixth derivative term is

$$y(x) = y_0 + (x - x_0)y'(x_0) + \frac{1}{2!}(x - x_0)^2 y''(x_0)$$
$$+ \frac{1}{3!}(x - x_0)^3 y'''(x_0) + \frac{1}{4!}(x - x_0)^4 y^{(4)}(x_0)$$
$$+ \frac{1}{5!}(x - x_0)^5 y^{(5)}(x_0) + \frac{1}{6!}(x - x_0)^6 y^{(6)}(x_0). \tag{9.9}$$

The true solution to the differential equation is given as

$$y_{true} = \frac{7}{5}x^5 - x^3 + 9x - \frac{27}{5}. \tag{9.10}$$

Using (9.8) and (9.9), the Taylor series solution to the given differential equation can be generated and compared with the true solution of (9.10) as shown below.

```
h = 0.05;
x = 1:h:1.3;
n = (1.3 - 1.0)/h;

x0 = 1; y0 = 4;

y1 = 7*x0^4 - 3*x0^2 + 9;
y2 = 28*x0^3 - 6*x0;
y3 = 84*x0^2 - 6;
y4 = 168*x0;
y5 = 168;
y6 = 0;

ytrue = 7/5*x.^5 - x.^3 + 9*x - 27/5;

for i = 1:n+1
    y(i) = y0 + (x(i) - x0)*y1 + 1/2*(x(i)-x0)^2*y2 + 1/6*(x
        (i)-x0)^3*y3 + 1/24*(x(i)-x0)^4*y4 + 1/120*(x(i)-x0)
        ^5*y5 + 1/720*(x(i)-x0)^6*y6;
```

```
       err(i) = (ytrue(i) - y(i))/ytrue(i)*100;
end

j = 1:1:7;
table(j',x',y',ytrue',err','VariableNames',{'i','x','y','
   ytrue','error'})
```

i	x_i	y	$ytrue$	%Error
1	1	4	4	0
2	1.05	4.6792	4.6792	3.7963e-14
3	1.1	5.4237	5.4237	-1.6376e-14
4	1.15	6.245	6.245	-1.4222e-14
5	1.2	7.1556	7.1556	-1.2412e-14
6	1.25	8.1693	8.1693	0
7	1.3	9.3011	9.3011	1.9098e-14

In what follows, several Taylor series solutions with varying number of terms are developed and compared in Figure 9.1 with the true solution. Notice that because the sixth derivative is zero, the six-term solution which is the same as the one with seven terms produces no error at all.

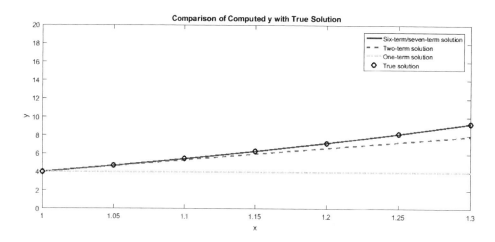

Fig. 9.1: Comparison of Taylor series solutions with true solution

```
Y1 = y0*(x-x+1);
Y2 = y0 + (x-x0)*y1;
Y6 = y0 + (x - x0)*y1 + 1/2*(x-x0).^2*y2 + 1/6*(x-x0).^3*y3
   + 1/24*(x-x0).^4*y4 + 1/120*(x-x0).^5*y5 + 1/720*(x-x0)
   .^6*y6;
```

```
p = plot(x,Y6,'blue',x,Y2,'red--',x,Y1,'green-.',x,ytrue,'
    blacko')
axis([1 1.3 0 20])
title('Comparison of Computer y with True Solution')
xlabel('x')
ylabel('y')
legend('Six-term/seven-term solution','Two-term solution','
    One-term solution','True solution')
p(1).LineWidth = 2;
p(2).LineWidth = 2;
p(3).LineWidth = 2;
p(4).LineWidth = 2;
```

Percentage errors for the various approximations are generated and compared in Figure 9.2. Notice that the error between the six-term/ seven-term approximation and the true solution is zero. In general, the error is sizeable in the range of interest if anything short of a five-term approximation is employed.

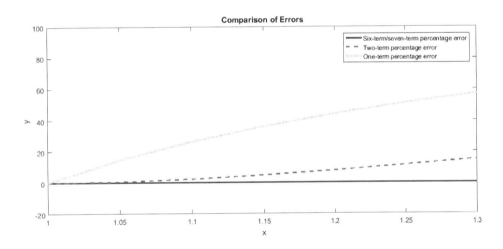

Fig. 9.2: Comparison of errors generated with varying number of terms in Taylor series

```
Err1 = (ytrue - Y1)./ytrue*100;
Err2 = (ytrue - Y2)./ytrue*100;
Err6 = (ytrue - Y6)./ytrue*100;

p = plot(x,Err6,'blue',x,Err2,'red--',x,Err1,'green-.')
axis([1 1.3 -20 100])
title('Comparison of Errors')
```

```
xlabel('x')
ylabel('y')
legend('Six-term/seven-term percentage error','Two-term
   percentage error','One-term percentage error')
p(1).LineWidth = 2;
p(2).LineWidth = 2;
p(3).LineWidth = 2;
```

9.3 Euler's Method

Euler's method is a simple, programmable, one-step method which uses information from the beginning of an interval to estimate the function value at the end of that interval. It is based on the forward difference equation for the first derivative only, without requiring the inclusion of higher order derivatives.

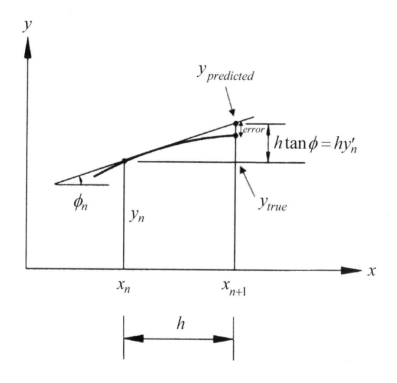

Fig. 9.3: Basis of Euler's method

Using the forward difference representation, the derivative of a function $f(x)$ is

$$\frac{d}{dx}f(x) = \frac{f(x+\Delta x)-f(x)}{\Delta x}. \qquad (9.11)$$

If the slope of a curve $y(x)$ at x_n is known, say y'_n, the function value y_{n+1} at an adjacent point x_{n+1} is given by

$$y_{n+1} = y_n + h y'_n \text{ with } h = x_{n+1} - x_n, \tag{9.12}$$

so long as h, which is the difference between x_{n+1} and x_n is small. See Figure 9.3.

If the problem to be solved is the following first-order initial value problem

$$\frac{dy}{dx} = f(x, y), \tag{9.13}$$

with initial condition

$$y(x_0) = y_0, \tag{9.14}$$

a numerical solution can be generated using (9.12) which gives

$$y_{n+1} = y_n + h f(x_n, y_n). \tag{9.15}$$

Now, given the initial condition (9.14), (9.15) can be used to do the computations one step at a time until the solution at a desired x value is generated, which is why this method is also referred to as Euler's one-step method. It is to be noted that for smaller h, the results will be more accurate and, clearly, the method is not very accurate for large values of h. Example 9.2 will illustrate the procedure of Euler's method.

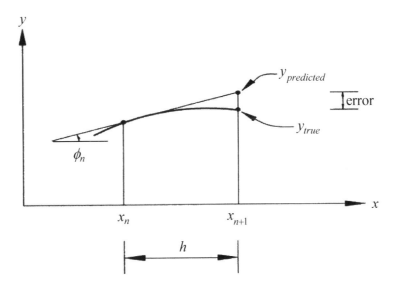

Fig. 9.4: Error of Euler's method

Because the relationship of (9.12) is based on a straight line segment between (x_n, y_n) and (x_{n+1}, y_{n+1}), the error due to the use of Euler's method is $y_{predicted} - y_{true}$, as shown in Figure 9.4. An approximate estimate of this error is given by the second order term of the Taylor series expansion which is

$$\varepsilon = \frac{(x - x_0)^2}{2!} \frac{d^2 y}{dx^2}. \tag{9.16}$$

Example 9.2. Solve:

$$\frac{dy}{dx} = y' = f(x, y) = -4x^3 + 18x^2 - 22x + 9$$

by Euler's method. The prescribed initial conditions are: $x_0 = 0$, $y_0 = 2$, and the range for the solution is to be $x = 0$ to 4.0 with a step size of $h = 0.5$.

By integrating the given equation, its true solution can be easily seen to be

$$y_{true}(x) = -x^4 + 6x^3 - 11x^2 + 9x + 2.$$

The procedure of Euler's method is utilized as shown below to generate solutions at $x = 0.5$ and 1.0.

n	x_n	$y_n = y_{n-1} + hf(x_{n-1}, y_{n-1})$	$f(x_n, y_n)$
0	0	2	9
1	0.5	6.5	2
2	1.0	7.5	1

The percentage errors between the true values at $x = 0.5$ and 1.0 and those computed by Euler's method are:

$$y_{true}(x_1) = 4.438, \quad \%\text{Error} = \frac{y_{true}(x_1) - y_1}{y_{true}(x_1)} 100 = -46.479\%$$

and

$$y_{true}(x_2) = 5, \quad \%\text{Error} = \frac{y_{true}(x_2) - y_2}{y_{true}(x_2)} 100 = -50\%.$$

Similarly, solutions as well as errors at $x = 1.5, 2.0, \ldots, 4$ can also be generated easily.

Alternatively, Euler solutions as well as the associated percentage errors at $x = 0.5, 1.0, 1.5, \ldots, 4.0$ can be generated by resorting to the following procedure.

```
h = 0.5;
x = 0:h:4;
n = (4 - 0)/h;

x0 = 0;
```

```
y = 2;
err = 0;
f =@(x,y) -4*x^3 + 18*x^2 - 22*x + 9;

ytrue = -x.^4 + 6*x.^3 - 11*x.^2 + 9*x + 2;

for i = 1:n
    y(i+1) = y(i) + h*f(x(i),y(i));

    err(i+1) = (ytrue(i+1) - y(i+1))/ytrue(i+1)*100;
end

table(x',y',ytrue',err','VariableNames',{'x','y','ytrue','
    error'})
```

The computed and true solutions and the error due to Euler's method for the range of interest are tabulated and shown in Table 9.1 below.

x	y	y_{true}	%Error
0	2	2	0
0.5	6.5	4.4375	-46.479
1	7.5	5	-50
1.5	8	5.9375	-34.737
2	9.5	8	-18.75
2.5	12	10.438	-14.97
3	14	11	-27.273
3.5	12.5	5.9375	-110.53
4	3	-10	130

Table 9.1: Comparison between true and computed solutions and error due to Euler's method

MATLAB's cubic spline interpolation can now be resorted to as shown below to generate a plot of the computed solution. This solution is compared with the true solution in Figure 9.5. The errors due to Euler's method for the range of interest are presented in Figure 9.6, which shows that the Euler error for this problem can be as large as 98%, thus making the method extremely inaccurate.

```
X = 0:0.05:4;
Euler = spline(x,y,X);
Ytrue = -X.^4 + 6*X.^3 - 11*X.^2 + 9*X + 2;
p = plot(X,Ytrue,'blue',X,Euler,'red--')
title('Comparison of Euler Solution with the True Solution')
```

```
xlabel('x')
ylabel('y')
legend('True solution','Euler solution')
p(1).LineWidth = 2;
p(2).LineWidth = 2;
```

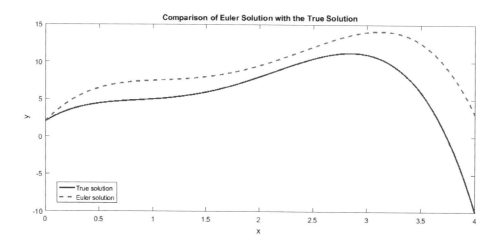

Fig. 9.5: Comparison of Euler solution with the true solution

```
Error = (Ytrue - Euler)./Ytrue*100;
p = plot(X,Error,'blue')
axis([0 3.5 -110 0])
title('Error vs. x')
xlabel('x')
ylabel('Percentage error')
legend('% Error')
p(1).LineWidth = 2;
```

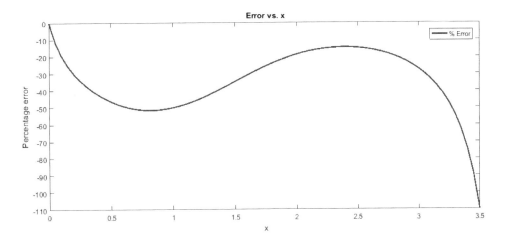

Fig. 9.6: Error due to Euler's method

9.4 Modified Euler's Method

Euler's method, which was discussed in the previous section, does not require the use of higher-order derivatives but apparently yields very inaccurate answers unless the step size used is very very small. The modified Euler's method, which is an attempt at improving the accuracy of the Euler solution, is quite similar and is still a one-step method but uses an average slope over the segment or step rather than that at the beginning of the segment. Thus, in this "modified" method, (9.15) is replaced by

$$y_{n+1} = y_n + h \frac{f(x_{n+1}) + f(x_n)}{2}. \qquad (9.17)$$

Another way to look at this method is to note that it employs the trapezoidal rule as shown in the sketch below to compute the integral $\int_{x_n}^{x_{n+1}} f(x)\,dx$.

The procedural steps to be followed in this method are given below.

1. Determine slope $\frac{dy}{dx}$ at the beginning of the interval, x_0.
2. Estimate y at x_1 using Euler's formula (9.15):

$$y_{n+1} = y_n + hf(x_n, y_n).$$

3. Evaluate slope $\frac{dy}{dx}$ at the end of the interval x_1, *i.e.*, evaluate $f(x_1, y_1)$.
4. Determine average of the slopes at the beginning and end of the interval, *i.e.*,

$$\frac{f(x_0, y_0) + f(x_1, y_1)}{2}.$$

5. Compute a revised estimate of y_1 using

$$y_1 = y_0 + h \frac{f(x_0, y_0) + f(x_1, y_1)}{2}.$$

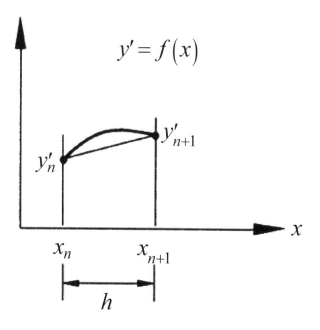

Fig. 9.7

6. Keep improving the estimate y_1 until convergence to a solution takes place.

Example 9.3. Using the modified Euler method, solve:

$$\frac{dy}{dx} = f(x,y) = -3x - y \quad y(0) = -1.5,$$

with $h = 0.1$, for $x = 0$ to 0.5.

The procedure of the modified Euler method is utilized as shown in the following steps to generate numerical solutions at $x = 0.1$ and 0.2. Solutions for $x = 0.3$, 0.4 and 0.5 are obtained in a similar manner. The quantity y_{1c} refers to the revised estimate of the solution in each iteration.

Given initial values:

$$x_0 = 0, \quad y_0 = -1.5, \quad f(x_0, y_0) = 1.5;$$

For x_1:

$$x_1 = 0.1, \quad y_1 = y_0 + hf(x_0, y_0) = -1.35, \quad f(x_1, y_1) = 1.05$$

Calculate average and evaluate:

$$\frac{f(x_1, y_1) + f(x_0, y_0)}{2} = 1.275 \quad \Rightarrow \quad y_{1c} = y_0 + h\frac{f(x_1, y_1) + f(x_0, y_0)}{2} = -1.373$$

Let $y_1 = y_{1c}$, and evaluate:

$$f(x_1, y_1) = 1.073.$$

Iterate calculations until convergence:

$$\frac{f(x_1, y_1) + f(x_0, y_0)}{2} = 1.286 \quad \Rightarrow \quad y_{1c} = y_0 + h\frac{f(x_1, y_1) + f(x_0, y_0)}{2} = -1.371$$

$$\Rightarrow \quad y_1 = y_{1c} \quad \Rightarrow \quad f(x_1, y_1) = 1.071.$$

For x_2:

$$y_1 = -1.371, \quad f(x_1, y_1) = 1.071$$

$$x_2 = 0.2, \quad y_2 = y_1 + hf(x_1, y_1) = -1.264, \quad f(x_2, y_2) = 0.664$$

Calculate average and evaluate:

$$\frac{f(x_2, y_2) + f(x_1, y_1)}{2} = 0.868 \quad \Rightarrow \quad y_{2c} = y_1 + h\frac{f(x_2, y_2) + f(x_1, y_1)}{2} = -1.285$$

Let $y_2 = y_{2c}$, and evaluate:

$$f(x_2, y_2) = 0.685$$

Iterate calculations until convergence:

$$\frac{f(x_2, y_2) + f(x_1, y_1)}{2} = 0.878 \quad \Rightarrow \quad y_{2c} = y_1 + h\frac{f(x_2, y_2) + f(x_1, y_1)}{2} = -1.284$$

$$\Rightarrow \quad y_2 = y_{2c} \quad \Rightarrow \quad f(x_2, y_2) = 0.684.$$

$$\frac{f(x_2, y_2) + f(x_1, y_1)}{2} = 0.878 \quad \Rightarrow \quad y_{2c} = y_1 + h\frac{f(x_2, y_2) + f(x_1, y_1)}{2} = -1.284$$

At x_3, x_4, and x_5, the solutions can be similarly generated as:

$$\begin{array}{l|l} x_3 = 0.3 & y_3 = -1.2328 \\ x_4 = 0.4 & y_4 = -1.2154 \\ x_5 = 0.5 & y_5 = -1.2283 \end{array}$$

The results obtained by this method are presented in Table 9.2 in a tabular format for x-values ranging from 0 to 0.5 with a step size of 0.1. Converged values of the solution are pointed out in the "Corrected y_n" column.

The x values and the computed y values are assembled in the form of vectors vx and vy in order to generate a cubic spline interpolation as follows which is presented as a plot of the solution in Figure 9.8.

```
vx = 0:0.1:0.5;
vy = [-1.5 -1.371 -1.284 -1.233 -1.215 -1.228];

X = 0:0.01:0.5;
ModEuler = spline(vx,vy,X);
```

x_n	y_n	$f(x_n, y_n)$	Average slope at beginning and end	Corrected y_n	
0	-1.5	1.5			
0.1	-1.35	1.05	1.275	-1.3725	
	-1.3725	1.0725	1.2862	-1.3714	
	-1.3714	1.0714	1.2857	-1.3714	(convergence)
0.2	-1.2643	0.6643	0.8679	-1.2846	
	-1.2846	0.6846	0.8780	-1.2836	
	-1.2836	0.6836	0.8775	-1.2837	
	-1.2837	0.6837	0.8776	-1.2837	(convergence)
0.3	-1.2153	0.3153	0.4995	-1.2337	
	-1.2337	0.3337	0.5087	-1.2338	
	-1.2328	0.3328	0.5082	-1.2338	(convergence)
0.4	-1.1996	-0.0004	0.1662	-1.2162	
	-1.2162	0.0162	0.1745	-1.2154	
	-1.2154	0.0154	0.1741	-1.2154	(convergence)
0.5	-1.2139	-0.2861	-0.1353	-1.2290	
	-1.2290	-0.2710	-0.1278	-1.2282	
	-1.2282	-0.2718	-0.1282	-1.2283	
	-1.2283	-0.2717	-0.1282	-1.2283	(convergence)

Table 9.2: Calculations by Modified Euler Method

A solution by the Euler method is also generated below in order to obtain a comparison between the Modified Euler solution and the not-so-accurate Euler solution.

```
h = 0.1;
x = 0:h:0.5;
n = (0.5-0)/h;

x0 = 0;
y = -1.5;
f =@(x,y) -3*x-y;

for i = 1:n
     y(i+1) = y(i) + h*f(x(i),y(i));
end

table(x',y','VariableNames',{'x','y'})
```

x_i	y_i
0.0	-1.5
0.1	-1.35
0.2	-1.245
0.3	-1.1805
0.4	-1.1525
0.5	-1.1572

MATLAB's cubic spline interpolation is now used below to generate a plot of the computed Euler solution, which is compared with the Modified Euler solution in Figure 9.8.

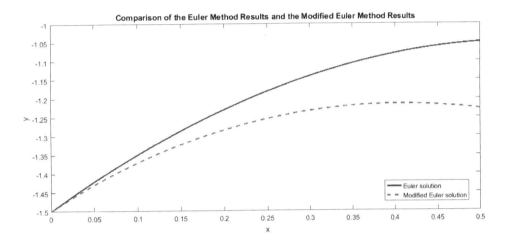

Fig. 9.8: Comparison of the modified Euler solution the Euler solution

```
Euler = spline(x,y,X);
p = plot(X,Euler,'blue',X,ModEuler,'red--')
title('Comparison of the Euler Method Results and the
    Modified Euler Method Results')
xlabel('x')
ylabel('y')
legend('Euler solution','Modified Euler solution')
p(1).LineWidth = 2;
p(2).LineWidth = 2;
```

9.5 Runge-Kutta Methods

Runge-Kutta methods are among the most popular techniques employed in the numerical solution of ordinary differential equations. These methods use the *y*-value at the beginning of an interval along with some representative slope over the interval to determine the y-value at the end of the interval. Special cases of the method are Euler's method, which uses the slope at the beginning of the interval and the modified Euler method which uses the average slope over the segment.

There are several orders of Runge-Kutta methods from the first order to the eighth depending on the number of iterations involved in the solution-generating process. However, only the fourth-order Runge-Kutta method will be discussed in detail in this chapter. All of these still resort only to the use of the first derivative and do not require the involvement of higher order derivatives. While the second-order Runge-Kutta method is essentially the same as the modified Euler method and offers the same order of accuracy, the main difference is that it resorts only to two iterations. The third-order Runge-Kutta method resorts to Simpson's one-third rule, which is a higher-order integration scheme than the trapezoidal rule and uses slopes at the beginning, middle, and end of the segment in order to estimate the y-value at the end of the segment. As its name clearly suggests, the fourth-order method does require four iterations to determine the y-value at the segment end. Because higher-order integration schemes are employed, the Runge-Kutta fourth-order method gives very accurate results. Orders of the method that are higher than fourth are not common.

Advantages of Runge-Kutta methods include ease of programming, good stability characteristics, flexibility of step size, and self-starting capability.

9.5.1 Fourth-Order Runge-Kutta Method

The fourth-order Runge-Kutta method comes in two popular versions. The first version is based on Simpson's one-third rule while the second is based on Simpson's three-eighth rule. The sequence of calculations to be used in these versions is given below.

Procedure for Version 1 - Based on Simpson's One-Third Rule:

Given: $\frac{dy}{dx} = f(x, y) = \text{Slope}$, $y = y_0$ at $x = x_0$ (initial condition), and $h = $ interval width.

Determine: y_1, which is $y(x_1)$. See Figure 9.9.

1. Compute h time slope k_1 at (x_0, y_0): $k_1 = h f(x_0, y_0)$.
2. Compute y at the midpoint of the interval (x_0, x_1) using the Euler formula

$$y_{mp} = y_0 + \frac{1}{2} k_1. \tag{9.18}$$

3. Compute k_2 at $x = x_{mp}$, $y = y_{mp}$: $k_2 = h f(x_{mp}, y_{mp})$.
4. Obtain a revised estimate of y_{mp} with y_0, k_2, and $\frac{1}{2}h$,

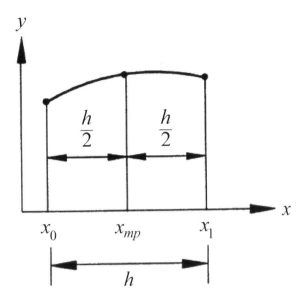

Fig. 9.9: Basis of the fourth-order Runge-Kutta method utilizing Simpson's one- third rule

$$y_{mp} = y_0 + \frac{1}{2}k_2. \tag{9.19}$$

5. Compute a revised estimate of k at mid-interval, using the above value of y_{mp}:

$$k_3 = hf(x_{mp}, y_{mp}). \tag{9.20}$$

6. Compute y_1 using:

$$y_1 = y_0 + k_3. \tag{9.21}$$

7. Compute k at the end of the interval:

$$k_4 = hf(x_1, y_1). \tag{9.22}$$

8. Compute a revised estimate of y_1 using:

$$y_1 = y_0 + \frac{1}{6}(k_1 + 2k_2 + 2k_3 + k_4) \tag{9.23}$$

per Simpson's one-third rule. Notice the four estimates of slope being used.

9. Repeat above steps for computing y_2, y_3, etc. For example, to compute y_2, repeat the procedure with (x_1, y_1) replacing (x_0, y_0) and (x_2, y_2) replacing (x_1, y_1).

Procedure for Version 2 - Based on Simpson's Three-Eighth Rule:

The procedure for Version 2 is very similar to Version 1, except that the range x_0 to x_1 is subdivided into three regions, the starting and ending points of which are x_0, x_{13}, x_{23}

and x_1. The slopes at these intermediate points within the range x_0 to x_1 are computed and revised until y_1 is determined as shown in the following summary of calculations.

Summary of Calculations for Versions 1 and 2:

Version 1 - Based on Simpson's One-Third Rule:

$$k_1 = hf(x_0, y_0)$$

$$y_{mp} = y_0 + \frac{1}{2}k_1$$

$$k_2 = hf(x_{mp}, y_{mp})$$

$$y_{mp} = y_0 + \frac{1}{2}k_2 \quad \leftarrow \quad \text{Revised } y_{mp} \text{ (using } h \text{ times the new slope)} \qquad (9.24)$$

$$k_3 = hf(x_{mp}, y_{mp})$$

$$y_1 = y_0 + k_3$$

$$k_4 = hf(x_1, y_1)$$

$$y_1 = y_0 + \frac{1}{6}(k_1 + 2k_2 + 2k_3 + k_4)$$

Version 2 - Based on Simpson's Three-Eighth Rule:

$$x_{13} = x_0 + \frac{1}{3}h, \quad x_{23} = x_0 + \frac{2}{3}h, \quad k_1 = hf(x_0, y_0)$$

$$y_{13} = y_0 + \frac{1}{3}k_1, \quad k_2 = hf(x_{13}, y_{13}), \quad y_{23} = y_0 + \frac{1}{3}k_1 + \frac{1}{3}k_2$$

Note that $y_0 + \frac{1}{3}k_1$ is, in fact, y_{13}.

$$k_3 = hf(x_{23}, y_{23})$$

$$y_{1adj} = y_0 + k_1 - k_2 + k_3 \qquad (9.25)$$

Note that "$k_1 - k_2 + k_3$" represents h multiplied by a representative average slope over segment (x_0, x_1).

$$k_4 = hf(x_1, y_{1adj})$$

$$y_1 = y_0 + \frac{1}{8}(k_1 + 3k_2 + 3k_3 + k_4)$$

Example 9.4. Solve $\frac{dy}{dx} = f(x, y) = -2x^2 - y$; Initial condition: $y(0) = -1.75$; $h = 0.1$; Range of x: 0 to 0.5.

Version 1 - Based on Simpson's One-Third Rule:

The given information is:

$$f(x, y) = -2x^3 - y, \quad h = 0.1, \quad x_0 = 0, \quad y_0 = -1.75.$$

We can implement Version 1 in MATLAB using a loop. Calculations for $x = x_1$ and $x = x_2$ are as follows.

```
h = 0.1;
x = 0;
y = -1.75;

f = @(x,y) -2*x.^2 - y;

for i = 1:5
    k1 = h*f(x,y)
    ymp = y + 0.5*k1
    xmp = x + 0.5*h
    k2 = h*f(xmp,ymp)
    ymp = y + 0.5*k2
    k3 = h*f(xmp,ymp)
    x1 = x + h
    y1 = y + k3
    k4 = h*f(x1,y1)
    x = x1
    y = y + 1/6*(k1 + 2*k2 + 2*k3 + k4)
    X1(i) = x;
    Y1(i) = y;
end

X1 = [0 X1];
Y1 = [-1.75 Y1];

k1 =
    0.1750

ymp =
    -1.6625
```

```
xmp  =

    0.0500


k2  =

    0.1658


ymp  =

   -1.6671


k3  =

    0.1662


x1  =

    0.1000


y1  =

   -1.5838


k4  =

    0.1564


x  =

    0.1000


y  =

   -1.5841


k1  =

    0.1564


ymp  =

   -1.5059


xmp  =

    0.1500


k2  =

    0.1461


ymp  =

   -1.5111


k3  =
```

```
      0.1466

x1 =
      0.2000

y1 =
     -1.4375
```

The remaining iterations for $x = 0.3, 0.4$ and 0.5 are completed yielding the following results:

i	x_i	y_i
0	0	-1.75 (given)
1	0.1	-1.5841
2	0.2	-1.4379
3	0.3	-1.3132
4	0.4	-1.2118
5	0.5	-1.1353

In order to generate a cubic spline interpolation for the Runge-Kutta solution, the x and y values are put into vectors $X1$ and $Y1$. The resulting y is plotted as a function of x in Figure 9.10.

Version 2 - Based on Simpson's Three-Eighth Rule:

```
h = 0.1;
x = 0;
y = -1.75;

f = @(x,y) -2*x.^2 - y;

for i = 1:5
    k1 = h*f(x,y)
    y13 = y + 1/3*k1
    x13 = x + 1/3*h
    k2 = h*f(x13,y13)
    x23 = x + 2/3*h
    y23 = y + k1/3 + k2/3
    k3 = h*f(x23,y23)
    x1 = x + h
    y1adj = y + k1 - k2 + k3
    k4 = h*f(x1,y1adj)
    y1 = y + 1/8*(k1 + 3*k2 + 3*k3 + k4)
    x = x1;
    y = y1;
```

```
    X2(i) = x;
    Y2(i) = y;
end

X2 = [0 X2];
Y2 = [-1.75 Y2];

k1 =
    0.1750

y13 =
   -1.6917

x13 =
    0.0333

k2 =
    0.1689

x23 =
    0.0667

y23 =
   -1.6354

k3 =
    0.1626

x1 =
    0.1000

y1adj =
   -1.5813

k4 =
    0.1561

y1 =
   -1.5843

k1 =
    0.1564
```

```
y13 =
   -1.5321

x13 =
    0.1333

k2 =
    0.1497

x23 =
    0.1667

y23 =
   -1.4822

k3 =
    0.1427

x1 =
    0.2000

y1adj =
   -1.4348

k4 =
    0.1355

y1 =
   -1.4382
```

The remaining iterations for $x = 0.3, 0.4$ and 0.5 are completed yielding the following results:

i	x_i	y_i
0	0	-1.75 (given)
1	0.1	-1.5843
2	0.2	-1.4382
3	0.3	-1.3136
4	0.4	-1.2124
5	0.5	-1.1361

Generation of the $X2$ and $Y2$ vectors as in Version 1, leads to the graph in Figure 9.10 which compares the two solutions of the fourth-order Runge-Kutta method. These plots definitely indicate that the two solutions are very very close to each other.

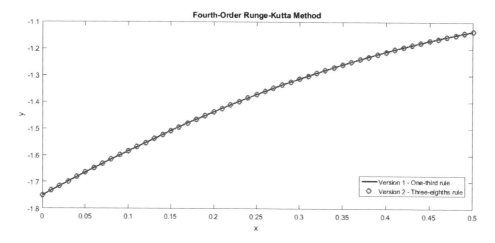

Fig. 9.10: Solution by fourth-order Runge-Kutta method

```
X = 0:0.01:0.5;
RKV1 = spline(X1,Y1,X);
RKV2 = spline(X2,Y2,X);


p = plot(X,RKV1,'blue',X,RKV2,'redo')
title('Fourth-Order Runge-Kutta Method')
xlabel('x')
ylabel('y')
legend('Version 1 - One-third rule','Version 2 - Three-
    eighths rule')
p(1).LineWidth = 2;
p(2).LineWidth = 2;
```

9.5.2 MATLAB Solutions to a First-Order Differential Equation

The MATLAB function *ode45* is a general-purpose Runge-Kutta solver. It is a single-step solver in computing $y(t_n)$; it needs only the solution at the immediately preceding time point, $y(t_{n-1})$.

The arguments to the function *ode45* are

$$[x, y] = ode45(f, [x0, x1], y0)$$

where f is such that $\frac{dy}{dx} = f(x, y)$, $[x0, x1]$ is the range of x, and $y0$ is the initial condition. Each row in the solution array y corresponds to a value returned in a column vector x.

To illustrate the use of this MATLAB function, the MATLAB solution to the problem of Example 9.1 presented in the section on the Taylor series method is outlined below.

Recall, we are to solve the differential equation $\frac{dy}{dx} = f(x, y) = 7x^4 - 3x^2 + 9$, with initial condition $y = 4$ at $x = 1$. In Example 9.1, we found the Taylor series expansion for $x = 1$ to $x = 1.3$.

Using *ode45*, we enter $f(x, y)$ as an anonymous function, then call the function *ode45* with the proper arguments. The solutions to the differential equation obtained with *ode45* are presented in Figure 9.11 and compared with the Taylor series solution, which is redone here in order to obtain its plot.

```
f = @(x,y) 7*x.^4 - 3*x.^2 + 9;
[X,Y] = ode45(f,[1,1.3],4);

h = 0.05;
x = 1:h:1.3;
n = (1.3 - 1.0)/h;

x0 = 1; y0 = 4;

y1 = 7*x0^4 - 3*x0^2 + 9;
y2 = 28*x0^3 - 6*x0;
y3 = 84*x0^2 - 6;
y4 = 168*x0;
y5 = 168;
y6 = 0;
y = y0 + (x - x0)*y1 + 1/2*(x-x0).^2*y2 + 1/6*(x-x0).^3*y3 +
    1/24*(x-x0).^4*y4 + 1/120*(x-x0).^5*y5 + 1/720*(x-x0)
    .^6*y6;

p = plot(X,Y,'blue',x,y,'redo')
axis([1 1.3 4 10])
title('Comparison of Solutions')
xlabel('x')
ylabel('y')
legend('ode45 solution','Taylor series solution')
p(1).LineWidth = 2;
p(2).LineWidth = 2;
```

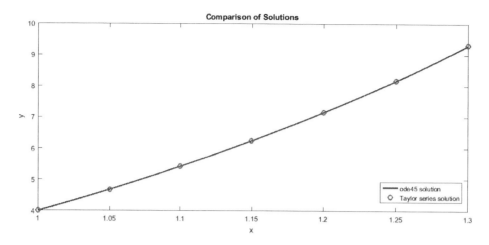

Fig. 9.11: Comparison of the MATLAB solution with the Taylor series solution

As can be seen from the solution plots, the MATLAB solution agrees well with the Taylor series solution.

Example 9.5. Using the MATLAB function, solve the problem of Example 9.3 presented in the section on the modified Euler method, namely,

$$\frac{dy}{dx} = f(x, y) = -3x - y; \quad y(0) = -1.5; \quad h = 0.1; \quad \text{Range of } x: 0 \text{ to } 0.5.$$

The modified Euler solution is partially redone here in the following steps in order to generate a solution plot.

```
f = @(x,y) -3*x-y';
[X,Y] = ode45(f,[0, 0.5],-1.5);

vx = 0:0.1:0.5;
vy = [-1.5 -1.371 -1.284 -1.233 -1.215 -1.228];
ModEuler = spline(vx,vy,X);

p = plot(X,Y,'blue',X,ModEuler,'redo')
title('Comparison of Solutions')
xlabel('x')
ylabel('y')
legend('ode45 solution','Modified Euler solution')
p(1).LineWidth = 2;
p(2).LineWidth = 2;
```

Figure 9.12 shows a comparison of the MATLAB solution with the modified Modified Euler solution. The agreement between the results is, clearly, very good.

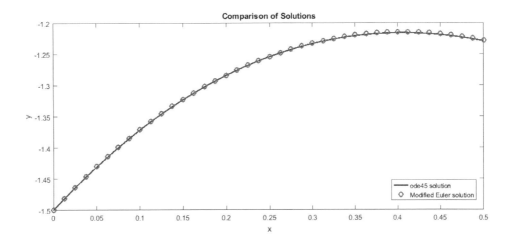

Fig. 9.12: Comparison of the MATLAB solution with the Modified Euler method

Example 9.6. Using the MATLAB function *ode45*, solve the problem of Example 9.4 presented in 9.5.1 on the Runge-Kutta fourth order method, which is repeated below.

Solve $\frac{dy}{dx} = f(x, y) = -2x^2 - y$; Initial condition: $y(0) = -1.75$; $h = 0.1$; Range of x: 0 to 0.5.

The Runge-Kutta solutions (Versions 1 and 2) are repeated here in the following steps in order to generate solution plots in Figure 9.13 for comparison with the solutions generated with the MATLAB function *ode45*.

```
f = @(x,y) -2*x.^2 - y;
[X,Y] = ode45(f,[0,0.5],-1.75);

h = 0.1;
x = 0;
y = -1.75;

for i = 1:5
    k1 = h*f(x,y);
    ymp = y + 0.5*k1;
    xmp = x + 0.5*h;
    k2 = h*f(xmp,ymp);
    ymp = y + 0.5*k2;
```

```matlab
    k3 = h*f(xmp,ymp);
    x1 = x + h;
    y1 = y + k3;
    k4 = h*f(x1,y1);
    x = x1;
    y = y + 1/6*(k1 + 2*k2 + 2*k3 + k4);
    X1(i) = x;
    Y1(i) = y;
end

X1 = [0 X1];
Y1 = [-1.75 Y1];

x = 0;
y = -1.75;

for i = 1:5
    k1 = h*f(x,y);
    y13 = y + 1/3*k1;
    x13 = x + 1/3*h;
    k2 = h*f(x13,y13);
    x23 = x + 2/3*h;
    y23 = y + k1/3 + k2/3;
    k3 = h*f(x23,y23);
    x1 = x + h;
    y1adj = y + k1 - k2 + k3;
    k4 = h*f(x1,y1adj);
    y1 = y + 1/8*(k1 + 3*k2 + 3*k3 + k4);
    x = x1;
    y = y1;
    X2(i) = x;
    Y2(i) = y;
end

X2 = [0 X2];
Y2 = [-1.75 Y2];

RKV1 = spline(X1,Y1,X);
RKV2 = spline(X2,Y2,X);

p = plot(X,Y,'blue',X,RKV1,'redo',X,RKV2,'green*')
title('Comparison of Solutions')
xlabel('x')
```

```
ylabel('y')
legend('ode45 solution','RK Version 1 - One-third solution',
   'RK Version 2 - Three-eights solution')
p(1).LineWidth = 2;
p(2).LineWidth = 2;
p(3).LineWidth = 2;
```

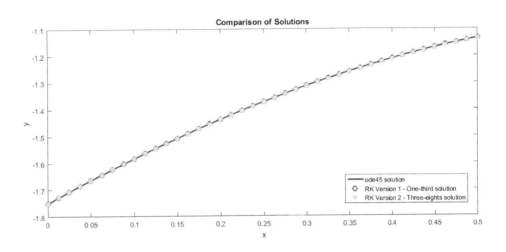

Fig. 9.13: Comparison of the MATLAB solution with Runge-Kutta fourth order methods

9.6 Systems of First Order Ordinary Differential Equations

Sometimes, in engineering and the physical sciences, the need to solve a system of first-order ordinary differential equations is encountered. Such a system is

$$
\begin{aligned}
\frac{dy_1}{dx} &= f(x, y_1, y_2, \ldots, y_n) \\
\frac{dy_2}{dx} &= g(x, y_1, y_2, \ldots, y_n) \\
&\vdots \\
\frac{dy_n}{dx} &= q(x, y_1, y_2, \ldots, y_n)
\end{aligned}
\tag{9.26}
$$

with n initial conditions specified at the starting value of the independent variable x. This system of equations can be easily solved using any of the methods discussed in Sections 9.2-9.5. However, here, the application of the fourth order Runge-Kutta procedure to obtain a solution to a problem involving a pair of first-order differential equations will be illustrated. Notice that in a problem involving a pair of differential equations, where x and y are the dependent variables and t is the independent variable, x and y calculations have to be alternately performed as illustrated in the following example.

Example 9.7. Using the Runge-Kutta fourth-order method, obtain a solution to

$$\frac{dx}{dt} = f(x, y, t) = xy^2 + t$$

and

$$\frac{dy}{dt} = g(x, y, t) = ty + x^2,$$

for $t = 0$ to $t = 0.5$ seconds. The initial conditions are given as: $x(0) = -1$; $y(0) = 1$. Use a time increment of $h = 0.1$ seconds.

Note that both x and y are functions of the independent variable t.

Version 1 of the Runge-Kutta Method, which utilizes Simpson's one-third rule, will then resort to the following sequential equations to compute x and y at t_1, where $t_1 = t_0 + h$ and h is the increment or step size.

$$k_1 = hf(x_0, y_0, t_0); \quad m_1 = hg(x_0, y_0, t_0);$$

$$t_{mp} = t_0 + 0.5h; \quad x_{mp} = x_0 + 0.5k_1; \quad y_{mp} = y_0 + 0.5m_1;$$

$$k_2 = hf(x_{mp}, y_{mp}, t_{mp}); \quad m_2 = hg(x_{mp}, y_{mp}, t_{mp});$$

$$x_{mp}^* = x_0 + 0.5k_2; \quad y_{mp}^* = y_0 + 0.5m_2;$$

$$k_3 = hf(x_{mp}^*, y_{mp}*, t_{mp}); \quad m_3 = hg(x_{mp}^*, y_{mp}^*, t_{mp});$$

$$x_1 = x_0 + k_3; \quad y_1 = y_0 + m_3; \quad t_1 = t_0 + h;$$

$$k_4 = hf(x_1, y_1, t_1); \quad m_4 = hg(x_1, y_1, t_1)$$

$$x_1 = x_0 + \frac{1}{6}(k_1 + 2k_2 + 2k_3 + k_4); \quad y_1 = y_0 + \frac{1}{6}(m_1 + 2m_2 + 2m_3 + m_4)$$

In order to compute the solution (x_1, y_1) at t_1, we start with known values x_0, y_0 and t_0 as shown above. Similarly, to compute the solution (x_2, y_2) at t_2, the above procedure needs to be repeated with (x_1, y_1, t_1) replacing (x_0, y_0, t_0) and (x_2, y_2, t_2) replacing (x_1, y_1, t_1).

We implement in MATLAB using a loop. Calculations for $t = t_1$ and $t = t_2$ are as follows.

```
f = @(x,y,t) x*y.^2 + t;
g = @(x,y,t) t*y + x.^2;

h = 0.1;
t = 0;
```

```
x = -1;
y = 1;

X(1) = x;
Y(1) = y;
T(1) = t;
for i = 1:5
    k1 = h*f(x,y,t)
    m1 = h*g(x,y,t)

    tmp = t + 0.5*h
    xmp = x + 0.5*k1
    ymp = y + 0.5*m1
    k2 = h*f(xmp,ymp,tmp)
    m2 = h*g(xmp,ymp,tmp)

    xmpast = x + 0.5*k2
    ympast = y + 0.5*m2
    k3 = h*f(xmpast,ympast,tmp)
    m3 = h*g(xmpast,ympast,tmp)

    x1 = x + k3
    y1 = y + m3
    t1 = t + h
    k4 = h*f(x1,y1,t1)
    m4 = h*g(x1,y1,t1)

    x = x + 1/6*(k1 + 2*k2 + 2*k3 + k4)
    y = y + 1/6*(m1 + 2*m2 + 2*m3 + m4)
    t = t1

    X(i+1) = x;
    Y(i+1) = y;
    T(i+1) = t1;
end

table(T',X',Y','VariableNames',{'t','x','y'})

k1 =
    -0.1000

m1 =
     0.1000
```

```
tmp =
    0.0500

xmp =
   -1.0500

ymp =
    1.0500

k2 =
   -0.1108

m2 =
    0.1155

xmpast =
   -1.0554

ympast =
    1.0578

k3 =
   -0.1131

m3 =
    0.1167

x1 =
   -1.1131

y1 =
    1.1167

t1 =
    0.1000

k4 =
   -0.1288

m4 =
    0.1351
```

```
x =
    -1.1127

y =
     1.1166

k1 =
    -0.1287

m1 =
     0.1350

tmp =
     0.1500

xmp =
    -1.1771

ymp =
     1.1841

k2 =
    -0.1500

m2 =
     0.1563

xmpast =
    -1.1878

ympast =
     1.1947

k3 =
    -0.1545

m3 =
     0.1590

x1 =
    -1.2673

y1 =
```

```
        1.2756

t1 =
        0.2000

k4 =
        -0.1862

m4 =
        0.1861

x =
        -1.2668

y =
        1.2752
```

The remaining iterations for $t = 0.3, 0.4$ and 0.5 are completed yielding the following results:

i	t_i	x_i	y_i
0	0	-1	1 (given)
1	0.1	-1.1127	1.1166
2	0.2	-1.2668	1.2752
3	0.3	-1.5058	1.4997
4	0.4	-1.9446	1.8483
5	0.5	-3.0248	2.5223

Plots of the results of the Runge-Kutta process can be obtained by an interpolation procedure involving the generation of the X, Y, and T vectors and the spline function. Both the spline and the MATLAB solution process using *ode45* is done below. Note that *ode45* handles systems of equations, but the anonymous function must be entered as a vector function as demonstrated.

```
F = @(t,x) [x(1).*x(2).^2 + t; t.*x(2) + x(1).^2];
[TM, XY] = ode45(F,[0, 0.5],[-1;1]);

xspl = spline(T,X,TM);
yspl = spline(T,Y,TM);

subplot(2,1,1)
p = plot(TM,xspl,'blue',TM,XY(:,1),'redo')
title('System of First-Order Differential Equations: t vs. x
    ')
```

```
xlabel('t')
ylabel('x')
legend('RK 4th-order solution ','ode45 solution')
p(1).LineWidth = 2;
p(2).LineWidth = 2;

subplot(2,1,2)
p1 = plot(TM,yspl,'blue',TM,XY(:,2),'redo')
title('System of First-Order Differential Equations: t vs. y
   ')
xlabel('t')
ylabel('y')
legend('RK 4th-order solution ','ode45 solution')
p1(1).LineWidth = 2;
p1(2).LineWidth = 2;
```

The MATLAB solution generated through the above procedure is compared with the analytical Runge-Kutta results in Figure 9.14. It is noted that the Runge-Kutta solution agrees reasonably well with the MATLAB solution.

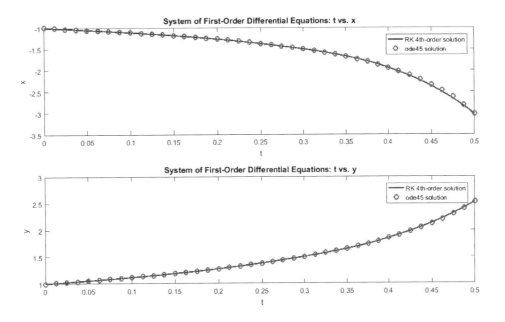

Fig. 9.14: Solutions to the differential equation

9.7 Solution of Higher-Order Differential Equations

In many areas of engineering and physics, the solution of higher-order differential equations is often required. Examples can be encountered in vibration engineering, control systems engineering, electrical circuit analysis etc.

The general form of a second-order differential equation is

$$\frac{d^2y}{dx^2} = f\left(x, y, \frac{dy}{dx}\right). \tag{9.27}$$

A more special form often encountered in vibrations, control systems, and electrical circuit analysis is

$$a\frac{d^2y}{dx^2} + b\frac{dy}{dx} + cy = q(x), \tag{9.28}$$

with initial conditions $y(0)$ and $\frac{dy}{dx}(0)$ specified.

Although any of the methods discussed in Sections 9.2-9.5 can certainly be used to obtain solutions to (9.28), it must first be converted to a system of first-order differential equations as follows,

$$\frac{dy}{dx} = z = f(x, y, z),$$
$$\frac{dz}{dx} = \frac{q(x) - bz - cy}{a} = g(x, y, z), \tag{9.29}$$

with the initial conditions now becoming $y(0)$ and $z(0)$. Thus, if a solution to the second-order differential equation, which is now represented by the two first-order equations of (9.29), is to be generated by Version 1 of the fourth-order Runge-Kutta method, the calculations shown in the following procedure must be resorted to.

$$k_1 = hf(y_0, z_0, x_0); \quad m_1 = hg(y_0, z_0, x_0);$$
$$y_{mp} = y_0 + 0.5k_1; \quad z_{mp} = z_0 + 0.5m_1; \quad x_{mp} = x_0 + 0.5h;$$
$$k_2 = hf(y_{mp}, z_{mp}, x_{mp}); \quad m_2 = hg(y_{mp}, z_{mp}, x_{mp});$$
$$y_{mp}^* = y_0 + 0.5k_2; \quad z_{mp}^* = z_0 + 0.5m_2; \tag{9.30}$$
$$k_3 = h(y_{mp}^*, z_{mp}^*, x_{mp}); \quad m_3 = hg(y_{mp}^*, z_{mp}^*, x_{mp});$$
$$y_1 = y_0 + k_3; \quad z_1 = z_0 + m_3; \quad x_1 = x_0 + h;$$
$$k_4 = hf(y_1, z_1, x_1); \quad m_4 = hg(y_1, z_1, x_1);$$
$$y_1 = y_0 + \frac{1}{6}(k_1 + 2k_2 + 2k_3 + k_4); \quad z_1 = z_0 + \frac{1}{6}(m_1 + 2m_2 + 2m_3 + m_4);$$

where h is the increment or step size. Note that in order to generate the solution (y_1, z_1), we started with known values (y_0, z_0, x_0). Similarly, to obtain (y_2, z_2), the above procedure must be repeated with (y_1, z_1, x_1) replacing (y_0, z_0, x_0) and (y_2, z_2, x_2) replacing (y_1, z_1, x_1).

Example 9.8. Using the Runge-Kutta fourth-order method, obtain a solution to

$$m\frac{d^2y}{dt^2} + c\frac{dy}{dt} + ky = F(t);$$

with $m = 1$ kg, $c = 3$ N-sec/m, $k = 9$ N/m, $F(t) = 9$ N, for $t = 0$ to $t = 3$ seconds. The initial conditions are given as $y(0) = 0$ and $\frac{dy}{dt}(0) = 0$. Use a time increment of 0.5 seconds.

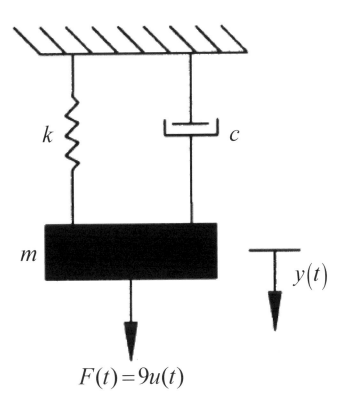

Fig. 9.15: Spring-mass-damper system

The above differential equation represents the equation of motion of a linear spring-mass-damper system subjected to a step forcing function as shown in Figure 9.15. As mentioned earlier, application of the fourth order Runge- Kutta Method to the solution of a second-order differential equation is quite similar to that of a first order differential equation, except that the following two first-order equations must now be considered.

$$\frac{dy}{dt} = z$$

and

$$m\frac{dz}{dt} + cz + ky = F(t).$$

Note that, now, both y and z are functions of the independent variable t.

Thus, in this case,

$$\frac{dy}{dt} = f(y, z, t) = z$$

and

$$\frac{dz}{dt} = g(y, z, t) = \frac{F(t) - (ky + cz)}{m}.$$

We implement in MATLAB using a loop. Calculations for $t = t_1$ and $t = t_2$ are as follows.

```
f = @(y,z,t) z;
g = @(y,z,t) (9 - 3*z - 9*y)/1;

h = 0.5;
t = 0;
y = 0;
z = 0;

Y(1) = y;
Z(1) = z;
T(1) = t;

for i = 1:5
    k1 = h*f(y,z,t)
    m1 = h*g(y,z,t)

    tmp = t + 0.5*h
    ymp = y + 0.5*k1
    zmp = z + 0.5*m1
    k2 = h*f(ymp,zmp,tmp)
    m2 = h*g(ymp,zmp,tmp)

    ympast = y + 0.5*k2
    zmpast = z + 0.5*m2
    k3 = h*f(ympast,zmpast,tmp)
    m3 = h*g(ympast,zmpast,tmp)

    y1 = y + k3
    z1 = z + m3
    t1 = t + h
    k4 = h*f(y1,z1,t1)
```

```
    m4 = h*g(y1,z1,t1)

    y = y + 1/6*(k1 + 2*k2 + 2*k3 + k4)
    z = z + 1/6*(m1 + 2*m2 + 2*m3 + m4)
    t = t1;

    Y(i+1) = y;
    Z(i+1) = z;
    T(i+1) = t;
end

table(T',Y',Z','VariableNames',{'t','y','z'})

k1 =
     0

m1 =
    4.5000

tmp =
    0.2500

ymp =
     0

zmp =
    2.2500

k2 =
    1.1250

m2 =
    1.1250

ympast =
    0.5625

zmpast =
    0.5625

k3 =
    0.2813
```

```
m3 =
     1.1250

y1 =
     0.2813

z1 =
     1.1250

t1 =
     0.5000

k4 =
     0.5625

m4 =
     1.5469

y  =
     0.5625

z  =
     1.7578

k1 =
     0.8789

m1 =
    -0.6680

tmp =
     0.7500

ymp =
     1.0020

zmp =
     1.4238

k2 =
     0.7119

m2 =
```

```
      -2.1445

ympast =
      0.9185

zmpast =
      0.6855

k3 =
      0.3428

m3 =
      -0.6614

y1 =
      0.9053

z1 =
      1.0964

t1 =
        1

k4 =
      0.5482

m4 =
      -1.2184

y =
      1.1519

z =
      0.5081
```

The remaining iterations for $t = 1.5, 2.0, 2.5$ and 3.0 can be performed in a similar way, giving the following results:

i	t_i	y_i	z_i
0	0	0	0 (given)
1	0.5	0.5625	1.7578
2	1.0	1.1519	0.5081
3	1.5	1.1657	-0.3425
4	2.0	1.0056	-0.2404
5	2.5	0.9555	0.0258
6	3.0	0.9856	0.0744

Plots of the results of the Runge-Kutta process can be obtained by an interpolation procedure involving the generation of the Y, Z, and T vectors and the spline functions. The MATLAB solution process using *ode45* is also done below.

```
F = @(t,y) [y(2); 9 - 3*y(2) - 9*y(1)];
[TM, YZ] = ode45(F,[0,3],[0;0]);


yspl = spline(T,Y,TM);
zspl = spline(T,Z,TM);


subplot(2,1,1)
p = plot(TM,yspl,'blue',TM,YZ(:,1),'redo')
title('Displacement as a Function of Time')
xlabel('t (time)')
ylabel('y (displacement)')
legend('RK 4th-order solution ','ode45 solution')
p(1).LineWidth = 2;
p(2).LineWidth = 2;


subplot(2,1,2)
p1 = plot(TM,zspl,'blue',TM,YZ(:,2),'redo')
title('Velocity as a Function of Time')
xlabel('t (time)')
ylabel('z (velocity)')
legend('RK 4th-order solution ','ode45 solution')
p1(1).LineWidth = 2;
p1(2).LineWidth = 2;
```

The displacement and velocity profiles generated are compared in Figure 9.16. It is noted that the Runge-Kutta Version 1 solution agrees reasonably well with the MATLAB solution.

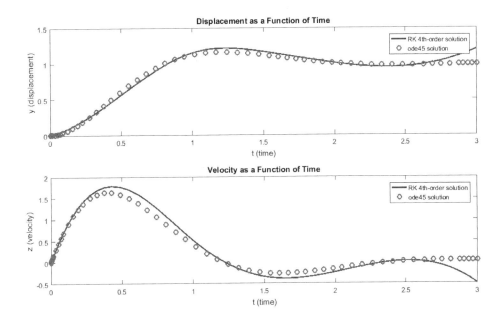

Fig. 9.16: Solution to the second-order differential equation

9.8 Boundary-Value Problems and the Shooting Method

As mentioned in the introduction, a boundary value problem is one in which conditions are prescribed at two different values of the independent variable. An example of a boundary-value problem is

$$\frac{d^2y}{dx^2} + Cy = F(x), \quad y(0) = 0, \quad y(L) = 2. \tag{9.31}$$

Because the two conditions given in (9.31) deal with different values of the independent variable x, this problem cannot be solved by the methods discussed so far. Other methods, therefore, have to be resorted to in order to obtain a solution. One such method is the Shooting Method in which a boundary-value problem is converted to a pseudo- initial-value problem involving a trial and error approach that can make use of any of the methods discussed in this chapter. Since only one initial condition is prescribed at $x = 0$, the second initial condition, which is not given, must be assumed at $x = 0$, in order to start the solution process. Upon completion of the solution process, a check must be made to determine if the condition prescribed at the point $x = L$ is satisfied or not. If not, a second guess must be made and the procedure redone. If the second guess still does not satisfy the prescribed end condition, a third guess has to be estimated. This can be accomplished by noting the difference between the given and the computed conditions at $x = L$ and resorting to a linear interpolation process that utilizes the results of the first two trials. This iteration process must be repeated until the prescribed end condition is, in fact, satisfied. In this method, it is important for the analyst to be skillful at estimating the unprescribed initial condition properly at the starting point in order to maintain efficiency and avoid divergence. Because the method is analogous to aiming properly and shooting at a given object, it has been appropriately labeled as the "shooting method". When higher-order differential equations must be solved involving several boundary conditions, this method has proven to be quite uncouth and laborious and, thus, inefficient.

Although any of the methods discussed in this chapter can be employed in the solution of a boundary-value problem by the shooting method, the following example will illustrate its application with MATLAB's *ode45* function.

Example 9.9. Solve

$$\frac{d^2y}{dx^2} = \frac{M}{EI} = \frac{30x - 1.5x^2}{EI},$$

where $EI = 121,500$ kips-ft^2.

The boundary conditions prescribed are

$$y(0) = 0 \text{ and } y(20) = 0.$$

This differential equation represents the relationship between the bending moment M and the deflection y at a distance x along the span from the left hand end of a 20 foot long simply supported beam loaded with a uniformly distributed load of 3 kips/ft. as shown in Figure 9.17. The slope and deflection at any point x can be obtained by solving the above differential equation.

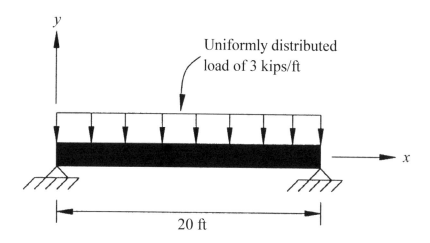

Fig. 9.17: A simply supported beam with a uniformly distributed load

Consider the two equations

$$\frac{dy}{dx} = z;$$

$$\frac{dz}{dx} = \frac{M}{EI} = \frac{30x - 1.5x^2}{EI}. \tag{9.32}$$

Note that both y and z are functions of the dependent variable x. Thus, in this case,

$$\frac{dy}{dx} = f(x, y, z) = z;$$

$$\frac{dz}{dx} = g(x, y, z) = \frac{30x - 1.5x^2}{EI}. \tag{9.33}$$

As said earlier, the shooting method is a trial-and-error method used in the solution of boundary-value problems. Although two boundary conditions are prescribed here, there is only one initial condition ($y(0) = 0$) provided to begin the solution process. The initial slope (derivative) at $x = 0$ is not known. Thus, the second initial condition, namely, the value of $\frac{dy}{dx}$ at $x = 0$ has to be assumed so that the solution process can be initiated. With these initial values of y and $\frac{dy}{dx}$, the solution y at $x = 20$ ft must then be computed by any appropriate method such as Modified Euler or Runge-Kutta. If this solution does not agree with the true value of y at $x = 20$ ft, which, in this case, is zero, the initial condition $\frac{dy}{dx}$ at $x = 0$ used must be revised and a new solution y at $x = 20$ computed. This process has to be repeated until the solution obtained at $x = 20$ ft agrees with the actual condition prescribed at that point on the beam.

In the following paragraphs, an iteration process utilizing MATLAB's *ode45* function is presented by which a solution to this boundary value problem is found.

Because the slope at $x = 0$ is not known, a reasonable starting value ($\frac{dy}{dx}(0) = -1$) has been assumed.

```
F = @(x,y) [y(2); (30*x - 1.5*x.^2)/121500];

guess1 = -1;
[X Y1] = ode45(F,[0,20],[0;guess1]);
y1 = Y1(end,1)

y1 =
  -19.8354
```

The command *Y(end,1)* extracts the solution to the differential equation obtained by using the MATLAB command *ode45* at the endpoint $x = 20$. This value is non-zero, therefore the initial guess of $\frac{dy}{dx}(0) = -1$ is incorrect. Therefore, we try a new value.

```
guess2 = -0.5;
[X Y2] = ode45(F,[0,20],[0;guess2]);
y2 = Y2(end,1)

y2 =
    -9.8354
```

The above analysis has yielded a deflection of 9.835 ft at the end $x = 20$ ft.

With the assumed value of $\frac{dy}{dx}(0)$, the deflection at the end is, clearly, still non-zero. Therefore, a third value of $\frac{dy}{dx}(0)$ must be tried which can be arrived at by a process of linear interpolation utilizing the results of the first two trials. The formula arrived at that must be used for estimating the next guess is the following.

New value of to be tried is the (second value of the first derivative assumed times the first deflection value at the end computed - first value of the first derivative assumed times the second deflection value at the end computed)/ (first deflection value at the end computed - the second deflection value at the end computed). That is,

```
guess3 = (guess2*y1 - guess1*y2)/(y1-y2)

guess3 =
    -0.0082
```

Then, the solution with the new guess is

```
[X Y3] = ode45(F,[0,20],[0;guess3]);
y3 = Y3(end,1)

y3 =
    1.5925e-15
```

Note the negligible deflection computed at the end with the current assumed value of the slope. The results of the above MATLAB computation are plotted in Figure 9.18.

```
subplot(2,1,1)
p = plot(X,Y3(:,1),'blue')
title('Beam Displacement')
xlabel('x (feet)')
ylabel('y (feet)')
p(1).LineWidth = 2;

subplot(2,1,2)
```

```
p1 = plot(X,Y3(:,2),'blue')
title('Beam Slope')
xlabel('x (feet)')
ylabel('dy.dx')
p1(1).LineWidth = 2;
```

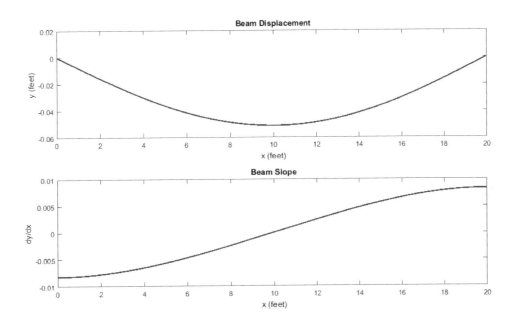

Fig. 9.18: Beam displacement and beam slope along span

9.9 Applications in Numerical Solution of Ordinary Differential Equations

9.9.1 Response of an Electric R-L Circuit to a Unit-Step Voltage Input

Consider the electric circuit shown in Figure 9.19 which is subjected to a unit step input voltage.

Summing voltages around the loop, the governing differential equation for the circuit can be seen to be

$$RI(t) = L\frac{dI}{dt} = u(t), \tag{9.34}$$

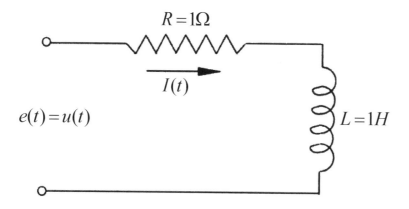

Fig. 9.19: *R-L* circuit with a unit-step voltage input

where *R* is the resistance of the circuit, *L* its inductance and $I(t)$ the current in it at any time *t*. With no initial energy in the network, the following initial condition is applicable

$$I(0) = 0. \tag{9.35}$$

The MATLAB statements that are needed to generate the solution using *ode45* are as follows.

```
f = @(t,I) (1 - I)/1;
[T I] = ode45(f,[0,6],0);

p = plot(T,I(:,1),'blue')
title('Current in an Electric Circuit')
xlabel('t (seconds)')
ylabel('Current (amperes)')
p(1).LineWidth = 2;
```

The MATLAB solution generated is shown in Figure 9.20. Notice how the current attains its steady-state value in a time *t* equal to 4τ, where τ is the system time constant, which, in this case, is L/R or 1 second.

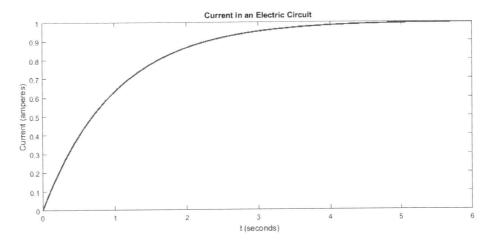

Fig. 9.20: Response of R-L circuit to unit step input voltage

9.9.2 Deflection Curve of a Cantilevered Beam with a Uniformly Distributed Load

Consider a uniform beam fixed at one end and free at the other, as shown, with a uniformly distributed load of w per unit length. The bending moment at a distance x from the left hand end of the beam is given by

$$M(x) = wLx - w\frac{L^2}{2} - w\frac{x^2}{2}. \qquad (9.36)$$

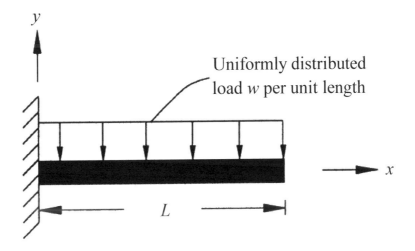

Fig. 9.21: Cantilevered beam with uniformly distributed load

The displacement at x is then given by

$$\frac{d^2y}{dx} = \frac{M(x)}{EI} \tag{9.37}$$

where E is Young's modulus of elasticity for the material of the beam, and I is the moment of inertia of the beam cross section about its neutral axis. In order to determine the deflection curve of the beam, (9.37) must be integrated and the appropriate boundary conditions applied, which are

$$y(0) = 0, \quad \frac{dy}{dx}(0) = 0. \tag{9.38}$$

For a beam of length $L = 165$ inches, $w = 12$ lb/in, $EI = 75 \times 10^6$ lb-in^2, (9.37) can be solved with MATLAB's *ode45* function as follows.

```
f = @(x,y) [y(2); (12*165*x - 12*(165)^2/2 - 12*x.^2/2)
    /(75*10^6)];
[X Y] = ode45(f,[0,165],[0;0]);

subplot(2,1,1)
p = plot(X,Y(:,1),'blue')
axis([0 165 -20 0])
title('Deflection Along Beam Span')
xlabel('Distance from left end (inches)')
ylabel('Deflection (inches)')
p(1).LineWidth = 2;

subplot(2,1,2)
p1 = plot(X,Y(:,2),'blue')
axis([0 165 -0.2 0])
title('Slope Along Beam Span')
xlabel('Distance from left end (inches)')
ylabel('Slope')
p1(1).LineWidth = 2;
```

The results of the MATLAB computation are shown in Figure 9.22, with the maximum deflection and slope occurring at the free end as anticipated.

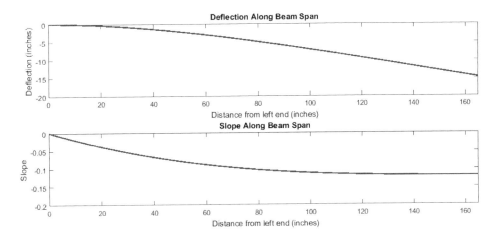

Fig. 9.22: Beam deflection curve and beam slope along span

9.9.3 Temperature Response of a Solid Steel Ball Placed in a Hot Stream of Air

When a body which is initially at a uniform temperature T_0 is suddenly placed in a hot fluid, the rate at which the temperature $T(t)$ of the body changes with time is given by the differential equation [9]

$$\rho c L_c \frac{dT}{dt} = h(T_{inf} - T(t)), \tag{9.39}$$

where ρ is the mass density of the body, c is its specific heat at constant pressure, T_{inf} is the temperature of the surrounding fluid, h is the average convection heat transfer coefficient, and L_c is the characteristic length. For a solid steel sphere of diameter 2 cm initially at 10°C, and placed in a stream of hot air at temperature, $T_{inf} = 75°C$, with $h = 25$ W/m²K, we have

$$d = 0.02 \text{ m}, \quad \rho = 7854 \text{ kg/m}^3, \quad c = 434 \text{ J/kg K}, \quad h = 25 \text{ W/m}^2\text{K}$$

$$T_{inf} = 75°\text{K}, \quad T_0 = 10°\text{K}, \quad V = \pi\frac{d^3}{6}, \quad A = \pi d^2$$

$$L_c = \frac{V}{A} = 3.3333333 \times 10^{-3} \text{ m},$$

and the MATLAB statements needed to generate the temperature response of the steel ball to the hot stream of air are as follows.

```
d = 0.02;
rho = 7854;
c = 434;
h = 25;
```

```
V = pi*d^3/6;
A = pi*d^2;
Lc = V/A;
const = h/(rho*c*Lc)

f = @(t,T) 0.002200293607179*(75 - T);
[t Temp] = ode45(f,[0,2000],10);

p = plot(t,Temp(:,1),'blue')
title('Temperature Response of Steel Ball')
xlabel('Time (seconds)')
ylabel('Temperature (deg C)')
p(1).LineWidth = 2;
```

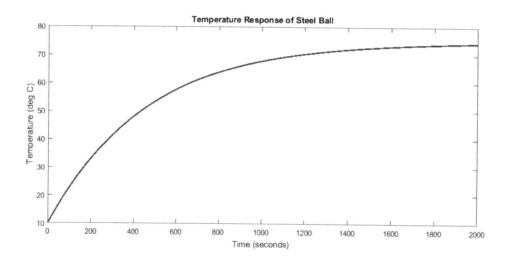

Fig. 9.23: Temperature response of steel ball

The MATLAB solution generated, which is plotted in Figure 9.23, shows how the steel ball attains its steady-state temperature of 75°C. in a time t equal to 4τ, where τ is the system time constant which, in this case, is $\rho c L_c / h = 454.5$ seconds.

9.9.4 Nonlinear Vibration of a Simple Pendulum

The natural frequency of large oscillation of a simple pendulum, which is a mass attached to one end of a light rigid rod, has been generated in Section 6 of Chapter 8 as a function of the maximum amplitude of the pendulum. The nonlinear behavior of the pendulum is governed by the differential equation [3, 5, 8, 12]

$$\frac{d^2\theta}{dt^2} + \frac{G}{L}\sin(\theta) = 0, \tag{9.40}$$

where L is the length of the pendulum and G is the acceleration due to gravity.

For a pendulum of length $L = 12$ inches, with a maximum initial amplitude of $A = 60$ degrees and zero initial velocity, the initial conditions are defined by

$$\theta(0) = 0, \quad \frac{d\theta}{dt}(0) = 0. \tag{9.41}$$

(9.40) can then be solved with MATLAB's *ode45* function as follows.

```
f = @(t,theta) [theta(2); -386.4/12*sin(theta(1))];

A1 = 10*pi/180;
A2 = 50*pi/180;
A3 = 90*pi/180;
A4 = 120*pi/180;

[t1 Theta1] = ode45(f,[0,5],[0;A1]);
[t2 Theta2] = ode45(f,[0,5],[0;A2]);
[t3 Theta3] = ode45(f,[0,5],[0;A3]);
[t4 Theta4] = ode45(f,[0,5],[0;A4]);

p = plot(t1,Theta1(:,1),'blue',t2,Theta2(:,1),'red--',t3,
    Theta3(:,1),'green',t4,Theta4(:,1),'magenta-.')
title('Nonlinear Pendulum Response')
xlabel('Time (seconds)')
ylabel('Angular position (degrees)')
legend('A = 10^\circ','A = 50^\circ','A = 90^\circ', 'A =
    120^\circ')
p(1).LineWidth = 2;
p(2).LineWidth = 2;
p(3).LineWidth = 2;
p(4).LineWidth = 2;
```

The graphs plotted in Figure 9.24 clearly indicate that there is an increase in the magnitude of the period of vibration of the nonlinear pendulum with increase in the oscillation amplitude. Also, as can be seen from the response plots, because there is no damping present in the system, the free vibration of the pendulum never decays out.

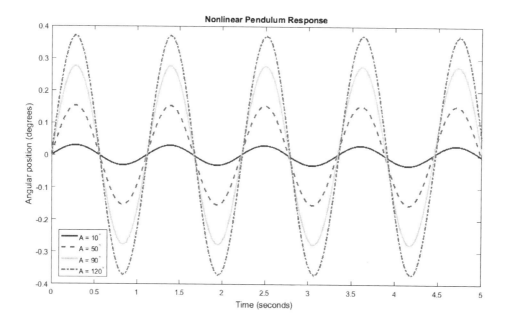

Fig. 9.24: Dynamic response of nonlinear pendulum

9.9.5 Transient Vibration of a Spring-Mass-Damper System Excited by a Pulse Function

The differential equation of the spring-mass-damper system of Figure 9.25 excited by the pulse function $F(t)$ shown is

$$M\frac{d^2x}{dt^2} + c\frac{dx}{dt} + kx = F(t). \tag{9.42}$$

For a system with $m = 3$ kg, $c = 12$ N-sec/m, $k = 120$ N/m, and initially at rest, the solution to (9.42) can be obtained using MATLAB as follows.

```
t1 = 0:0.001:0.5;
G1 = polyfit([0,0.5],[0,2],1);

t2 = 0.5:0.001:1.0;
G2 = polyfit([0.5,1.0],[2,0.5],1);

t3 = 1.0:0.001:2;
G3 = polyfit([1.0,2],[0.5,0],1);

f = @(t,y,G1,G2,G3) [y(2); 1/3*(((G1(1)*t + G1(2)).*(t <=
    0.5) + (G2(1)*t + G2(2)).*(0.5 < t).*(t <= 1.0) + (G3(1)*
```

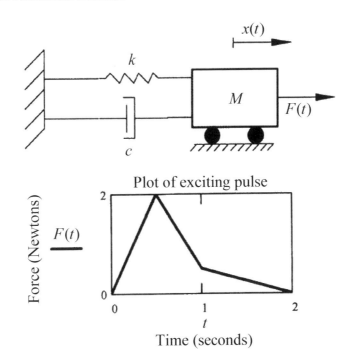

Fig. 9.25: Spring-mass-damper system excited by pulse function

```
   t + G3(2)).*(1.0 < t).*(t <= 2.0)) - 12*y(2) - 120*y(1))
   ];

[t x] = ode45(@(t,x) f(t,x,G1,G2,G3),[0,4],[0;0]);

subplot(2,1,1)
p = plot(t,x(:,1),'blue')
axis([0 4 -0.001 0.02])
title('Displacement Time History Obtained with ode45')
xlabel('Time (seconds)')
ylabel('Displacement (m)')
p(1).LineWidth = 2;

subplot(2,1,2)
p1 = plot(t,x(:,2),'blue')
axis([0 4 -0.05 0.05])
title('Velocity Time History Obtained with ode45')
xlabel('Time (seconds)')
ylabel('Velocity (m/sec)')
p1(1).LineWidth = 2;
```

Note, the first section of MATLAB code uses *polyfit* to create the forcing function $F(t)$ that is then implemented using conditional statements in the derivative vector function.

The displacement and velocity time histories plotted in Figure 9.26 indicate that, because of the presence of damping in the system, the response, which is in fact transient in nature, dies out soon after the forcing function is withdrawn at $t = 2$ seconds.

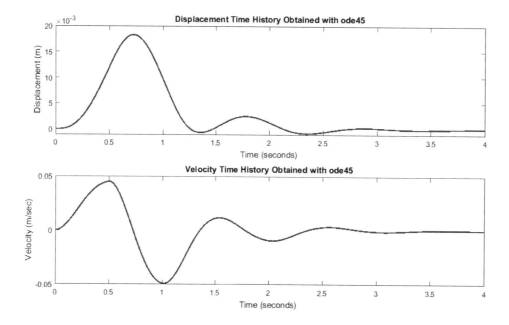

Fig. 9.26: Displacement and velocity response of the spring-mass-damper system

9.9.6 Nonlinear Vibration of a Damped System with a Hardening Spring

Consider the following nonlinear equation known as Duffing's equation [3, 8, 12, 13], which is the differential equation of motion of a spring-mass-damper system with a hardening spring

$$M\frac{d^2x}{dt^2} + c\frac{dx}{dt} + kx + \mu x^3 = F(t), \qquad (9.43)$$

where the last term on the right hand side of the equation is due to the effect of the hardening spring in which the spring stiffness increases as the load on it increases. The term $F(t)$ on the right hand side of the equation is the exciting force to which the system is subjected. We will utilize MATLAB to obtain solutions to (9.43) for $m = 1.2$ kg, $c = 0.6$ N-sec/m , $k = 1.2$ N/m and $F(t) =$ (a) a unit-step function and then (b) a unit-ramp function for values of μ ranging from 0.01 to 1.0. The results will then be compared with those for $\mu = 0$. The results are plotted in Figures 9.27 and 9.28.

(a) Step input with $\mu = 0, 0.01, 0.1, 1.0$:

```
f = @(t,y,mu) [y(2);1/1.2*(1 - 0.6*y(2) - 1.2*y(1) - mu*y
    (1).^3)];

[t F] = ode45(@(t,y) f(t,y,0),[0 20],[0;0]);
[t1 F1] = ode45(@(t,y) f(t,y,0.01),[0 20],[0;0]);
[t2 F2] = ode45(@(t,y) f(t,y,0.1),[0 20],[0;0]);
[t3 F3] = ode45(@(t,y) f(t,y,1.0),[0 20],[0;0]);

p = plot(t,F(:,1),'blue',t1,F1(:,1),'red--',t2,F2(:,1),'
    green--',t3,F3(:,1),'magenta-.')
axis([0 20 0 1.5])
title('Step Response')
xlabel('Time (seconds)')
ylabel('Displacement (m)')
legend('\mu = 0','\mu = 0.01', '\mu = 0.1', '\mu = 1')
p(1).LineWidth = 2;
p(2).LineWidth = 2;
p(3).LineWidth = 2;
p(4).LineWidth = 2;
```

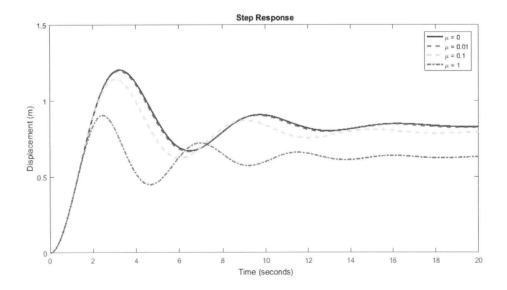

Fig. 9.27: Response of system with hardening spring to unit step input

(b) Ramp input with $\mu = 0, 0.01, 0.1, 1.0$:

```
f = @(t,y,mu) [y(2);1/1.2*(t - 0.6*y(2) - 1.2*y(1) - mu*y
    (1).^3)];
[t F] = ode45(@(t,y) f(t,y,0),[0 20],[0;0]);
[t1 F1] = ode45(@(t,y) f(t,y,0.01),[0 20],[0;0]);
[t2 F2] = ode45(@(t,y) f(t,y,0.1),[0 20],[0;0]);
[t3 F3] = ode45(@(t,y) f(t,y,1.0),[0 20],[0;0]);


p = plot(t,F(:,1),'blue',t1,F1(:,1),'red--',t2,F2(:,1),'
    green--',t3,F3(:,1),'magenta-.')
axis([0 20 0 20])
title('Response to Ramp Input')
xlabel('Time (seconds)')
ylabel('Displacement (m)')
legend('\mu = 0','\mu = 0.01', '\mu = 0.1', '\mu = 1')
p(1).LineWidth = 2;
p(2).LineWidth = 2;
p(3).LineWidth = 2;
p(4).LineWidth = 2;
```

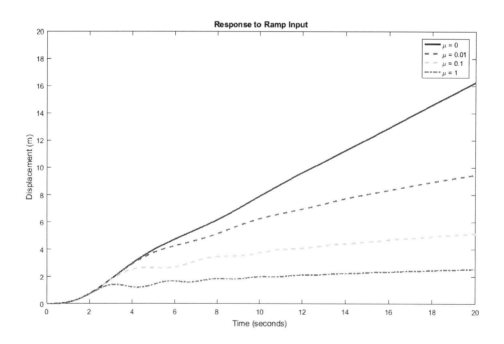

Fig. 9.28: Response of system with hardening spring to a unit ramp input

9.9.7 *Temperature Distribution in the Wall of a Pipe Carrying a Hot Fluid*

The differential equation relating temperature in the wall of a metal pipe to radial distance is [9]

$$r\frac{d^2T}{dr^2} + \frac{dT}{dr} = 0, \tag{9.44}$$

where $T(r)$ is the temperature in the pipe wall at a radial distance r from the pipe centerline. The inner radius of the pipe is r_i and the outer radius is r_o. The temperature of the fluid inside the pipe is T_f while the temperature of the outer wall of the pipe is T_o. Although two boundary conditions are prescribed here, namely the temperatures at the inner and outer walls of the pipe, there is only one initial condition available, that is, $T(r_i) = T_f$ to begin the solution process. The initial temperature gradient, namely, dT/dr, is not known. Thus, in order to resort to the Shooting Method, this initial temperature gradient must be assumed so that the process of generating a solution may be initiated. The solution T at r_o must then be determined with these initial values of T and dT/dr (at r_i). If the solution obtained does not match up with the given condition at $r = r_o$, the assumed initial condition must be revised and a new solution $T(r_o)$ determined. This process must be repeated until the solution obtained at r_o agrees with the prescribed condition. As discussed in Section 9.7, (9.44) must first be converted to the following two first-order differential equations before a solution can be obtained,

$$\frac{dT}{dr} = 0, \quad \frac{dz}{dr} = -\frac{1}{r}z. \tag{9.45}$$

In the following, an iteration process utilizing MATLAB's *ode45* function is presented by which a solution to this boundary value problem is arrived at for $r_i = 1$ cm, $r_o = 2$ cm, $T_f = 650°$ C and $T_o = 10°$ C.

```
f = @(r,T,initgrad) [initgrad; -1./r*initgrad];


ri = 1; ro = 2;
Tf = 650; To = 10;


initgrad1 = -100;

[r T1] = ode45(@(r,T) f(r,T,initgrad1),[ri, ro],[650;
   initgrad1]);
Temp1 = T1(end,1)


Temp1 =
  550.0000
```

The use of the MATLAB function *ode45* is demonstrated above. Because *initgrad* which is the temperature gradient at $r = r_i$ is not known, a reasonable starting value has been assumed. The following command generates the solution to the differential equation at the endpoint $r = r_o$. The computation indicates that, with the assumed dT/dr value at $r = r_i$, a temperature of 550° C is generated at $r = r_o$, which is not the prescribed temperature. Therefore, try a new value of initgrad:

```
initgrad2 = -200;


[r T2] = ode45(@(r,T) f(r,T,initgrad2),[ri, ro],[650;
    initgrad2]);
Temp2 = T2(end,1)


Temp2 =
   450.0000
```

The above analysis has yielded a temperature of 450° C at the outer wall of the pipe. With the second assumed value of *initgrad*, the temperature of the outer pipe wall is, clearly, still not what it should be. Therefore, a third value of *initgrad* must be tried which can be arrived at by a process of linear interpolation utilizing the results of the first two trials. The formula generated that must be used for estimating the next guess is given below.

```
initgrad3 = (initgrad2*(Temp1-To) - initgrad1*(Temp2-To))/(
    Temp1 - Temp2)

initgrad3 =
 -640.0000
```

Then, the solution with the new *initgrad* is:

```
r T3] = ode45(@(r,T) f(r,T,initgrad3),[ri, ro],[650;
    initgrad3]);
Temp3 = T3(end,1)


Temp3 =
   10.0000
```

The results of the above MATLAB computation are plotted in Figure 9.29.

```
subplot(2,1,1)
p = plot(r,T3(:,1),'blue')
axis([1 2 0 600])
title('Temperature in Pipe Wall')
xlabel('r (cm)')
ylabel('Temperature (deg C)')
```

```
p(1).LineWidth = 2;


subplot(2,1,2)
p1 = plot(r,T3(:,2),'blue')
axis([1 2 -800 0])
title('Temperature Gradient in Pipe Wall')
xlabel('r (cm)')
ylabel('dT/dr (deg C/cm)')
p1(1).LineWidth = 2;
```

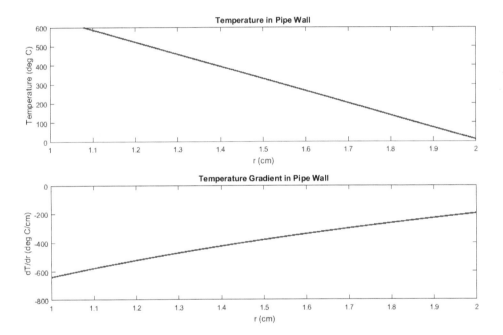

Fig. 9.29: Temperature and temperature gradient in pipe wall

9.9.8 Response of an R-L Circuit with a Nonlinear Resistor

Consider a series R-L circuit having a nonlinear resistor R with the voltage drop across it is given by

$$V_R = R(I(t) - I^3(t)), \tag{9.46}$$

Summing voltages around the loop, the governing differential equation for the circuit is

$$R(I(t) - I^3(t)) + L\frac{dI}{dt} = 0, \tag{9.47}$$

where R is the resistance of the circuit, L its inductance and $I(t)$ the current in it at any time t. If $R = 2.25\,\Omega$, $L = 1.10\,H$ and the initial current in the circuit is $I(0) = 0.75$ amperes, the following MATLAB statements will be needed to generate the solution using *ode45* and compare it with that for the corresponding linear problem.

```
R = 2.25;    L = 1.10;    I0 = 0.75;

f1 = @(t,I,R,L) (0 - R*(I - I.^3))/L;
[t1,I1] = ode45(@(t,I) f1(t,I,R,L),[0 3],I0);

f2 = @(t,I,R,L) (0 - R*I)/L;
[t2,I2] = ode45(@(t,I) f2(t,I,R,L),[0 3],I0);

p = plot(t1,I1(:,1),'blue',t2,I2(:,1),'red--')
title('Current in R-L Circuit')
xlabel('Time(seconds)')
ylabel('Current (amperes)')
legend('Nonlinear resistor','Linear resistor')
p(1).LineWidth = 2;
p(2).LineWidth = 2;
```

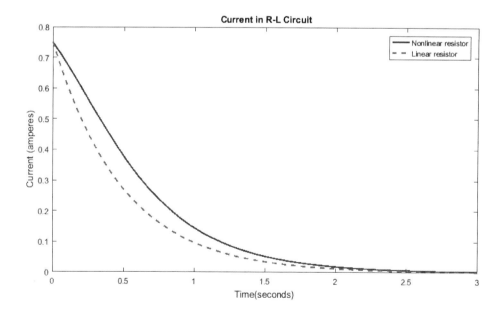

Fig. 9.30: Response of *R-L* circuit with a nonlinear resistor

The MATLAB solutions generated are shown in Figure 9.30. Notice how the current decays down to a zero value in a time t approximately equal to 4τ, where τ is the system time constant, which, in this case, is L/R or 0.5 seconds.

9.9.9 The Effect of Damping on the Step Response of a Second-Order Control System

The general differential equation governing the behavior of a second-order control system subjected to a unit step input is [7]

$$\frac{d^2 y}{dt^2} + 2\zeta\omega_n \frac{dy}{dt} + \omega_n^2 y = \omega_n^2, \tag{9.48}$$

where $y(t)$ is the system response to the unit step input, ζ is the system damping ratio, and ω_n is the natural frequency of the undamped system. We want to investigate the dynamic response of the system to different levels of damping obtained by varying ζ. If $\omega_n = 5$ rad/sec and ζ is varied from 0.1 to 1.4, the following MATLAB statements will be needed to generate the responses.

```
omegan = 5;
f = @(t,y,omegan,zeta) [y(2);omegan^2 - 2*zeta*omegan*y(2) -
    omegan^2*y(1)];

[t1 y1] = ode45(@(t,y) f(t,y,omegan,0.1),[0 10],[0;0]);
[t2 y2] = ode45(@(t,y) f(t,y,omegan,0.2),[0 10],[0;0]);
[t3 y3] = ode45(@(t,y) f(t,y,omegan,0.6),[0 10],[0;0]);
[t4 y4] = ode45(@(t,y) f(t,y,omegan,0.8),[0 10],[0;0]);
[t5 y5] = ode45(@(t,y) f(t,y,omegan,1.0),[0 10],[0;0]);
[t6 y6] = ode45(@(t,y) f(t,y,omegan,1.4),[0 10],[0;0]);

p = plot(t1,y1(:,1),'blue',t2,y2(:,1),'red--',t3,y3(:,1),'
    green-.',t4,y4(:,1),'magenta:',t5,y5(:,1),'cyan',t6,y6
    (:,1),'black--')
title('Second-Order System Response')
xlabel('Time(seconds)')
ylabel('Response')
legend('\zeta = 0.1','\zeta = 0.2','\zeta = 0.6','\zeta =
    0.8','\zeta = 1.0','\zeta = 1.4')
p(1).LineWidth = 2;
p(2).LineWidth = 2;
p(3).LineWidth = 2;
p(4).LineWidth = 2;
```

```
p(5).LineWidth = 2;
p(6).LineWidth = 2;
```

The response of the second-order system to a unit step input, which is plotted in Figure 9.31 for varying levels of damping, indicates that as ζ varies from 0.1 to 1.0, the peak overshoots as well as the time to achieve steady-state diminish, with the transient oscillations dying down faster as the system damping is increased. An overdamped system ($\zeta > 1.0$), however, is the most sluggish in attaining steady-state.

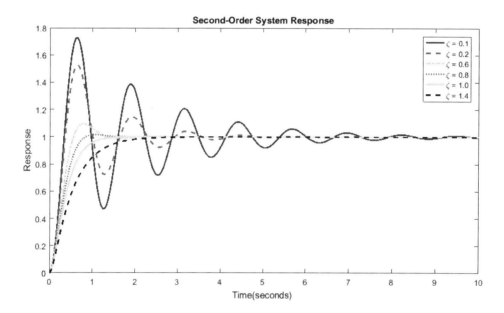

Fig. 9.31: Response of *R-L* circuit with a nonlinear resistor

Problems

9.1. Given the differential equation

$$\frac{dy}{dx} = (1 - 2x)e^{-2x},$$

with initial condition: $y = 3$ at $x = 0$, estimate values of the function using a Taylor series expansion for $x = 0.1$, that is, take Δx to be 0.10. Then, generate a MATLAB script for $x = 0$ to $x = 0.5$. Using MATLAB, compare results with the true solution which is $y = 3 + xe^{-2x}$ and with MATLAB's *ode45* solution by drawing appropriate graphs with proper labels and titles. Also plot the percentage error as a function of x.

9.2. Given the differential equation

$$\frac{dy}{dx} = e^x + xe^x + 2x,$$

with boundary condition $y = 0$ at $x = 0$, estimate values of the function using a Taylor series expansion for $x = 0.2$, that is, take Δx to be 0.20. Then, generate a MATLAB script for $x = 0$ to $x = 1.0$. Using MATLAB, compare results with the true solution which is $y = xe^x + x^2$ and with MATLAB's *ode45* solution by drawing appropriate graphs with proper labels and titles. Also plot the percentage error as a function of x.

9.3. Given the differential equation

$$\frac{dy}{dx} = x + y + xy,$$

with boundary condition $y = 1$ at $x = 0$, estimate values of the function using a 5-term Taylor series expansion for the range $x = 0.1$ to $x = 0.5$. Take Δx to be 0.10.

9.4. Solve Problem 9.1 using Euler's method. Do a hand-calculation for $x = 0.10$, that is, take the step size to be $h = 0.1$. Then generate a MATLAB script for $x = 0$ to $x = 1.0$. Using MATLAB, compare results with the true solution which is $y = 3 + xe^{-2x}$ and with MATLAB's *ode45* solution by drawing appropriate graphs with proper labels and titles. Also plot the percentage error as a function of x.

9.5. Using Euler's method, solve

$$\frac{dy}{dx} = y' = f(x, y) = \frac{3x^2}{2y}.$$

The initial condition given is $y = 3$ at $x = 2$, and the step size, h, is to be 0.1. Do a hand calculation for $x = 2.1$. Then, generate a MATLAB script for $x = 2$ to $x = 3$. Using MATLAB, compare results with the true solution which is $y = \sqrt{1 + x^3}$ and with MATLAB's *ode45* solution by drawing appropriate graphs with proper labels and titles. Also plot the percentage error as a function of x.

9.6. Given the following information:

$$\frac{dy}{dt} = -y^2 + 2, \quad y(0) = 10, \quad h = 0.1,$$

(a) Determine $y(0.1)$, using the modified Euler method. The answer should be correct to 3 decimal places.
(b) Continue the computation process until $t = 0.5$ is reached.
(c) Then, generate a MATLAB script for $t = 0$ to $t = 0.5$. Using MATLAB, compare results with MATLAB's *ode45* solution by drawing appropriate graphs with proper labels and titles.

9.7. Given the differential equation

$$\frac{dy}{dt} = y^2 + t^2,$$

with initial condition $y = 0$ at $t = 1$, determine:

(a) $y(1.1)$ and $y(1.2)$ by Euler's Method using an interval size $h = 0.1$.
(b) $y(1.1)$ and $y(1.2)$ by Modified Euler's Method, using an interval size $h = 0.1$ again.

9.8. Given the differential equation

$$\frac{dy}{dt} = y^2 + t^3,$$

with initial condition $y = 1$ at $t = 2$, determine:

(a) $y(2.1)$ and $y(2.2)$ by Euler's Method using an interval size $h = 0.1$.
(b) $y(2.1)$ by Modified Euler's Method, using an interval size $h = 0.1$.

9.9. Given the differential equation

$$\frac{dy}{dt} = y + t^2,$$

with initial condition $y = 2$ at $t = 1$, determine:

(a) $y(1.1)$ and $y(1.2)$ by Euler's Method using an interval size $h = 0.1$.
(b) $y(1.1)$ by Modified Euler's Method, using an interval size $h = 0.1$.

9.10. Given the differential equation

$$\frac{dy}{dx} = y + x^5,$$

with initial condition $y = 3$ at $x = 2$, determine:

(a) $y(2.1)$ and $y(2.2)$ by Euler's Method using an interval size $h = 0.1$.
(b) $y(2.1)$ by Modified Euler's Method, using an interval size $h = 0.1$.

Obtain answers that are good to at least three decimal places.

9.11. Given the differential equation

$$\frac{dy}{dx} = \frac{4x}{y} - xy^3,$$

with initial condition $y = 3$ at $x = 0$, determine:

(a) $y(0.1)$ and $y(0.2)$ by Euler's Method using an interval size $h = 0.1$.
(b) $y(0.1)$ by Modified Euler's Method, using an interval size $h = 0.1$.

Obtain answers that are good to at least three decimal places.

9.12. Given the differential equation

$$\frac{dy}{dx} = y + x^2,$$

with initial condition $y = 0.515$ at $x = 1$, determine y at $x = 1.2$ by Modified Euler's Method, using an interval size of $h = 0.2$.

9.13. Given the differential equation

$$\frac{dy}{dt} + y = 1,$$

with initial condition $y = 0$ at $t = 0$, determine:

(a) $y(0.10)$ and $y(0.20)$ by Euler's Method using an interval size $h = 0.10$.
(b) $y(0.10)$ by Modified Euler's Method, using an interval size $h = 0.10$. You will require about four to five iterations to converge to a solution.

Obtain answers that are good to at least three decimal places.

9.14. Given the differential equation

$$\frac{dy}{dx} = y + 2x^5,$$

with initial condition $y = 3.525$ at $x = 2$, determine:

(a) $y(2.1)$ and $y(2.2)$ by Euler's Method using an interval size $h = 0.1$.
(b) $y(2.1)$ by Modified Euler's Method, using an interval size $h = 0.1$.

Obtain answers that are good to at least three decimal places.

9.15. Given the differential equation

$$\frac{dy}{dx} = -xy^2,$$

with initial condition $y = 2$ at $x = 1$, determine:

(a) $y(1.1)$ and $y(1.2)$ by Euler's Method using an interval size $h = 0.1$.
(b) $y(1.1)$ by Modified Euler's Method, using an interval size $h = 0.1$.

Obtain answers that are good to at least three decimal places.

9.16. Given the differential equation

$$\frac{dy}{dx} = -xy^2,$$

with initial condition $y = 0.3333$ at $x = 2$, determine:

(a) $y(2.2)$ and $y(2.4)$ by Euler's Method using an interval size $h = 0.2$.

(b) $y(2.2)$ by Modified Euler's Method, using an interval size $h = 0.2$.

Obtain answers that are good to four decimal places.

9.17. Given the initial-value problem

$$\frac{dy}{dx} = f(x, y) = x^3 - 2y^2,$$

with initial condition: $y(0) = 1$ and step size $h = 0.3$, obtain the solution at $x = 0.3$, using Version 1 of the Runge-Kutta method, which is based on Simpson's one-third rule.

9.18. Given the initial-value problem

$$\frac{dy}{dx} = 4x^3 - 9x^2 + 4x - 1,$$

with $y = 5$ at $x = 1$, $h = 0.2$, obtain a solution by the Runge-Kutta fourth-order method (both versions) for the range $x = 1$ to 2. Do a hand calculation for $x = 1.2$ only. Then, generate a MATLAB script for $x = 1$ to $x = 2$. Using MATLAB, compare results with the true solution which is $y = x^4 - 3x^3 + 2x^2 - x + 6$ and with MATLAB's *ode45* solution by drawing appropriate graphs with proper labels and titles. Also plot the percentage error as a function of x.

9.19. Using the Runge-Kutta fourth order method (Version 2- that employs Simpson's three-eighth rule), obtain a solution at $x = 0.1$ and $x = 0.2$ to the differential equation

$$\frac{dy}{dx} = \frac{4x}{y} - xy,$$

with initial condition $y(0) = 3$. Use a step size of $h = 0.1$.

9.20. Given

$$\frac{dy}{dx} = \frac{3x^3 + 6xy^2 - x}{2y},$$

with $y = 0.707$ at $x = 0$, $h = 0.1$, obtain a solution by the fourth-order Runge-Kutta method for the range $x = 0$ to 0.5. Do a hand calculation for $x = 0.1$ only. Then, generate a MATLAB script for $x = 0$ to $x = 0.5$. Using MATLAB, compare results with the true solution which is $\ln(x^2 + 2y^2) - 3x^2 = 0$ and with MATLAB's *ode45* solution by drawing appropriate graphs with proper labels and titles. Also plot the percentage error as a function of x.

9.21. The governing differential equation of a series R-L circuit with a nonlinear resistor is

$$L\frac{dy}{dt} = -R(y - y^3),$$

where R and L are the resistance and inductance in the circuit and $y(t)$ is the current. The prescribed initial condition is: at $t = 0$, $y = 0.75$ (ampere). Using Version 1 (that employs Simpson's one-third rule), as well as Version 2 (that employs Simpson's three-eighth rule) of the Runge-Kutta fourth order method, obtain solutions at $t = 0.5$ seconds, that is, determine $y(0.5)$ and $dy/dt(0.5)$. Use a step size of $h = 0.5$ seconds. Take $R = 2.25$ Ohms, and $L = 1.10$ Henries. Obtain answers that are good to at least two decimal places.

9.22. Given the initial value problem

$$c\frac{dy}{dt} + ky = F(t),$$

with $c = 0.4$, $k = 1$, $F(t) = 1$ and initial condition $y(0) = 0$. Using Version 1 (that employs Simpson's one-third rule) as well as Version 2 (that employs Simpson's three-eights rule) of Runge-Kutta's fourth order method, obtain solutions at $t = 0.5$ sec, *i.e*, find $y(0.5)$ and $dy/dt(0.5)$. Use a step size of $h = 0.5$.

9.23. Using the Runge-Kutta fourth-order method, obtain a solution to

$$\frac{dx}{dt} = f(t, x, y) = xy^3 + t^2; \quad \frac{dy}{dt} = g(t, x, y) = ty + x^3,$$

for $t = 0$ to $t = 1$ second. The initial conditions are given as: $x(0) = 0$, $y(0) = 1$. Use a time increment of 0.2 seconds. Do hand calculations for $t = 0.2$ sec only. Then, generate a MATLAB script for $t = 0$ to $t = 1$ sec. Using MATLAB, compare results with MATLAB's *ode45* solution by drawing appropriate graphs with proper labels and titles.

9.24. Given the initial value problem

$$\frac{d^2y}{dt^2} = \frac{y}{e^t + 1}, \quad y(0) = 1, \text{ and } \frac{dy}{dt}(0) = 0,$$

obtain a solution at $t = 0.1$, *i.e.*, find $y(0.1)$ and $dy/dt(0.1)$, using Version 1 of Runge-Kutta's fourth order method . Use a step size of 0.1.

9.25. Given the initial value problem

$$\frac{d^2y}{dt^2} + 2\frac{dy}{dt} + 4y = 0, \quad y(0) = 2, \text{ and } \frac{dy}{dt}(0) = 0,$$

obtain a solution at $t = 0.1$, *i.e.*, find $y(0.1)$ and $dy/dt(0.1)$, using Version 1 of Runge-Kutta's fourth order method. Use a step size of 0.1.

9.26. Given the initial value problem

$$m\frac{d^2y}{dt^2} + c\frac{dy}{dt} + ky^3 = F(t),$$

with $m = 1$, $c = 0.5$, $k = 9$, and $F(t) = 9t$ and initial conditions: $y(0) = 0$ and $dy/dt(0) = 1$, obtain a solution at $t = 0.5$ seconds, *i.e.*, find $y(0.5)$ and $dy/dt(0.5)$ using Runga-Kutta's fourth order method. Use a step size of $h = 0.5$.

9.27. Given the initial value problem

$$\frac{d^2y}{dt^2} + 3\frac{dy}{dt} + 4y = 3,$$

and initial conditions $y(0) = 0$, $dy/dt(0) = 1$, obtain a solution at $t = 0.5$ seconds, *i.e*, determine $y(0.5)$ and $dy/dt(0.5)$ using Runge-Kutta's fourth order method. Use a step size of $h = 0.5$. Obtain answers that are good to at least three decimal places.

9.28. Given the initial value problem

$$\frac{d^2y}{dt^2} + 4\frac{dy}{dt} + 6y = 6,$$

and initial conditions $y(0) = 0$, $dy/dt(0) = 2$, obtain a solution at $t = 0.5$ seconds, *i.e*, determine $y(0.5)$ and $dy/dt(0.5)$ using Runge-Kutta's fourth order method. Use a step size of $h = 0.5$. Obtain answers that are good to at least three decimal places.

9.29. Given the initial value problem

$$\frac{d^2y}{dt^2} + 2\frac{dy}{dt} + 3y = 3,$$

and initial conditions $y(0) = 0$, $dy/dt(0) = 1$, hand calculate a solution at $t = 0.5$ seconds, *i.e*, determine $y(0.5)$ and $dy/dt(0.5)$ using Runge-Kutta's fourth order method, with a step size of $h = 0.5$. Obtain answers that are good to at least three decimal places. Then generate a MATLAB script for $t = 0$ to $t = 3$ sec using a step size of $h = 0.5$ sec. Using MATLAB, compare results with MATLAB's *ode45* solution by drawing appropriate graphs with proper labels and titles.

9.30. Given the initial value problem

$$\frac{d^2y}{dt^2} + 4\frac{dy}{dt} + 6y = 0,$$

and initial conditions $y(0) = 0$, $dy/dt(0) = 2$, obtain a solution at $t = 0.1$ seconds, *i.e*, determine $y(0.1)$ and $dy/dt(0.1)$ using Runge-Kutta's fourth order method. Use a step size of $h = 0.1$.

9.31. The differential equation for a series R-C circuit with an applied voltage $v(t)$ is

$$Ri(t) + \int \frac{1}{C}i(t)\,dt + v_C(0) = v(t),$$

where $v_C(0)$ is the initial voltage across the capacitor and $i(t)$ is the resulting current in the circuit.

Using MATLAB, obtain a numerical solution to this differential equation for $R = 1\Omega$, $C = 1$ F, and $v(t) = u(t)$, a unit step function. Assume that there is no initial energy in the network.

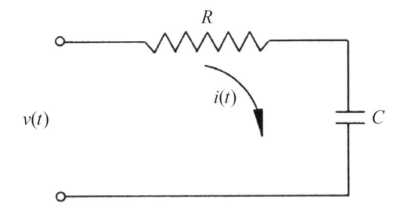

Fig. 9.32: Problem 9.31

9.32. The differential equation governing the vertical fall of an object in air from a height is

$$M\frac{dv}{dt} + Cv^2(t) = MG,$$

where M is the mass of the object, C is a proportionality constant that defines the aero-dynamic drag on the object which is proportional to the square of the velocity, $v(t)$ is the vertical velocity (positive downward) the object acquires at time t measured from the start of the fall and G is the acceleration due to gravity. Using MATLAB, obtain and plot the numerical solution of this differential equation over 30 seconds for $M = 100$ kg, and $C = 0.30$ N-sec^2/m^2. Assume that the initial vertical velocity of the object at $t = 0$ is zero.

9.33. In a tank with inflow as well as outflow, the relationship between the liquid level or head $h(t)$ and the rate of inflow $q_{in}(t)$ is given by the following differential equation,

$$A\frac{dh}{dt} + \frac{h(t)}{R} = q_{in}(t),$$

where A is the cross sectional area of the tank and R is the hydraulic resistance which is the change in head required to cause a unit change in the rate of outflow.
If the hydraulic resistance is given by $R = C\sqrt{h(t)}$, where C is a constant, use MATLAB to obtain a numerical solution to the differential equation for $A = 0.04$ m^2, $q_{in} = 5 \times 10^{-4}$ m^3/sec and $C = 3500$. The initial level in the tank is $h = 0$ at $t = 0$. Plot h versus time and determine how long it will take for the level in the tank to rise to 2.5 m. Also determine the steady state value of h and the time taken to achieve it.

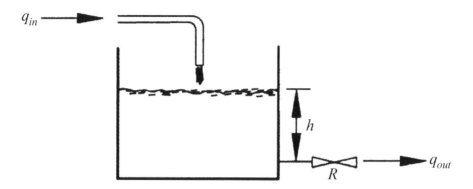

Fig. 9.33: Problem 9.33

9.34. The large-angle deflection of a cantilevered beam of length L loaded with a vertical load P at the free end is given by

$$\frac{d^2y}{dx^2} = \frac{-P(L-x)}{EI}\left[1+\left(\frac{dy}{dx}\right)^2\right]^{3/2},$$

where $y(x)$ is the beam deflection at a distance x from the left hand end which is the cantilevered end, L is its length, I is the moment of inertia of the cross-section about the neutral axis, and E is the modulus of elasticity. Using MATLAB, obtain numerical solutions to this differential equation and generate deflection curves for a beam with a load $P = 10$ kips, length $L = 15$ feet, and moment of inertia $I = 200$ in^4 in the following cases.

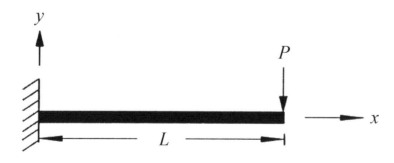

Fig. 9.34: Problem 9.34

(a) The beam is made of steel, with modulus of elasticity $E = 30 \times 10^6$ psi.
(b) The beam is made of wood, with modulus of elasticity $E = 1.8 \times 10^6$ psi.

Compare your results in the two cases with those for small-angle bending (linear beam theory) generated by ignoring the effect of the nonlinearity in the right hand side of the equation.

9.35. The differential equation governing the behavior of a control system is

$$\frac{d^2y}{dt^2} + 6\frac{dy}{dt} + 9y = u(t).$$

Using MATLAB, obtain and plot the numerical solution to the differential equation for zero initial conditions. What is the steady-state value of the response and how long does it take to achieve it?

9.36. A spring-mass-damper system is subjected to a force pulse $F(t)$ which is one half of a sine wave. The governing differential equation is, thus,

$$M\frac{d^2x}{dt^2} + C\frac{dx}{dt} + kx = F(t),$$

where M is the mass, C is the damping coefficient, k is the spring constant and $x(t)$ is the displacement of the mass at time t. The forcing function $F(t)$ is $F(t) = F_0\sin(\omega_f t)$ for $0 \le t \le 1$ and $F(t) \equiv 0$ for $t \ge 1$.

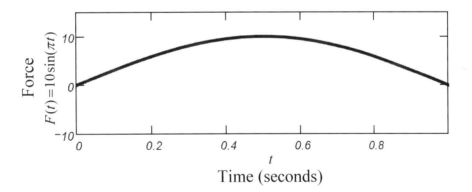

Fig. 9.35: Problem 9.36

Using MATLAB, obtain and plot the numerical solution (displacement and velocity) to the above differential equation for $M = 1$ kg, $C = 1.25$ N-sec/m, $K = 10$ N/m , $F_0 = 10$ N, $\omega_f = \pi$, and zero initial conditions. How long does it take for the transient vibration to die out?

9.37. The system of Problem 9.36 is now excited by the trapezoidal pulse $F(t)$ shown. Using MATLAB, obtain and plot the numerical solution (displacement and velocity). How long does it take for the transients to die out?

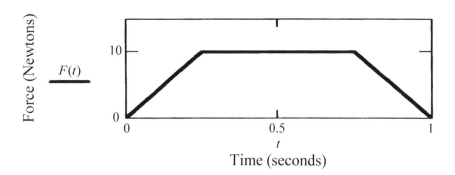

Fig. 9.36: Problem 9.37

9.38. The Van der Pol oscillator is a spring-mass system with a damping mechanism that depends on position, as well as velocity. The motion of this system is a sustained oscillation that is independent of initial conditions and is governed by the following differential equation,

$$\frac{d^2x}{dt^2} - \mu\frac{dx}{dt}(1 - x^2) + x = F(t).$$

Using MATLAB, obtain numerical solutions to this equation for $\mu = 0.01, 0.1$, and 1, when $F(t)$ is a unit step function, and the initial conditions are zero.

9.39. Verify, using MATLAB, that the motion of the Van der Pol oscillator of Problem 9.38 subjected to a unit step forcing function is a sustained oscillation that is independent of initial conditions. Consider four sets of initial conditions as follows:

1. $t = 0$, $x = 0$, $dx/dt = 0$;
2. $t = 0$, $x = 0$, $dx/dt = 10$;
3. $t = 0$, $x = 2$, $dx/dt = 0$;
4. $t = 0$, $x = 2$, $dx/dt = 10$.

Obtain numerical solutions for $\mu = 1$ only.

9.40. The differential equation for a series R-L-C circuit with an applied voltage $v(t)$ is

$$Ri(t) + L\frac{di}{dt} + \int \frac{1}{C}i(t)\,dt + v_C(0) = v(t),$$

where $v_C(0)$ is the initial voltage across the capacitor and $i(t)$ is the resulting current in the circuit.

Using MATLAB, obtain a numerical solution to this differential equation for $R = 1\Omega$, $L = 1H$, $C = 0.04F$, and $v(t) = u(t)$, a unit step function. Assume that there is initially no current in the circuit.

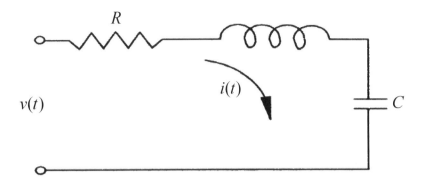

Fig. 9.37: Problem 9.40

9.41. A simply supported steel beam of length L is loaded with a distributed load that increases from zero at the left hand end to a maximum value of w_0 at the right hand end. Its deflection curve is given by the following differential equation,

$$\frac{d^2y}{dx^2} = \frac{M(x)}{EI},$$

where EI is the bending stiffness of the beam and the bending moment $M(x)$ at x is

$$M(x) = \frac{w_0 x}{6L}(L^2 - x^2).$$

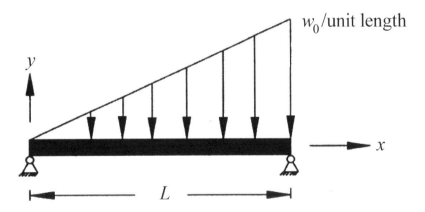

Fig. 9.38: Problem 9.41

Generate a MATLAB script to obtain a numerical solution by the *Shooting Method* to this boundary value problem in the form of deflection and slope curves for $w_0 = 2.5$ kips/ft, $L = 15$ ft, $EI = 2.5 \times 10^9$ lbs-in^2.

9.42. A cylindrical metal pipe of inner radius r_i and outer radius r_o transports cold air at T_f° C in a building which has a room temperature of T_R° C. The differential equation that relates the temperature in the pipe wall to radial distance is known to be

$$r\frac{d^2T}{dr^2} + \frac{dT}{dr} = 0.$$

Generate a MATLAB script to obtain a numerical solution by the *Shooting Method* to the differential equation in the form of temperature and temperature gradient profiles in the pipe wall for $T_f = 2^\circ$ C, $T_R = 30^\circ$ C, $r_i = 2$ cm and $r_o = 4$ cm.

References

1. Chapra, S.C. and Canale, R.P.: Numerical Methods for Engineers, Fourth Edition. McGraw Hill (2002)

2. Cernica, J.J.: Strength of Materials. Holt, Rinehart and Winston, Inc. (1966)

3. Dimargonas, A.D.: Vibration for Engineers, Second Edition. Prentice-Hall, Inc. (1996)

4. Hibbeler, R.C.: Engineering Mechanics, Eleventh Edition. Pearson Prentice-Hall (2007)

5. Inman, D.J.: Engineering Vibration, Second Edition. Prentice-Hall Inc. (2001)

6. Irwin, J.D., and Graf, E.R.: Industrial Noise and Vibration Control. Prentice-Hall, Inc. (1979)

7. Nise, N. S.: Control Systems Engineering, Seventh Edition. John Wiley and Sons, Inc. (2015)

8. Rao, S.S.: Mechanical Vibrations, Fourth Edition. Pearson Prentice-Hall (2004)

9. Schmidt, F.W., Henderson, R.E., Wolgemuth, C.H.: Introduction to Thermal Sciences. John Wiley and Sons, Inc. (1984)

10. Shigley, J.E., Mischke, C.R.: Mechanical Engineering Design, Fifth Edition. McGraw-Hill Book Company (1989)

11. Spotts, M.F., Shoup, T.E. and Hornberger, L.E.: Design of Machine Elements, Eighth Edition. Pearson Prentice-Hall (2004)

12. Thomson, W.T., Dahleh, M.D.: Theory of Vibration with Applications, Fifth Edition. Prentice-Hall, Inc. (1998)

13. Volterra, E., Zachmanoglou, E.C.: Dynamics of Vibrations. Charles E. Merrill Books, Inc. (1965)

14. Wilson, J.F., Ed.: Dynamics of Offshore Structures. John Wiley and Sons (1984)

Index